.

THE
OLD FAITH
& THE NEW

THE
OLD FAITH
& THE NEW

TWO VOLUMES IN ONE

DAVID FRIEDRICH STRAUSS

With an introduction & notes by

G. A. WELLS

WESTMINSTER COLLEGE–OXFORD: CLASSICS IN THE STUDY OF RELIGION

Amherst, New York • Oxford, England

Published 1997 by Prometheus Books
59 John Glenn Drive, Amherst, New York 14228–2197,
716–691–0133. FAX: 716–691–0137.

Library of Congress Cataloging-in-Publication Data

Strauss, David Friedrich, 1808–1874.
  [Alte und der neue glaube. English]
  The old faith & the new / David Friedrich Strauss ; translated by
Mathilde Blind ; with an introduction and notes by G. A. Wells.
      p.   cm. — (Westminster College–Oxford: classics in the
study of religion)
  Originally published: New York : H. Holt, 1873.
  Includes bibliographical references.
  ISBN 1–57392–118–1 (cloth : alk. paper)
  1. Rationalism. 2. Religion—Controversial literature.
3. Christianity—Controversial literature. 4. Evolution. 5. Liberal-
ism (Religion) I. Title. II. Series.
BL2775.S7513 1997
210—dc21   96–37772

Printed in the United States of America on acid-free paper.

Contents

Introduction[*]

G. A. Wells

(1) Strauss's Work on Christianity and Its Reflection in His Final Book

The literary career of David Friedrich Strauss began with his *Life of Jesus Critically Examined* (1835) and ended with the work here introduced, published in 1872 (two years before his death) which he called a "Confession," a statement of his religious, moral and political credo. Both books were great publishing successes—the latter went through six large editions in as many months—and both evoked a storm of incensed criticism. Strauss's purpose in both books was to state his case to those who would hear it while leaving undisturbed those to whom enjoyment of the Christian faith brings peace and happiness. And he stressed in the final book (I, 3) that he spoke as a private indi-

---

*References to Strauss in this Introduction which give only a volume number (I or II) and a page or pages are to the English version of his text as printed in this volume.

vidual, not with the authority which might go with any professional position. The publication of his 1835 book had led to his prompt dismissal from his junior post at Tübingen University. In 1839 he was elected to a chair of theology in the University of Zürich, but there was such a storm of clerically organized protest that the authorities would not let him take up the appointment.

In his valuable historical survey, J. M. Robertson noted that, before Strauss, "all destructive analysis of the gospel records had been regarded by the mass even of educated Christians as a continuation of the work of the 'infidel' deists of France in the previous century," except in "the curiously detached academic world of Germany."[1] The political disunity of Germany entailed many universities, all independent of any overall national or central authority, whereas in England the only two were still controlled by an established church. Hence in Germany, Strauss's standpoint—that many gospel stories are myths based on Old Testament expectations and motivated by Christian desire to represent Jesus as in no way inferior to Moses and the prophets—was already (albeit tentatively) represented among university teachers before he wrote, and even in some few cases (mostly under the cloak of anonymity) in print. He himself refers to an anonymous book on *Revelation and Mythology* published at Berlin in 1799, whose author "contends that the whole life of Jesus, all that he should and would do, had an ideal existence in the Jewish mind long prior to his birth."[2] In the same context, he alludes to an article of 1816 (also anonymous) in a theological journal, which pointedly observed that Elisha raises someone from the dead, feeds a multitude with a small amount of bread, cures leprosy and passes through water.[3]

It is not surprising that such parallels with Jesus should have aroused suspicion among scholars whose speciality was investigation of the relevant texts and who were free to treat these critically. It is equally unsurprising that this fact was adduced to belittle Strauss's achievement in setting out the relevant evidence in full detail and in pressing home its consequences for the traditional faith. Carlyle, for instance, called Strauss's 1835 book "a revolutionary and ill-advised enterprise, setting forth in words what all wise men had had in their minds for fifty years past, and thought it fittest to hold their peace about."[4] Yet even Ferdinand Christian Baur, who in 1847 accused Strauss of lack of originality, had to allow that it was this book which "for the first time worked out in detail" the view that gospel stories are myths.[5] And, as Schopenhauer insisted when his own originality was queried, although the development of knowledge achieved at a certain time makes it likely that a great truth will have been indistinctly observed before its full import is decisively stated, it is the man who recognizes this import and presses it home on the public in all its consequences who is to be considered its true originator.[6]

Strauss's achievement is best appreciated by comparing him with his major and well-known predecessors. Prominent among them was Hermann Samuel Reimarus who, as Strauss observes (I, 40), had demonstrated that the gospel resurrection narratives contradict each other in important respects, which Reimarus explained by supposing that Jesus' disciples stole his body from his tomb and then circulated stories, not consistent with each other, of his having risen from the dead. Morgan and Barton allow that this "fraud hypothesis is less far-fetched than it initially appears," for the discrepancies (which amount to glaring contradictions) would look very suspicious to anyone who retained, as Reimarus did, the traditional view that the gospels were written by eyewitnesses of the events reported in them.[7]

Strauss realized the absurdity of supposing that the apostles knew that there was no word of truth in their proclamation of their master's resurrection, and yet spread this story with a fire of conviction that sufficed to change the world.[8] He also realized that it will not do to surrender miraculous features in a narrative and yet assume that what remains represents eyewitness reporting of some kind of real occurrences. Reimarus had done this with both Old and New Testament stories, arguing, for instance, that Moses had created sham thunder and lightning on Sinai so as to impress his audience. Strauss commented:

If it was not God who thundered at the law-giving, . . . who is it who
tells us that there was any thunder and lightning at all? It is the same
writer who tells us that it was God, and we are not entitled uncritically to accept the one affirmation while discounting the other.
Again, if Jesus did not rise miraculously on the third day, who gives
us guarantees that his body was at that time sought in the grave and
no longer found there?[9]

If Reimarus invoked conscious deceit, the "rationalists," as
Strauss calls them, among early nineteenth-century German theologians supposed instead that misunderstanding on the part of Jesus'
entourage underlies the gospel miracle stories (I, 41–42). Jesus, it was
held, did not die on the cross, recovered consciousness in the cool
tomb, crept out of it and was then occasionally seen by his followers,
who took these appearances for a resurrection. Strauss traced the
absurdity of such argumentation to the same factor that had vitiated
Reimarus's reasoning, namely, rejecting the miracles while retaining
the eyewitness origin of the stories. His own explanation imputed neither fraud nor stupid misunderstanding to their originators. Since, he
argued, the early Christians believed that Jesus was the Messiah, they
will also have believed that he must have been, have said and have
done all that was expected of the Messiah. He must, for instance, have
been descended from David and born in David's city of Bethlehem.
Hence the origin of stories giving him these qualifications—stories
which, as they were not based on fact, varied between each other, so
that what one evangelist says on the subject is excluded by the narrative of another. Again, Isaiah spoke of a time when the eyes of the
blind would be opened, and to early Christians this could only be the
time of Jesus, whom they accordingly represented as curing blind-
ness. Jesus had also to be portrayed as a man of no less power than
Elijah and Elisha, and as a second and greater Moses (I, 57–59). Old
Testament material does not, of course, account for the crucifixion,
and Strauss accepted it as historical and confirmed by the evidence of
Tacitus (I, 27).

Strauss and Baur realized that any reconstruction of the development of Christianity must start with the Pauline letters as the earliest extant documents. Baur saw the great issue in the early church to have been the conflict between the original Jewish-Christian party, led by Peter and James, and the circumcision-free missionary work of Paul—this conflict being most clearly evidenced in Paul's epistle to the Galatians. From this starting point, Baur took Matthew as the earliest of the four gospels, as it seemed to him the most Jewish. He regarded Luke as dependent on Matthew and as showing some compromise between the two opposed factions. Mark was, in his view, later still, and rearranged the gospel material when the controversy between Pauline and strictly Jewish Christians had died down. Acts he also thought late, for it minimizes the conflict by making Paul look as Petrine as possible and Peter as Pauline as possible. The fourth gospel he considered quite incompatible with the others, and also as betraying gnostic influences which date it as late as the middle of the second century.[10]

Strauss accepted all this (I, 46, 57, 62–65). He held that, if any of the Johannine literature is truly 'apostolic,' then this honor must be assigned to the despised final book in the canon, the apocalypse entitled Revelation (where the original Jewish standpoint of earliest Christianity is all too much in evidence) and certainly not to the gospel, which is quite incompatible with it. In this connection Strauss alludes jocularly to "malicious criticism" (I, 46 and 52), meaning articles by Schnitzer and Zeller in the first volume of the *Theologische Jahrbücher*, 1842, where Zeller declared that their rehabilitation of Revelation at the expense of the much prized fourth gospel showed once again that the first shall be last and the last first.

The distinction between the historical Jesus and Jesus as represented in the gospels is now a commonplace; but critics of Baur and Strauss called it a delusion dependent on their implausibly late datings of the gospels. Obviously, the later these gospels were, the more would a gulf between them and the original eyewitnesses seem likely; and Baur put even his earliest gospel, Matthew, well into the second century. Even today, there are still writers who suppose that disposing of this chronology disposes likewise of Baur's fundamental thesis concerning the conflicts from which the doctrines of the early Catholic church in time emerged.[11] The Durham theologian C. K. Barrett gives a juster assessment when he notes that "the historical study of the last hundred years has not shown that the conflicts, tensions and resolutions described by Baur are imaginary; it has shown that they belong to earlier dates than those to which Baur assigned them."[12] We must, he says elsewhere, "accept Baur's observation that the gospels reflect the concerns of those who wrote them."[13]

The growing consensus on the priority of the gospel of Mark also compromised Baur and Strauss. Lachmann, Wilke and Weisse had already argued this before Holtzmann gave it classic expression in 1863. The priority of this simple gospel, which many took as an unadorned 'transcript from life,' seemed to strengthen the eyewitness hypothesis. Not until 1901 did William Wrede show that Mark was largely shaped by theological interests.

To sum up so far, one may justly say, with J. M. Robertson, that "it is only in the light of the labors of the hundreds of scholars who have since explored the ground" that Strauss's views on the New Testament can finally be seen to be "at important points inadequate or inconclusive."[14] This is very obviously true of the other major weakness in Strauss's view of earliest Christianity, namely, his undervaluation of the Judaism in which it originated (I, 67f.). G. F. Moore's 1921 survey of "Christian writers on Judaism" showed that for some fifty years the misconception had been current among them that the Judaism of the first century was a barren 'legalism,' justly criticized by the strictures of the gospels and the Pauline letters.[15] A full fifty years later, E. P. Sanders found that Moore's attempt to correct such a distorted view had still not been fully effective, and he called Moore's article "required reading for any Christian scholar who writes about Judaism."[16]

Strauss was visibly sickened by the centuries of theological strife that went with the doctrines which emerged from the conflicts of New

Testament times—centuries when it was endlessly debated which propositions about these doctrines were to bring death to their proponents. He notes that, at his time of writing, one cannot even state the traditional formulas about baptism, eucharist and Trinity without making them seem ridiculous (I, 14f., 34f., 104f.). Subsequent developments have done nothing to lessen this truth. Hence the Cambridge theologian J. S. Bezzant had to concede in 1963 that numerous traditional Christian doctrines have been "so shattered" that the bare recital of them "has the aspect of a malicious travesty."[17] But whereas Bezzant, with many others who have made like concessions, remained within the church, Strauss resolutely refused to prop up these ancient structures with some sort of compromise views (I, 102), even though in his day, as he notes in his "Prefatory Postscript," the churches, having dropped the weapon of theological murder, still wielded that of ostracism. Hence his scorn of what he considered the absurd half measures of the "Protestant League," founded in 1863 by liberal elements in the Lutheran and Reformed Churches, and of the "Old Catholic" party, formed by Catholics who felt that the decrees of the Vatican Council of 1870, defining the dogma of papal infallibility, had gone just a little too far. He was equally critical of the "German Catholics," a group which was trying to unite the various confessions by basing the faith on moral principles and not on doctrines. Gladstone saw well enough—specifically with reference to Strauss's final book—that "in no part of his writings, perhaps, has he been so effective as where he assails the inconsistency of those who adopt his premises but decline to follow him to their conclusions."[18] It was perfectly clear to Strauss that you cannot have anything that may with propriety be called Christianity without the kind of high Christology that had been thoroughly discredited by historical criticism. It was equally clear to him that, while compromise is essential in political action, compromise in our beliefs is not possible without insincerity, and that, although in individual cases it may be expedient to be silent, it is usually better to be perfectly frank and open about what one believes. There are of course cases where misery can be avoided by ignorance, but it can hardly be claimed that any *systematic* propagation of error or concealment of truth is overall beneficial.

(2) Theism and Immortality: Man and the Cosmos

From his critique of Christianity,which concludes with his statement that he is no longer a Christian, Strauss turns to a critique of theism in general. When the application of the idea of God to an ever widening range of experience exposed its inadequacy, attempts were made to redefine it. But new definitions of long-established terms cannot get rid of their existing associations; they can only add new ones, so that if the term was inadequate before, it is still more so after (I, 124).

Strauss makes short shrift of the argument that God must exist because "everything must have a cause," noting that, if this were so, then God himself must have a cause, and we are landed in an infinite regression (I, 131). Schopenhauer had already written: "The law of causation is not so amenable as to allow itself to be used like a cab, which can be sent off home when one has got where one wanted to go."[19] Strauss finds the argument that the imperious commands of our moral consciousness must derive from Deity equally unimpressive, and regards moral precepts as dependent on the nature of man and the needs of society (I, 134f.). Schleiermacher, he notes (I, 52), had regarded human nature as base and sensual, and hence a hindrance to religious life. In our own day, J. A. T. Robinson's *Honest to God* equally one-sidedly called it fundamentally loving and caring. Strauss saw it as comprising both egoistic and social impulses, and implied (II, 41f.) that the self-preserving tendency is the older and more fundamental of the two, and the other produced by the pressure of hostile forces too strong for the individual to resist, but capable of being defeated by common action.

Along with the ideas of Deity, belief in immortality is traced to emotional needs—to dread of annihilation, to desire for reunion, and to the sense of justice that requires the unfair balance of happiness here to be redressed hereafter. A weak point surfaces in this context in the form of a strangely naive optimism: anyone who thinks that the evil-doer is happy and the good person miserable in this life (and so in need of future recompense) does not know how to distinguish appearances from reality (I, 145f.). Strauss's vehement rejection of the pessimistic views of Schopenhauer and Eduard von Hartmann (I, 165ff.) seems to have led him here to a position akin to that of the theodicies of the eighteenth century, to which he is otherwise quite opposed. For him, if we can be said still to have a religion, it consists in acknowledging our dependence on the cosmos—but on a basically rational and beneficent cosmos to be accepted with piety (I, 161, 164, 168). It was this kind of statement that led Nietzsche to dub his book mere "philistine optimism."[20] Strauss's view is of course not an endorsement of providential rule in history. He acknowledged no higher power which ruled or whose rule could be influenced by prayer[21]; and he marveled (I, 125) that prayer and fasting had only recently been urged upon the British government as an influence on Deity by educated speakers in the House of Lords.

In the two final parts of his book, Strauss is concerned to trace the origin of the world and the development of life to natural causes, and human actions to their natural motives. For the first of these tasks he utilizes the ideas of Kant and Laplace concerning the origin of the solar system.[22] As to human nature, he has already asked with what right we refuse to acknowledge the obvious facts of death by positing the persistence of a part of our being of which there is in any case no ascertainable trace (I, 143f.); and he has insisted on the physical basis of mind, in that mental capacities develop and decline with the body (I, 150). Hence it comes as no surprise that he does not find it humiliating to be related to the monkey (II, 4f.). The fossil record, he says, gives strong support to Darwin's theory, from which man cannot be arbitrarily exempted. Man and the higher apes differ in their capacities only in degree, and it is man's development of language that has done so much to elaborate his brain (II, 11, 13). Strauss obviously realized that to regard structure and function as developing progressively and simultaneously is the rational alternative to a theory of divine intervention.[23]

In sum, Strauss wished to substitute the nebular hypothesis and geology for the fables of Genesis, and Darwinism for the biblical or deistic conception of a special creation—this at a time when there was considerable opposition to Darwin. Haeckel had found all the eminent German authorities contemptuously hostile in 1863.[24]

(3) Patriotism, Conservatism and Sincerity

Strauss began his book (I, 1) with patriotic allusions to Bismarck's three recent, swift and decisive wars against Denmark, Austria and France successively, which led to the proclamation of the King of Prussia as German Emperor in 1871. Also, it was patriotism as much as his standpoint on religion which led Strauss to deplore current "menacing" Catholic encroachments (I, 2), an allusion to the recently proclaimed doctrine of papal infallibility which, in Bismarck's view, reduced bishops to mere functionaries of a foreign sovereign.[25] Strauss attributed the war with France to "passion and unreason" on the part of the French—a "vain and restless people"—whereas the German decision to fight had been purely rational (II, 75). For Nietzsche such statements merely exemplified the deplorable complacency engendered by the German success. It is, however, juster to regard Strauss's exaggerated patriotism as an example of the natural willingness of innovators to be on a friendly footing with the majority, at least on some questions, and hence unduly to stress what notions they do happen to have in common with that majority. As Strauss says in his "Prefatory Postscript," he had found in the German cause a ground of union with his countrymen which for the first time put him into sympathetic relation with them after his long exposure to their Christian wrath. The open letters he wrote to Renan about the war aroused jubilation throughout the whole country.

After Bismarck's successes, Strauss was not inclined to regard war as undesirable (II, 72ff.). Those who see in this just one more example of "German militarism" should be given pause by Walter Bagehot's *Physics and Politics* (London, 1872), where it is alleged that Western Europe was early in advance of other countries because there "the contest of races," involving "constant war," was "exceedingly severe," whereas "the 'protected' regions of the world—the interior of continents like Africa, outlying islands, like Australia or New Zealand—are of necessity backward" (p. 82). In fact, of course, the "contest of races," or of tribes of the same race, has been—and in the case of Africa still is—as murderous in all these places as elsewhere. Those who think that the gospel of militarism was distinctively German need to be reminded how the whole of Europe was engulfed by disastrous patriotism in 1914.

Persons critical of religion tended in Strauss's day as now to be well to the left of the political center; and so his strongly conservative views alienated many who might otherwise have welcomed his book. Seeing that human progress depends on cooperation, he inferred that it is essential to support existing institutions of family and state (II, 63). To this we may reply that, if customs are to be modified to suit changed conditions, there must exist in the community some possibility of questioning traditions and discrediting those which have become obsolete. But Strauss feared that to allow such a mechanism would result in chronic instability: hence his advocacy of monarchy and rejection of republicanism (II, 84, 87f.). He dreaded demagogy and was frightened by the rising power of the working class, whose heads had been turned by "French quacks"—St. Simon and others. And he was appalled by the excesses of the Paris Commune (II, 94f.). Alarmed memory of similar social convulsion had inspired similar support of the existing state by Hegel, Schopenhauer and others.

Although Strauss's views on theism, on the cosmos and man's place in it, and on moral and political issues are of interest both historically and in themselves, it is his New Testament scholarship that constitutes his principal claim to lasting fame; and so to conclude I revert to that. Albert Schweitzer assessed him as "the most absolutely sincere" of theologians[26]; and in my own (1988) account I found myself in hearty agreement.[27] Like that of any other pioneer, his work needed subsequent correction. All scientific inquiry is essentially provisional and consists of hypotheses which draw attention to the very facts which do not fit them, and which can thus point the way to better theories. But pioneers are, in their day, often resisted because they require their audiences to give up so much of what has long been accepted as assuredly true. Strauss knew that his work would for this reason be called "negative" (I, 9). But the Finnish theologian Heikki Räisänen has noted that "the history of biblical study is full of examples"—Galileo, Wellhausen, Schweitzer as well as Strauss—which "demonstrate that it is the 'negative' results which have most forcefully driven research forwards."[28] Once Strauss, in his very first book, had made it unavoidable—even before Baur—to distinguish what was claimed as the Jesus of history from Jesus as represented in the gospels, there inevitably followed fierce and continuing controversy as to which items in the 'ministry' and the 'passion' belong in which of these two categories. And so by now we are faced with what the New Testament scholar Christopher Evans has called "a curious feature of some of the theological writing of our time," namely, "combining an emphatic insistence in general on the historical element as the hallmark of Christianity as a religion with an uncertainty about the historical authenticity of any one element in it in particular."[29]

The positive effect of negative criticism comes only after some considerable time. Strauss lived to see it in the case of his 1835 *Life of Jesus,* but he knew that he would not do so in the case of his 1872 book.

The present publication reprints the English translation of 1874 and is complete except for Strauss's two appendices (on German poets and German musical composers).

Notes to Introduction

1. J. M. Robertson, *A History of Freethought in the Nineteenth Century* (London:Watts, 1929), pp. 151f.

2. Strauss, *The Life of Jesus Critically Examined,* English translation (from the fourth German edition of 1840) in three volumes by George Eliot, London, 1846, I, 47.

3. These and further details in Horton Harris, *D. F. Strauss and His Theology* (Cambridge: Cambridge University Press, 1973), pp. 268f.

4. See *A Diary,* by the poet and man of letters William Allingham (1824–1889), edited by H. Allingham and D. Redford (London: Macmillan, 1907), p. 211.

5. Quoted from Baur's *Kritische Untersuchungen über die kanonischen Evangelien,* Tübingen, 1847, pp. 46–47, by Harris, *D. F. Strauss and His Theology,* p. 107.

6. A. Schopenhauer, "Fragmente zur Geschichte der Philosophie," para. 14 ("Einige Bemerkungen über meine eigene Philosophie") in volume 1 of *Parerga und Paralipomena: Sämtliche Werke,* edited by J. Frauenstädt (Leipzig: Brockhaus, 1864), V, 144.

7. R. Morgan, with J. Barton, *Biblical Interpretation* (Oxford: Oxford University Press, 1988), pp. 52–57.

8. See Strauss's 1861 essay on Reimarus in E. Zeller's edition of the *Gesammelte Schriften,* volume 5, Bonn, 1877, p. 402.

9. Ibid., p. 401. C. H. Talbert includes a translation of this part of Strauss's essay in his edition of Reimarus's *Fragments* (London: SCM, 1971).

10. For Baur's views, see the extracts given by W. G. Kümmel, *The New Testament. The History of the Investigation of Its Problems,* English translation (London: SCM, 1973), pp. 127–43.

11. This dismissive attitude to Baur is taken, for instance, by C. Stephen Evans, *The Historical Christ and the Christ of Faith* (Oxford: Oxford University Press, 1996), p. 32, where he uncritically follows Stephen Neill's *The Interpretation of the New Testament, 1861–1961* (Oxford: Oxford University Press, 1964).

12. C. K. Barrett, "Pauline Controversies in the Post-Pauline Period," *New Testament Studies* 20 (1973/74): 243.

13. C. K. Barrett, "Joseph Barber Lightfoot" (Bishop of Durham and critic of Baur), *Durham University Journal* 64 (New Series 33) (1972): 203.

14. Robertson, *A History of Freethought in the Nineteenth Century,* p. 153.

15. G. F. Moore, in *Harvard Theological Review* 14 (1921): 197–254.

16. E. P. Sanders, *Paul and Palestinian Judaism* (London: SCM, 1977), p. 33.

17. J. S. Bezzant in *Objections to Christian Belief* by several hands, with an introduction by A. R. Vidler (London: Constable, 1963), p. 84.

18. W. E. Gladstone, *Address Delivered at the Liverpool Collegiate Institution* (London: Murray, 1873), p. 25.

19. A. Schopenhauer, "Essay on the Four-Fold Root of the Principle of Sufficient Reason," para. 20, in *Sämtliche Werke,* I, 38.

20. F. Nietzsche, "David Strauss der Bekenner und der Schriftsteller" (1873), the first of Nietzsche's *Unzeitgemässe Betrachtungen* (Thoughts out of Season) in *Werke,* ed. A. Baeumler, Leipzig, 1913, I, 38.

21. In his discussion of prayer Strauss follows (I, 127) Ludwig Feuerbach, on whom see Van A. Harvey's recent book *Feuerbach and the Interpretation of Religion* (Cambridge: Cambridge University Press, 1995).

22. Kant's *Natural History and Theory of the Heavens* (1755), edited in English translation by W. Hastie (Glasgow: Maclehose, 1900), with a long introduction. This translation has been revised and edited with a new introduction by W. Ley, *Kant's Cosmogony* (New York: Greenwood, 1968).

23. Strauss is not fully consistent on this matter, and in some passages (e.g., I, 108) represents nonhuman animals as devoid of reason. Darwin had already observed—in *The Descent of Man,* 1871 (chapter 3), which Strauss knew and quotes (II, 5) on another matter—that "only a few persons now dispute that animals possess some power of reasoning. Animals may constantly be seen to pause, deliberate, and resolve." The classic demonstration of the truth of this was later given in Wolfgang Köhler's *The Mentality of Apes* (English translation 1925).

24. E. Haeckel, *Last Words on Evolution,* English translation, London, 1906, p. 29.

25. Details in W. E. H. Lecky, *Democracy and Liberty,* 2nd edition (London: Longmans, Green, 1896), II, 31f.

26. A. Schweitzer, *The Quest of the Historical Jesus,* English translation by W. Montgomery, 3rd edition (London: Black, 1954), p. 68.

27. See my account of Strauss in *Religious Postures* (La Salle, Ill.: Open Court, 1988), pp. 34–57.

28. H. Räisänen, *Beyond New Testament Theology* (London: SCM, 1990), p. 97.

29. C. F. Evans, "Is 'the Jesus of History' Important?" in Evans, *Is "Holy Scripture" Christian?* (London, SCM: 1971), p. 57.

PREFATORY POSTSCRIPT.

(*Translated by J. Fitzgerald.*)

THE little book which three months after its first appearance is now about to come before the world in a fourth edition, was originally left, and still remains, without a preface. It must speak for itself, thought I; and in point of fact it left very little room for doubt whether as to its motive or its object. But so much has been said against it in several quarters, and that with such vehemence, and in some cases with such force, that some reply will be expected from the author. There is material enough at hand for a whole series of polemical works on subjects the most dissimilar—philosophy and theology, natural and political science. Still, not alone the vastness of such an undertaking but also the very nature of the matter in hand, requires that I should restrict myself to a narrower field. This is a Confession; it does not assail the position held by others, but only defends its own. Meanwhile, however briefly I may express what I have to say, these pages, if appended to my purposely compendious work, would weight it down, and therefore I

let it go forth by itself. It will serve not only as a
preface to the new edition, but also as a postscript
to the readers of the earlier ones.*

Lessing, as we know, was content to be less be-
praised than Klopstock, provided he was more dili-
gently read.

Indeed we know that he made no objection, if
lack of approval now and then was changed into
hearty disapprobation. In such a frame of mind as
that, I should be perfectly satisfied with the reception my Confession of Faith has met with. Strike,
but listen, exclaimed the Athenian general and
statesman to his opponent. In truth, when a man
has been condemned not without a hearing the pre-
sumption that he is innocent is so far lessened. If I
had been condemned by all who have read my book,
I should be without excuse. But I have reasons
for believing that such is not the case. Over against
the thousands of my readers stand a score or so of
my public accusers—an inconsiderable minority—
and it would be hard for them·to show that they are
exactly the faithful interpreters of the former. If in
a matter like this persons who do not understand the
question have been foremost in crying aloud while
those who do understand have been content with
quiet acquiescence, the reason is to be found in certain circumstances with which we are all familiar. It

---

* The German edition of this postscript was issued in a
small pamphlet.

is all very well to ask in derision who are the *we* of whom I speak; but my questioners know as well as as I do how the matter stands.

Here again I make no account of an expedient which I might turn to good use; and such neglect might well appear to be unpardonable in a literary veteran. The apostle Paul (at least as he is represented in the Acts) used other strategy. When standing in presence of the High Council at Jerusalem, so soon as he saw before him the Pharisees and Sadducees, whilom enemies, now brethren, banded together against him, he contrived to break up this ominous coalition and to bring the Pharisees over to his side, by throwing out the assertion that his offence was only this, that he taught the resurrection of the dead. If one were to-day, in imitation of the Apostle of the Gentiles, to declare before the theological world : " It is because of my denial of Christ's godhead that these men condemn me, notwithstanding that I have no hesitation in acknowledging the man Jesus as Redeemer and Eternal Head of the Church : " he would secure himself against attack from the side of the Orthodox * of the Protestant League. In like manner he who, disregarding the reproach of materialism, upholds the right of Science to explain the universe, man included, has merely to avoid mention of certain topics, certain measures, if he has nothing to say in favor of them, and he will

* So the author. *Qu* What then is heterodoxy ?—Trans.

have nearly all the democrats and socialists on his side.
But what is to be thought of that man's judgment
who on every occasion knowingly incurs the displeasure of both sides and exposes himself to the
cross-fire of orthodox and progressive theologians;
of conservatives and socialistic democrats? Well, be
the estimate of his judgment what it will, his candor is not to be questioned.

According to a reviewer in the *Weser-Zeitung*,
my book is like a declaration of war against the
Protestant League and the Old Catholics. This accusation is as unjust as it well could be, and I will
come back to it again, but it was quite natural that
when once the book was regarded in that light,
thereafter all those who are of one mind with the
Protestant League, viz. the writers in the *Deutsche
Allgemeine* and the *Weser-Zeitung*, as also the Old-
Catholic professor who opened out on me in the
Augsburg *Allgemeine Zeitung* (to say nothing of the
Protestantische Zeitung) should pass as unfavorable
a sentence upon it as the *Kreutz-Zeitung* itself or the
Orthodox *Kirchen-Zeitungs*. In this respect some
Socialist-democratic periodicals were fairer, inasmuch
as they did not suffer the indignation they felt at my
political principles to prevent their appreciation of
the critical and philosophical portion of my book.
And if the writers and publicists of that party are
prone to employ in controversy a style of language
which is hardly what you might suppose to be dic-
tated by good taste or by etiquette, at least such

manners are not in contradiction with their fundamental principles. On the other hand, we have grown
accustomed to similar language on the part of the
Clericals; but then we can conceive how in their
eyes courtesy and respect shown to one who is held
to be damned everlastingly, must appear to be simple
hypocrisy. Contrariwise the educated middle party
are wont to claim the credit of complying with the
usages of respectable society even in controversy. If
on the present occasion even they have departed from
this policy in their treatment of me, there must be
some special reasons for the phenomenon.

When I compare the tone in which most of the
criticisms of my latest work are expressed, with that
in which for some years past it has been usual in German literature to make reference to me, it is not surprising that I should be profoundly pained at the
sudden change that has come about. After the tu-
mults of former contests had subsided, people had
gradually accustomed themselves to meet me with
some degree of respect; on many sides even I was
done the unsolicited honor of being ranked as a sort
of classical writer of prose. This esteem it appears
I have now forfeited for good and all by my latest
work; the newspapers think they must address me
with a lofty air, as though I were some beginner, some
chance comer. But fortunately this new tone of the
press is nothing new at all to me : rather is it the very
first greeting I received when I entered on my literary
career with the " Life of Jesus." That I observe that

same tone now, when I am approaching the goal, is for me a sign that, unlike many a literary veteran, I am unchanged, and that I have persisted in the line of my vocation.

It were affectation in me to deny the profound gratification I felt at the applause bestowed in all quarters upon my books on Ulrich von Hutten and Voltaire, or at the warm approval with which my letters to Ernest Rénan were greeted in every part of the German Fatherland ; it was a great satisfaction to me to find myself in harmony with my contemporaries and countrymen—a thing which after all is the object of all honorable literary ambition. And yet—people may believe it or not as they please, but the event shows that I was not mistaken—I had ever with me an inward monitor that said to me, " such trifling is not for you ; others can do it better." I do not mean to belittle those writings which have brought me so much valued sympathy. It were ingratitude towards my genius, were I not glad that in addition to a remorseless spirit of criticism there was also given me an innocent delight in artistic forms. But my proper calling lies not in the latter province, and when by returning to the former I forfeited those sympathies, I had only to take things as they came, in the full consciousness that I had but done my duty.

It is in truth an ungracious and thankless office to have to tell the world what it least wishes to hear. The world lives with no end of outlay, like some

grand lord ; takes and spends so long as there is anything to spend ; but let somebody reckon up the cost
and call attention to the balance, and he is regarded as
a mischief-maker.   And precisely to such office as that
have I ever been inclined by natural disposition and
by mental constitution.   Forty years ago, before my
Life of Jesus appeared, the impression had long been
looming up before the minds of thoughtful students
of theology, that no such supernatural things could
have occurred in Jesus' career as were narrated in the
gospels and had been believed by the church down
to that period; neither could they believe in the un-
naturally-natural interpretations offered by the rationalistic expositors of scripture ; doubts too as to the
apostolic origin of the gospels and as to the historical
character of these writings in general had sprung up
here and there.   And yet when I brought these
fragments of thought together and showed that the
evangelic narratives are neither apostolical nor historical ; that the miracles they recount belong to Myth
rather than to History ; that everything about Jesus
was in reality perfectly natural, albeit we can not now
give an account of every circumstance of his life—
when in my Life of Jesus I put all these things together in consecutive order, every one, young and old,
was indignant, and the author's name " the synonym
for ev'ry deed accurst."

Upwards of a generation passed away, and the
matter of that work, after having been in many respects more accurately determined, but yet on the

whole simply confirmed, by the investigations of others, had forced its way not only into theological science, but also into the convictions of educated people in general. People began to leave me and my infidelity alone, as I left the world and its self-destroying belief in peace, and the fruits of my taste for description and narration newly awakened during this period of calm, were received with pleasure. But the further development of Science again placed me in a position to gather up the fragmentary thoughts and so give offence again, for progress' sake. I had now no longer to deal with merely theological questions, but to see how I might combine the conclusions reached in that field with the results especially of Natural Science. On the one hand was a Christ, no longer son of God, but purely and simply man, who notwithstanding was in a fair way to be honored forevermore in the church established for the God-man. On the other hand men were feeling themselves more and more impelled from day to day, to explain the origin of the Universe in all its complexity and in its entire comprehension up to Man himself, without the aid of a Creator, and without the intervention of miracle. Sundry investigators and amateurs of science have accepted these scientific results, without a thought of the consequences they must have for religion and theology; while on the other hand theologians of modern views have looked with all the indifference of laymen, on the rising flood of scientific investigation, and cared not for their ecclesiastical

groundwork which was imperilled. Now surely was
the time to gather together all these scattered thoughts
—a piece of work possessed of such attractions for me
that I could no more forego it than I could my previous work. When day by day the prospect grows
brighter for our eventually demonstrating the conditions under which life has been developed in accordance with natural laws out of what was lifeless, and
consciousness out of the unconscious; when furthermore everything leads us more and more to conceive
of the Universe, Being, as a primitive *datum*, which
we cannot do away with even in thought; what then
becomes of the personal Creator, who is supposed to
have miraculously called into being the Universe,
and then the various orders of living things? Then,
in view of this theory of a strictly natural evolution
of things, what becomes of the church, whose whole
system of faith is based upon a miraculous beginning, (creation) a violent interruption, (fall of man)
and a specially miraculous resumption of the development of the world and of the human race? (redemption).

There is doubtless many a one who, while noting
the problem here presented, and perhaps solving it
for himself, has passed it by quietly, and therein
shown his prudence. One must not rouse the sleep-
ing lion, unless one is ready to fight with him for life
and death. Mankind have no doubt made great
advances in civilization. Not only may one now-a-
days affirm the revolution of the earth around the

sun without being imprisoned and put to the torture, but one may even deny the divinity of Christ without any risk of being burned at the stake. There is a limit however. No man is now burned alive for seeing in Jesus only a mere man, for refusing to acknowledge God's personality, for not believing in a future life, or for declining to attach himself in the present life to any christian organization of what creed soever: but yet these things are noted down against him, and when he brings his views and the arguments for them before the public, he finds himself in disgrace. He has set himself above the conventional fashions of thought and life, has offended against good taste, and must not be surprised if people in dealing with him leave good taste out of consideration. As an author he is thenceforth outlawed; he must not expect ever again to have shown him what under any other circumstances would be his right by a sort of *Jus gentium* in literary warfare. This I learned by experience after the publication of my Life of Jesus, and this I am now learning again.

Here is seen again how much of our modern civilization is made up merely of forms of speech. Is there anything that we have heard oftener repeated, or with greater emphasis, for some years past, than this, that now-a-days the point is not what a man believes, but how he behaves; as regards the writer, not what he teaches men to believe, but how he instructs them to act? Very well; but now comes one

who takes all this in earnest, and who sincerely
believes that a man's creed is no longer taken into
account. He removes certain pillars of the Faith,
which he has found to be in a state of decay, without
however offering to mankind anything new with
regard to moral conduct; simply exhorting them
to the practice of much the same virtues they regarded as sacred before, though from somewhat less
selfish motives. Surely the man will not be molested
on account of what he has said, but will be treated
with as much respect as ever before. Undoubtedly
he would, if our boasted liberality were anything
more than a mere phrase! On the public highway
of literature, whoever will may load him with abuse.
I make no complaint, however, against the gentlemen who write literary criticisms. Accustomed and
necessitated as they are to live from hand to mouth,
they commonly think more of delivering a brilliant
judgment about a particular point, than of appreciating a coherent system of the universe; old and
new, faith and enlightenment, are in their minds
sometimes wonderfully harmonized; and owing to
the press of occupations their brains become as contracted as their closets. Then, too, from year's end
to year's end they find themselves tied down to all
sorts of considerations—deference to eminent Masters,
or to influential cliques, or to dominant prejudices,
etc., and it must be a real pleasure for them to ccme
across a writer whom they may treat *sans ceremonie*,
whom they may abuse to their hearts' content, with

the full consent of the mass of their readers. But as I have said, I do not complain of these gentlemen, though I cannot esteem it either brave or generous, to attack a man just because the bystanders will not lift a hand to save him.

Thus then a number of critics have again enjoyed hearty satisfaction at my expense. Their contest with me exalts them into the cheeriest frame of mind, so easily is it carried on under existing circumstances. One need not be particular as to the thrusts he makes at his adversary, when partial galleries are the judges of the combat. For instance, when I observe, with regard to Jesus' teaching, among other points this, that instead of ennobling the acquisition of wealth by subordinating it to higher aims, it spurns it in advance, and evinces no conception of·its agency in promoting civilization and enlightenment— one has only to say with Herr Dove that I "expect the founder of a religion to give counsel about money-matters," or, with still finer wit, to speak of "Jesus' hopeless unfitness to be a dealer in stocks;" and then of course I am sent to the ground amid the boisterous applause of the upper tier. Another case: the man who does not see that what I say about Lessing in section 86 comes warm from the heart, must be very obtuse. I will venture to say, Herr Dove is nothing of the kind, and yet he has the face, while enjoying a little sport at my expense, to talk of my "bowing and scraping before Lessing." And not alone the promising young man who in such sprightly fashion handles the helm of the *Im Neuen Reich*, but even the sedate old-catholic professor of Philosophy who writes for the *Allgemeine Zeitung* adopts the same tone when dealing with me. When, with a view to deter men from the commission of certain crimes, I favor the retention of the death penalty, the professor playfully insists that the same argument would justify the barbarous practice of putting criminals to death slowly—a punishment which would inspire far greater terror than instantaneous death. I am confident that in his heart Herr Huber knows very well that this does not follow, and that besides death, that *ultima linea rerum*, nothing more is needed to inspire fear—least of all anything which, by blunting human feeling, would produce as much mischief in the contrary direction, as simply capital punishment could produce good : all this, I say, Herr Huber of course knows perfectly well, but still he judges the argument good enough to employ against his esteemed adversary. If my memory is not at fault it is the reviewer of the Hamburg *Correspondent* who has so low an opinion of my book that he says it is just the thing to read over your coffee and cigar. Well, it was never composed amid such surroundings, and I will not venture to decide whether they would help a man in the understanding of it ; but the utterances of the critics are to a great extent of such a kind as to justify one in thinking that they are not unconnected with coffee and cigars. The English Premier does not appear to have taken

up my book in so trifling a spirit, for not long
since he found it worth his while, in a speech delivered at Liverpool, to controvert its positions at
length. Mr. Gladstone has not understood me quite
correctly, and attacks me after a fashion which even
to many of my German critics will appear weak;
but my countrymen might learn from this foreigner
how the earnest candid statesman recognizes earnestness and candor even in a writer whose work he regards as pernicious, and how the true gentleman speaks
of a man who, as he must admit, has devoted a long
life to the investigation of truth and sacrificed to the
profession of what appears to him to be truth, all his
prospects in life. In like manner, what the *Daily
News* says in opposition to Gladstone's speech, shows
more understanding and more genuine tact than anything that has yet appeared in German publications
with reference to my book.*

Inasmuch as my renunciation of the current religion is based, indirectly at least, on the data of Natural Science, the aim of my opponents must be to
remove that ground from under me and to show that
the great authorities in that department of knowledge
are by no means on my side. Almost simultaneously
with my work appeared Dubois-Reymond's essay on
the Limits of Natural Science, and in various quarters this was held up before me like Minerva's shield

* The "Kritik gegen Kritik" (*criticism* vs. *criticism*) of the
Allgemeine Zeitung, and the notice in the *Deutsche Presse* came
to hand only after these pages were written.

with the Gorgon's head. Herr Dove, in allusion to that work, adopts for his review of my book, the motto, "Confession or Discretion ?"—as though he should say : Look, good reader : on the one side you have a great Student of Nature, who is so modest and discreet as to say that his knowledge extends to a certain point, and who lets you believe as you please beyond that limit ; and on the other side a reputed philosopher who, regardless of such limitations, would push his confession of infidelity out beyond. This limitation established by Dubois-Reymond Herr Dove holds himself justified in calling by the flattering title of "a Kantian performance." In Kant's times too, there were not wanting individuals who welcomed the critical limitation of the Reason, in hopes that now on the outer side of the boundary they could without hindrance chase every phantom of ancient faith and superstition. Of course Kant himself would have nothing to do with this kind of adherents ; the Critic of Reason had no thought of ever promoting the interests of stagnant reason. In like manner I doubt if Dubois-Reymond ever intended to leave room outside of the line he has drawn, not only for ancient dualism, but also for his young admirer's dreams about the pre-existence and transmigration of souls.

At least the fundamental proposition of all Dualism viz.: the regarding of body and soul as two different substances appears to our Scientist as purely erroneous. In conclusions so utterly at variance with

the reality as the Cartesio-Leibnitzian theories with
regard to the concurrence of mind and body he recognizes "an apagogical demonstration against the correctness of the suppositions which led to them."
With Fechter he thinks that in his simile of two
watches Leibnitz forgot one very simple supposition,
viz: that possibly the two watches whose concordant
motion is to be explained, are after all only one.
The derivation of the organic from the inorganic Dubois-Reymond holds to be scientifically demonstrable,
as I gather from his earlier writings. "It is a mistake," says he in his latest essay, "to see in the first
appearance of living beings on the earth anything
supernatural or indeed anything more than an extremely difficult problem in mechanics." So then
the limit of our knowledge of Nature is not here;
but there is a point where the thread is broken, where
we must acknowledge our ignorance, our enduring
ignorance even. That point is, where consciousness
comes in ; not the consciousness of the human mind,
but consciousness in its widest sense, including its
lowest grades.

"Essentially," says he, almost in the words of
Voltaire, "it is no more difficult to conceive of the
most exalted mental activity, than of the lowest
grade of consciousness, sensation, as being the result
of material conditions: with the first feeling of pleasure or pain experienced at the beginning of animal
life by the most elementary creature, an impassable
chasm was made."

There are three points in the ascending evolution of Nature to which more particularly the note of the Inconceivable appears to attach. They are the three questions: How did the living spring from the lifeless, the sensible from the senseless, the reasoning from the irrational?—and they all three equally baffle the mind, and extort from it the old explication for all perplexities, God. The scientist of whom we are speaking, holds as we have seen, that the difficulty as to the first point is not insuperable—the evolution of the organic out of the inorganic appears to him conceivable. At one time, as he tells us, he thought he recognized the limit of our knowing only in the third point, i. e., in the problem of free-will, which would be a corollary of Reason. At that time therefore, the second problem, that of consciousness or sensation, must have been held by him capable of solution.

I am very sure that a man of science like Dubois-Reymond, would never consent to be made an *authority* of as he is by Herr Dove. The true thinker is always pleased when others too *think* over his words. I would therefore say candidly, that as far as I can see, these three questions are alike as regards their being solvable or insolvable. If faith is justified in bringing in God and miracle in all three cases, then science has the right to try and make this intervention unnecessary. Nor does Dubois-Reymond after all controvert this position: all he says is, that Science can aid us in the first, and in the third point, but that she can give us no assistance nor ever even expect to, as regards the second. I confess, I could more readily understand what was meant, were some one to say; A (*i. e.* life) is, and must ever be inexplicable; but supposing A once granted, B and C (i. e., sensation and thought) follow of course, that is to say by natural development. Or suppose it read : A and B are conceivable, but at C (self-consciousness) our understanding fails us. Either of these statements, as I have said, appears to me to be more tenable at first sight and in general, than the other which would make the middle stadium only impassable.

The first of the three problems *i. e.* the origin of Life is held by the Natural Science of our day to be solvable, it being, in the words of Dubois-Reymond, a difficult problem, yet simply a mechanical one. It involves a mode of motion different from any we are acquainted with, and far more complex, but yet simply motion, and so involves nothing that is absolutely new or fundamentally different from known modes of motion. As for the third problem—that of Reason and freedom of the will—our author appears to find its solution in the fact that it is most intimately connected with the second, Reason being only the highest stage of consciousness.

But as regards the insolvability of that second problem he expresses himself thus: The most accurate knowledge of the essential soul-organism reveals to us only matter in motion: but be-

tween this material movement and my feeling pain
or pleasure, experiencing a sweet taste, seeing red,
etc., with the conclusion *"therefore I exist,"* there is a
profound gulf; and it remains " utterly and forever
inconceivable why to a number of atoms of carbon,
hydrogen, etc., it should not be a matter of indifference how they lie, or how they move : nor can we in
any wise tell how consciousness should result from
their concurrent action." Whether these *Verba
Magistri* are indeed the " last word" on the subject,
time only can tell. I can accept the doctrine provisionally without essential injury to my position, for
what says Dubois-Reymond further ?

The question, says he, whether mental operations
will ever be for us intelligible by means of material
conditions is a very different one from that other,
whether these operations are not in themselves the results of material conditions. Now even if you with our
author reply to the first question in the negative, still
the other remains unanswered, as it is by no means
negatived with the first. On the contrary, in accordance with the familiar principle of investigation, that
the simplest theory as to the cause of a phenomenon is
to have the preference until proved false, our thought
will ever incline to an affirmative answer to the question. For if we had but a conception of the essential
nature of Matter and Force—which according to Dubois-Reymond constitutes the second, or rather the first
limit of Natural Science—then too should we understand " how the substance underlying them might

sense, and desire and think." We shall of course
never clear up these matters ; but the more absolutely the investigator of Nature recognizes this double
limitation of his science, the freer will he be, without
the illusions of dogmas and philosophemata, to construct his notions of the relations between mind and
matter inductively. He will clearly perceive the
multifarious dependences of man's mental life on his
organic constitution : no theological prejudice will
hinder him, like Descartes, from seeing in the souls
of brutes souls kindred to that of man, members of
the same evolutionary series, though standing at a
lower level. Finally he would be led by the Theory
of Descent, coupled with the Doctrine of Natural Selection, to hold that what is called Soul, came into
existence as the gradually resulting effect of certain
material conditions and that, like other heritable gifts
of service in the struggle for existence, it has gone
on advancing and perfecting itself through a long series of generations.

Here the question arises, can it be the intention
of a scientist who uses this language, that obsolete
hypotheses and defunct dogmas should find a new
resting-place beyond the limits of exact Natural
Science, as placed by him? Why he fires a regular
bomb-shell into these regions out beyond the signal-
lights! Even in his famous Leipsic discourse, he says
that no man must reproach the investigator of Nature
with recognizing in plants no soul-life, on the ground
that they possess no nervous system. " But what,"

continues the orator, " if before assenting to the notion of a World-Soul, he were to demand that you point out to him somewhere in the Universe a system of ganglia and nerves, imbedded in neurilemma, and nourished with arterial blood under due pressure, and corresponding in its comprehensiveness to the mental power of such a soul?" I am very careful not to attribute to any one, least of all to so distinguished a man as Dubois-Reymond, a thought which he does not distinctly avow; but he can make no objection if I on my own account make an application of his sentence to the question of a Personal God.

The remaining objections brought on scientific grounds against my work, are of minor importance. As for the scientific specialists, none of them have as yet expressed an opinion, and I confidently await their judgment. But whatever further objections have been urged, have chiefly to do with certain breaks in the demonstration of Nature's gradual evolution—a circumstance which is to be accounted for, partly by the unavoidable brevity of my exposition, partly by the insufficiency of the observations hitherto made, and partly too, by the imperfection of all human knowledge. Sometimes also, instances have been cited as disregarded by me, though in fact I had *not* overlooked them at all, but simply regarded them as of no special importance. Thus Olbers's assertion that supposing the number of worlds, of fixed stars, to be infinite, then the whole

firmament would radiate as much light and heat as
the sun.   Here, however, even the man who is no
astronomer, Prof. Huber, for instance, can see quite as
well as I, that though the number be infinite, the infinite distance of the stars diminishes their light.   As
for Clausius's calculation, that eventually all the
motion in the Universe will suffer impairment, I
am not in " direct contradiction" with it, as this critic
affirms; I contradict it only indirectly, for in my
view cessation of movement is on the one hand an
incident of the individual worlds, and on the other, is
but a transition state   like everything else in
the Universe that is conditioned.   Certain more or
less gross misconceptions entertained by my critics,
particularly with regard to the Darwinian Theory, I
leave to the special expounders of that theory for
correction.   For the rest, it was not without a purpose that in the title of my work, I opposed to the
old Faith not a new knowledge, but a new Faith.
In constructing a comprehensive view of the Universe, which shall take the place of the church's
equally comprehensive Faith, we not only may take
what is inductively demonstrable, but to this we
must append whatever postulates or consequences
the mind requires to complete the system.   With
the like intent I called my book a Confession, and
this affords me opportunity for bestowing some
attention on the theological objections that have
been urged against the work.

First then it is charged—particularly by Herr

Huber in the Allgemeine Zeitung—that in this later work I have "apostatized" from my earlier and higher estimate of the person of Jesus and of Christianity. Now apostasy, as this lively champion of Old Catholicism must know from home experience, usually is the result of very definite motives. It commonly takes a direction the reverse of that taken by me, retreating from some extreme and exposed ground to one that is more defensible and less dangerous. My apostasy, therefore, which took the contrary direction, could find its extrinsic motive only in the fact that, at most, certain considerations which once restrained me had now lost their force. But in fact the case was otherwise; in the composition of those earlier writings I enjoyed the same complete independence as I do to-day. The supposed apostasy must therefore proceed from purely intrinsic grounds, in consequence of a change in my convictions; and here was no occasion for self-reproach. But the simple fact is that there is no apostasy in the case at all.

True, in my earlier writings and also particularly in the new revision of the Life of Jesus, I was at great pains to collect into one image the scattered touches found in the gospels, so as to present a picture of Jesus possessing a human interest. My adversaries found the likeness I drew faint and shadowy, and demanded more life-like and definite lineaments, while I on the other hand was fain to confess to myself that, considering how little we really know of

Jesus, the lines were far too bold and distinct. Therefore was it that in the last part of my book I com-
plained of the meagreness and uncertainty of our historical information about Jesus, and said that no well
instructed and candid person would say me nay when
I affirmed that "there are but few great historical
personages of whom we have such unsatisfactory information as of him." Even at that period Jesus'
discourses about his return in the clouds annoyed me,
nor could I but with labored and specious argument
defend him against the reproach of fanaticism and
self-glorification. Finally, when in my latest work I
consider Jesus in the light of the Centre and Stay of
our religious life, I find there are chiefly two reasons
why he cannot be so regarded : first, he cannot be
the centre, for our knowledge of him is too fragmentary ; then he cannot be the stay, for what we do
know about him indicates a person of fantastic fanaticism. In all this there is clearly no apostasy but only
the normal result attending the development of scientific convictions, viz. that now I gave full swing to
certain reflections which previously I thought I
could push aside.

For some people you cannot repeat a thing too
often, and so I recur again to a point already referred
to. I have no intention of disputing that Jesus was
an extraordinary man. What I hold is only this : It
is not because of what he was, but because of what
he was not; not because of the truth he taught, but
on the strength of a prediction which was not fulfilled,

and which therefore was not true, that he has been made the central point of a church, of a cult. So soon as we see that he was not that because of which he was raised to such a position, then we have no further ground, nor even, if we would be truthful, any right to belong to such a church. Mere human excellence even at its highest perfection—sinlessness disappeared simultaneously with supernaturalism and is henceforth to be classed as fraud—gives no title to ecclesiastical veneration ; least of all can it give such title when, having its root in conditions and in spheres of thought which are remote from ours, and to some extent the reverse of ours, it grows daily less fitted to be the pattern for our lives and our thoughts.

That with such views in regard to the person of Jesus that person can no longer be the object of religious faith, was my conviction full thirty years ago, as expressed in my " Dogmatik." Even so early as then I held it to be an error to " suppose that the mere moral teaching of Jesus, including his doctrine concerning God and retribution, constitutes Christianity ; for it is an essential character of that system to regard us as in relation with these ideas only through the mediation of Christ, and to resign into his hands every thing noble that adds dignity to man, and every suffering that afflicts him, in order to get them back again in the shape of grace and mercy. He who has outgrown this idea of self-abnegation, which is the essence of Christianity, may have *his reasons*

indeed for calling himself a Christian, but *reason* for
the name he has none." The question as to our relation to Christianity, Herr Dove puts in this form,
whether the religious movement which began with
Jesus still extends so unmistakably to our views of
the world and of life as to justify us in coupling with
his name our religious principles. But this is not
one but two questions, one of which may be answered affirmatively, the other negatively. That the religious movement which began with Jesus goes on in
our own time, no one will deny—though with every
decade of years it comes in conflict more and more
plainly with the truths of Science and with the practical maxims of modern times. The phrase "coupling with his name our religious principles," is far
from saying all that is required in this case. The
question is whether we can still honor him with a
cultus, or consider him as the head of a special arrangement for procuring salvation : and I hold that,
from our standpoint, such views are no longer justifiable.

When the author of the notice in the *Allgemeine
Zeitung* perceives that I do not bestow praise on
some special good quality of the Christian system,
he is ready with the explanation that I have no
capacity for appreciating it. For example, the services rendered by Christianity in the moral culture
of the race. But I have not failed to speak of these
services ; and if I did not treat of them at greater
length, it was because the object of my work did not

require it. The book is, as I have said, a Confession, not a historical essay. The question I had to do with was not, What has Christianity done for the race? but, Be its past action what it will—and it will act on in any case—can one who is possessed of certain convictions continue to adhere to it as to a church? I might make a similar reply to the charge brought against me by the critic of the Cologne *Zeitung*, viz. that I make no account of the importance of the imagination in religion. As to whether I am capable of appreciating this importance, I would refer Herr Bacmeister to one work of mine among others, that on Reimarus. But he who has seen what an important *rôle* the imagination plays in religion, has left religious illusion far behind; and whether now those who are freed from such illusions, are forever to go on acting as though they were under their influence, is the question raised in my book.

As has been already observed, the reviewer in the *Weser Zeitung* looks on my book as a declaration of war against the Protestant League and Old-Catholicism. He even adds that I " very categorically deny the right of either to exist." And yet I had to do with either the League or with Old Catholicism only incidentally; and when in the Introduction I admitted that the vast majority of the malcontents, and of those who are striving to advance, belong to these two parties, I think that by that very admission, I conceded their historic right to exist. This right can only rest on the fact that, for a large number of people in these days, the force of advancing knowledge on the one hand, and on the other the weight of old convictions and habits, find their equilibrium just at the point which answers to Old-Catholicism and the Protestant League. But if I do not place myself and those of one mind with me at either of these stand-points, the reason simply is that I deny to both the logical right to exist, *i. e.*, I hold them to be only transition stages beyond which we have passed as our views developed.

The objection is urged that while all this may be true enough of individuals, it does not hold for the majority; that we must not break with this majority of our fellow-men, must not sever the sacred tie of religious association which binds us to them. " Why" asks Herr Dove, " Why do we, who have banished far away from us every phantom of Revelation and Miracle, attach so much importance to the name of Christian? The reason is, says he, " because we would not break away from those of our brethren who still anxiously cling to all these phantoms as though they were something real; and because we see in them Christians still, not in that they believe in these phantoms, but in spite of such belief." But once make the experiment of addressing those Christian brethren in that strain; tell them candidly and plainly that you regard Revelation and Miracle to be phantoms; that you hold themselves however to be Christians "notwithstanding" their beliefs--

and see if they will thenceforth reckon you as of their Church. In short, unless backed by *accomodatio*, by disguise and secrecy, by manifold deception, in a word by falsehood, such compromises are bound to fail ; but if honesty and truthfulness must rule any where, surely it must be in the domain of religion. In politics compromise is indispensable ; but there it does not of necessity imply deceit or falsehood, because in political affairs we are not concerned about convictions but about measures, not about the true but about the useful.

" I can understand," wrote Dahlmann to Gervinus, on occasion of the latter's work on the Mission of the German Catholics.* " I can understand how one might live without a church ; I so live myself, although I would it were otherwise. But how one can build up a church simply on Christian morals, I cannot so readily understand. It appears to me that those (clergymen) who themselves cleave to Christ ; who preach about the mysteries of his birth and resurrection and about his promises ; and the believing multitude who listen, constitute the church ; and when we others go in and out we cause a draught, but bring no warmth." This is precisely what I myself think, all but the wish it were otherwise. We have quit the church in a perfectly honorable way, and here outside of it we lack nothing : why then should we complain that we are not within ? This very thing, viz., the desire of firmly impressing on

---

* Seceders from Roman Catholic Church (1845).

our minds what we possess even without a Church, and so counteracting that "wish it were otherwise," was my chief motive in the composition and publication of my Confession. To the same end I recounted the incredible and contradictory dogmas we left behind when we quit the church, and the crucifixion of reason and truthfulness which we escaped when we took that step. But still these arguments were, as I have declared over and over again, never intended to make living in the church unpleasant to any man who chooses to remain there. We only desired to form a definite and coherent idea for ourselves as to the grounds of our separation from her. The purpose was, not controversy with those who differ, but an understanding with those who agree with us.

I wanted however, to make those who agree with me recognize not alone what we have, but also what we still lack. In laying before them a statement of our then possessions in the way of knowledge and opinions, of excitements and appeasements, I wished to call their attention to points where there is need of further light, and to induce them, on their part, to contribute to the common stock of knowledge. Not only are there still great gaps in our theory of the universe, we are still more backward in our doctrine of duty and virtue. Here I could only indicate the places where the foundation stones are to be laid, rather than point to a completed structure. The reason of this is that we are in practice accustomed to fall back upon our old notions, and half unconsciously to derive from them the motives of our conduct. But we must become and remain clearly conscious of the untenable character of these notions, so that we shall be compelled to look for and find the firm grounds of our moral conduct in man's nature as known to us, and not in any pretended superhuman revelation.

The natural effort of our times to sever the tie between church and state; the inevitable breaking up of state churches into sects and free societies, must at no distant period make it possible for numbers of citizens to belong to no church at all, even externally. The course of mental development especially for the past ten years has favored the formation of such groups; and the more purely they act out themselves, and the less they stultify themselves by concessions to others' views, the more beneficial will be their influence on mental and moral culture in general. There is no necessity in the world for our interfering with one another: there is nothing to hinder our standing up like men and getting our rights. The right to do just this was all I demanded in my Confession, with regard to which I still hold that in it I did a good work and earned the thanks of a less biased future. The day will come, as it came for the Life of Jesus, when my book shall be understood,—only this time I shall **not live** to see it.

THE OLD FAITH AND THE NEW.

1.

THE great politico-military movement which, in the course of the last six years, has transformed the internal and external relations of Germany, has been promptly followed by one of an ecclesiastical character, which evinces tendencies scarcely less militant.

In the accession of power which seemed to accrue to Protestantism in consequence of Austria's exclusion by Prussia and the formation of the North German Confederation, Roman Catholicism recognized a summons to declare the Pope infallible and to concentrate in his hands its entire ecclesiastico-secular authority. Within the pale of the Catholic Church itself, however, the new dogma encountered resistance, which has since assumed distinct shape in the party of the so-called Old Catholics; while the recently founded

German Executive seems determined at last, after a too protracted *laissez faire,* inherited from the Prussian policy of the last thirty years, vigorously to repel these menacing ecclesiastical encroachments.

In view of this perturbation in the Catholic Church, the Protestant may for the moment appear the more stable of the two. Nevertheless, it is not without an internal fermentation of its own; the difference consisting in the fact that, from the nature of its creed, this partakes more of the character of a religious than of a politico-ecclesiastical movement. At bottom, nevertheless, a dogmatic and religious difference of opinions underlies the antagonism between the hierarchical tendency of the old consistorial government on the one hand, and the democratic character of those efforts which aim at establishing a synodical constitution on the other. The contest between Lutheran orthodoxy and the Unionists, and still more, the men of the Protestant League, is, in fact, one concerning religious questions, concerning irreconcilable conceptions of Christianity and of Protestantism itself. If this Protestant agitation does not attract as much notice as the Catholic, it is solely due to the fact that questions directly bearing on political power naturally make more ado than those which concern faith, so long as the latter continue merely subjects of theological dispute.

Be this as it may : on every side people are at least stirring, speaking out, preparing for conflict; only we, it seems, remain silent and look on with folded arms.

What means this We ? For at present surely it is but a simple *I* which speaks, and one which, moreover, so far as yet appears, without allies, without adherents, occupies a singularly isolated position.

Oh, much less than that; this *I* has not even a position, and exercises only the degree of influence which the world may be willing to concede to its mere word. And this again applies only to the written and printed word; for it has neither the ability nor the inclination to address meetings, or become the itinerant missionary of its convictions. But it is possible to be without position and yet not prostrate; to belong to no society and yet not to stand alone. If I say We, I know that I am entitled to do so. The We I mean no longer counts only by thousands. True, we do not constitute a church, a congregation, or even a society ; but we know the reason why.

Innumerable assuredly is the multitude of those

who are no longer satisfied with the old faith, the old church, be it Protestant or Catholic; of those who either dimly apprehend, or distinctly perceive, the contradiction into which both are forced more and more with the knowledge, the view of life and the world, the social and political growths of the present age, and who in consequence regard a change, a modification, as an urgent necessity.

At this point, however, the mass of the dissatisfied and the progressive divide. One party—and undeniably it forms the great majority in both confessions—considers it sufficient to lop off the notoriously decayed branches of the ancient tree in hopes of thereby imparting to it fresh vitality and fruitfulness. Here people will let the Pope pass, only he must not be infallible; there they are quite ready to keep fast hold of Christ, but let him no longer be proclaimed the Son of God. In the main, however, both churches are to continue as they were: the one shall retain its priests and bishops set apart from the laity as consecrated dispensers of the ecclesiastical means of grace; the other, although with an elective clergy and a constitution prescribed by itself, must continue preaching Christ, the distribution of the sacraments as by him ordained, the celebration of the festivals, which serve to retain the chief events of his life in our memory.

Side by side with this majority there exists, however, a minority not to be overlooked. These lay great stress upon the mutual dependence of parts in the ecclesiastical system, in short, on logical sequence. They consider that if you once admit a distinctive difference between clergy and laity, if you admit a need inherent in mankind of always obtaining infallible teaching in religion and morals, from an authority instituted by God himself through Christ, you must likewise be prepared to give your adherence to the dogma of an infallible pope, as one equally required by this need. And in like manner, if you no longer consider Jesus as the Son of God, but as a man, however excellent, they think that you are no longer justified in praying to him, in cleaving to him as the centre of a cultus, in year after year preaching about his actions, his fortunes, and his utterances; more especially when you discern the most important of these actions and incidents to be fabulous, while those utterances and teachings are recognized by you as for the most part irreconcilable with our actual views of life and the universe. And if this minority thus notes the giving way of the close circle of ecclesiastical dogma, it confesses to not seeing what further needs a *cultus* still subserves, and proceeds to call in question the use of a distinct society like the church existing by the side of the state and the school, of science and art, the common property of all.

The minority which holds these opinions constitutes the We in whose name I undertake to speak.

2.

But it is a fact that no influence can be exercised on the world if we do not hold together, arrive at the knowledge of each other's convictions, and act according to these convictions with united strength. We ought thus, it would seem, in opposition to the old and new ecclesiastical societies, to found a non-ecclesiastical, a purely humanitarian or rationalistic one. This, however, we have not done, and where a few try to effect something of the kind they make themselves ridiculous. *We* need not be scared at this, as we have but to do better. Such is the opinion of many, but it is not ours. We rather recognize a contradiction in the idea of abolishing one society by instituting another. If we would demonstrate the inutility of a church, we must not establish a something which would itself be a sort of church.

Nevertheless, we would and should come to a mutual understanding. This, however, we can effect in our time without a distinct organization.

We have public speaking, and above all, we have the press. It is through this latter medium that I now try to come to an understanding with the rest of those I call *We*. And this medium is quite sufficient for all those purposes which we at present can have in view. For the present we wish no change whatever in the world at large. It does not occur to us to wish to destroy any church, as we know that a church is still a necessity for a large majority. For a new constructive organization (not of a church, but after the latter's ultimate decay, a fresh co-ordination of the ideal elements in the life of nations), the times seem to us not yet ripe. But neither do we wish to repair or prop up the old structures, for we discern in these a hindrance to the process of transformation. We would only exert our influence so that a new growth should in the future develop of itself from the inevitable dissolution of the old. For this end — mutual understanding without formal organization — the inspiriting power of free speech will be found to suffice.

I am well aware that what I purpose delineating

in the following pages is known to multitudes as well as to myself, to some even much better. A few have already spoken out on the subject. Am I therefore to keep silence ? I think not. For do we not all supply each other's deficiencies ? If another is better informed as regards many things, I may perhaps be as to some; while others again are known and viewed by me in a different light. Out with it, then ! let my colours be displayed, that it may be seen whether they are genuine or not.

To this I may add something more as regards myself personally. It is now close upon forty years that as a man of letters I have laboured in the same direction, that I have fought on and on for that which has appeared to me as truth, and still more perhaps against that which has appeared to me as error ; and in the pursuit of this object I have attained, nay, overstepped the threshold of old age. I have reached the time when every earnest-minded man hears the whisper of an inner voice : " Give an account of thy stewardship, for thou mayest be no longer steward."

Now I am not conscious of having been an unjust steward. An unskilful one at times, too probably also a negligent one, I may, heaven knows, have been ; but on the whole I have done what the strength and

impulse within prompted me to do, and have done
it without looking to the right or left, without
currying the favour or shunning the displeasure of
any. But what is it that I have done? No doubt
one has in one's own mind a certain unity of conception, but usually this finds only a fragmentary
kind of expression: now do these fragments also necessarily cohere from some inherent connection? In
the ardour of the moment we shatter much that is
old, but have we something new in readiness which
we can substitute in place of it?

This accusation of merely destroying without
reconstructing is perpetually cast in the teeth of
those who labour in this direction. In a certain
sense I care not to defend myself against this accusation; only that I do not acknowledge it as
such. For I have already pointed out that it never
lay in my intention to immediately construct anything external, simply because I do nót judge the time
for such action to have arrived. Our concern for
the moment is with an inward preparation, a preparation moreover of those who feel themselves no longer
satisfied with the old, no longer to be appeased by
half measures.

I have never desired, nor do I now desire to
disturb the contentment or the faith of any one.

But where these are already shaken, I desire to point out the direction in which I believe a firmer soil is to be found.

This, as I take it, can be no other than that which we call the modern Cosmic conception, the result painfully educed from continued scientific and historical research, as contrasted with that from Christian theology. But it is precisely this modern Cosmic conception, as it commends itself to me, to which I have hitherto given fragmentary and allusive expression, but never as yet an ample and explicit one. I have not yet adequately endeavoured to prove whether this conception is possessed of a firm basis, of the capacity of self-support, of unity and consistency with itself. The effort to do this I acknowledge to be a debt which I owe, not only to others, but to myself. We are apt to combine many things half-dreamily in our own minds which, when called upon to give them distinct outlines in the form of words and sentences, we discover to be wholly incoherent. Neither do I, by any means, pledge myself that this attempt will prove successful throughout, that some gaps, some contradictions will not remain. But from the fact that I shall not try to hide these latter, the inquirer may recognise the honesty of my purpose, and by reflecting on

these matters himself he will be in a position to
judge on which side exist more of the obscuri-
ties and insufficiencies unavoidable in human
speculation, whether on the side of the ancient
orthodoxy or on that of modern science.

3.

I shall, therefore, have a double task to perform;
first, to expound our position towards the old
creed, and then the fundamental principles of that
new Cosmic conception which we acknowledge as
ours.

The creed is Christianity. Our first question
therefore resolves itself into how and in what
sense we still are Christians. Christianity is a
definite form of religion, the generic essence of
which is distinct from any form; it is possible to
have severed oneself from Christianity and still to be
religious. Out of this first question therefore arises
the next, whether we still possess religion. Our
second leading question concerning the new Cosmic conception also, upon examination, resolves
itself into two. In the first place, we would know
in what this Cosmic conception consists, on what
evidence it rests, and what especially, as compared with the old ecclesiastical view, are its

characteristic principles. And in the second place we would learn whether this modern Cosmic conception performs the same services as did the Christian dogma for its votaries, whether it performs them better or worse, whether it is more or less adapted to serve as a basis on which to erect the structure of a life truly human, that is to say truly moral, and because moral, happy.

We ask, therefore, in the first place :

ARE WE STILL CHRISTIANS?

4.

CHRISTIANS in what sense? For the word at present has a diverse meaning, not only in regard to the confessions themselves, but still more in view of the various gradations now extant between faith and rationalism. It will be taken for granted, after what has been said, that we are no longer Christians in the sense attached to the term by the ancient creed of any denomination; and whether we shall be able to yield our assent to any of the diverse *nuances* assumed by the Christianity of the day, can with us be a question only in so far as it has reference to the most advanced and enlightened among them. Nevertheless, even as to this many things would remain incomprehensible if we had not, at least in its outlines, first brought the old Christian faith before our mind's eye; as only by aid of the pure aboriginal form will mixed forms be found possible of comprehension.

Would we know the nature of the old, unadulterated creed, and the effect it would produce upon us to-day, then let us not go to a modern theologian, even an orthodox one, with whom it already invariably appears in a diluted form; but let us draw it at the fountain-head, from one of the old confessions of faith. We will take that which is fundamentally the most ancient, and which still continues to be used by the Church, the so-called Apostles' Creed, while occasionally supplementing and elucidating it by later doctrinal definitions.

The Apostles' Creed is divided into three articles, according to the pattern of the Divine Trinity, the fundamental dogma of ancient orthodoxy. This Trinity itself it does not further express; but the later confessions of faith, the Nicene and the so-called Athanasian Creed, do this all the more. " The Catholic Faith," says the latter, " is this: That we worship one God in Trinity, and Trinity in Unity; neither confounding the Persons, nor dividing the Substance. For there is one Person of the Father, another of the Son, and another of the Holy Ghost: and yet all three are but one God."

It would really seem as if the more ignorant those old Christians were of all the facts of nature, the more brain-force they possessed for such like transcendental subtleties; for the kinds of claims on their reasoning faculties, which it simply paralyzes ours to recognize, such as conceiving of three as one and one as three, were a trifle to them, nay, a favourite pursuit, in which they lived and had their being, about which they could fight for centuries with all the weapons of acumen and of sophistry, but at the same time with a passion which did not shrink from violence and the shedding of blood.

One of the reformers even condemned to the stake a meritorious physician and naturalist, whose only weakness was that he could not let theology alone, for holding heretical notions as to this doctrine.

We moderns can no longer either excite or even interest ourselves about such a dogma; nay, we are only capable of conceiving the matter at all when we conceive something else in regard to it, *i.e.,* put an interpretation of our own upon it; instead of which, however, we shall do better to make clear to ourselves how the ancient Christians gradually came by so strange a doctrine. This, however, belongs to the church history, which also shows us in what manner Christians of more recent times again drifted away from this belief, for if still outwardly professed, it has nevertheless lost its former vitality even in circles otherwise orthodox.

5.

The first article of the Apostles' Creed simply
declares at once the belief in God the Almighty
Father, the maker of heaven and earth. We shall
have occasion to recur to this general conception
of a world-creating Deity, as being a primitive religious conception; now let us cast a glance at those
more particular definitions which the ecclesiastical
idea of creation derived from the biblical narrative
in the first chapter of Genesis, and which forthwith
became stereotyped articles of faith.

This is the famous doctrine of the six days' work,
according to which God did not create the world by
one simple act of volition once for all, but little by
little, according to the Jewish division of a week into
six days. If we accept this narrative as it stands,
if we conceive of it as a product of its time, comparing it with the traditions of creation or cosmogonies
which obtained among the ancients, then with all its
childishness we shall find it pregnant with sugges-
tion, and regard it with a mixture of pleasure and
respect. Nor shall we make it a reproach to the
old Hebrew prophet that he was ignorant of the
system of Copernicus, of the modern discoveries in
geology. How unjust to such a biblical narrative,

in itself dear and venerable, to thus petrify it into a dogma! For it becomes then at once a barrier, an obstructive rampart, against which the whole onset of progressive reason and all the battering rams of criticism now strike with passionate antipathy. So especially has it fared with the Mosaic cosmogony, which, once erected into a dogma, arrayed all modern science in arms against itself.

The order in which, according to its version, the creation of the various heavenly bodies succeeds each other, met with the strongest opposition. These, according to it, appear too late on the scene of action in every respect. The creation of the sun takes place on the fourth day only, when the changes of day and night, inconceivable with the sun omitted, are stated to have already taken place for three days. Moreover, the creation of the earth precedes that of the sun by several days, and to the latter as well as to the moon is ascribed a subordinate position with regard to the earth, while only casual mention is made of the stars : a perversion of the true relations governing heavenly bodies unbecoming a divinely-inspired account of the creation. A fact no less striking is the statement that God took no less than five days to create and fashion forth the earth, while for the making of

the sun, the whole starry host as well as the planets
—not such in the biblical narrative, it is true, but
merely lighted candles,—he allowed himself only
one day.

If such were the scruples of astronomy, geology
soon added others of no less moment. The sea
and earth are said to have been divided from
each other on the third day, and vegetation moreover created in all its forms; whereas our geologists now no longer speak of thousands but of
hundreds of thousands of years as having been
required by formative processes of this nature. On
the sixth day—excepting the fowl, which were made
on the one preceding it—all the beasts of the earth,
not omitting every creeping thing, and man himself
at the last, are said to have been called into being;
processes of growth for which, as shown by modern
science, periods of immeasurable duration were no
less requisite.

6.

Now there exist, it is true, not only theologians but
even naturalists of our own time who are prepared
with all sorts of little nostrums for cases of this sort.
That God made the sun three days after he had
already made the earth means, according to them,

that then for the first time it became visible to the
cloud-environed globe of earth; and the days,
although included unmistakably between sunset
and dawn, are explained as referring not to days
of twelve or twenty-four hours each, but as being
geological periods, capable of being extended to any
length that may be considered requisite.

He, however, who is seriously convinced of the
old Christian belief, ought on the contrary to say:
"A fig for science; thus it stands in the Bible, and the
Bible is the word of God." The Church, and more
especially the Protestant Church, takes this designation *au pied de la lettre*. The various books of
Holy Scripture were, it is admitted, written by
men, but these were not abandoned to their own
imperfect memory and fallacious reason, but God
himself (*i.e.* the Holy Spirit) was the inspirer
of these writings; and what God inspires must
be infallible truth. The narrative of these books is
therefore to be accepted with unqualified historical
assent, their teaching is no less unreservedly to be
received as the standard by which our actions and
our faith are to be regulated. There can be no
question in the Bible of false and contradictory
statements, of mistaken opinions and judgments.
Let reason recoil ever so much from what it relates

or would enjoin on us; when God speaks, then a modest silence can alone befit the mere human understanding.

"But what if Scripture were not the word of God?" Indeed; then explain how Isaiah could by merely human knowledge have predicted that Jesus should be the offspring of a virgin; how Micah could have foretold that he would be born at Bethlehem. How could the same Isaiah, a century and a half before the Persian Cyrus, have named him as the deliverer of the Jews from the Baby. lonian captivity, which had not then taken place ? How, without divine inspiration, could Daniel, in the days of Nebuchadnezzar and Cyrus, have foretold so many particular incidents in the history of Alexander the Great and his successors down to Antiochus Epiphanes ?

Alas! all this has now found but too satisfactory a solution—satisfactory for science that is to say, very unsatisfactory indeed for the old religion. Isaiah prophesying of the virgin's son, Micah with his ruler from Bethlehem, had not the most remote idea of our Jesus. The last third-part of the so-called prophecies of Isaiah proceeds from a contemporary of Cyrus, the entire book of Daniel from a contemporary of Antiochus, of whom therefore they could prophesy in a very human manner indeed, after or during the fulfilment of their predictions. Facts of a similar nature have long since been ascertained in regard to other books of the Bible: we no longer reckon a Moses, a Samuel, amongst its authors; the writings bearing their names have been recognized as compilations of much later date, into which older pieces of various epochs have been inserted with but small discernment and much deliberate design. It is known that in regard to the writings of the New Testament there has been a like result in the main, and of this we shall presently have occasion to give a more detailed account.

7.

We have already been led far away from the Apostles' Creed, but its first article is really too concise. Let us rather therefore take one more step in Genesis, the second and third chapters of which have, like the first, served as a basis for the Christian dogma. The history of creation is succeeded by the so-called Fall of Man: a point of far-reaching importance, as, in order to abolish its consequences, the Saviour was, in the course of time, to be sent into the world.

Here, as in the history of creation, we shall find

that in the ancient story we have to deal with a didactic poem, which, of itself deserving our esteem, has, on account of its erection into a dogma, had the misfortune to incur much misinterpretation, then censure and antagonism. The poet wishes to explain how all the evil and misery under which man suffers at present came into a world which God must undoubtedly have created good. The fault of God it cannot be, entirely man's it must not be. A tempter, therefore, is introduced, who persuades our first parents to transgress the divine commandment. This tempter is the serpent.

By it the author of the story simply meant the well-known mysterious animal of which remote antiquity could relate so many marvels; but subsequent Judaism and Christendom understood by it the devil, who having emigrated from the Zend religion into the Jewish, was destined to play so important a part in it, and one still more so in Christianity.

Only think of Luther, who lived and had his being in the doctrine of demonism. At every step he took, he fell foul of the arch-fiend. Not only evil thoughts and temptations, nay, even outward misfortunes to which man is subject, such as disease and sudden death, destructive fires and hailstorms, were ascribed by him to the immediate influence of the devil and his infernal crew. However undeniably this proves the low state of his scientific knowledge, as well as of his general culture, nevertheless the delusions of great men may occasionally assume grand proportions. Everybody knows Luther's utterance about the devils at Worms: " Were there as many of them as tiles upon the houses;" but on his way thither he had already had a tussle with the old enemy of mankind. While he was preaching, on his passage through Erfurt, the overcrowded church-gallery began to crack. Great was the dismay, a sudden panic and a consequent catastrophe might be apprehended. Then Luther from his pulpit began to thunder at the devil, whose hand he clearly recognized in the mischief, but whom he would counsel to bide quiet for the future ; and behold quiet is restored, and Luther able to conclude his sermon.

But who sups with the devil should have a long spoon. He could not be burned, fire being his element; but it was quite otherwise with those poor old women, who were reported to have wrought by his aid those very evils, such as maladies, hailstorms, etc., which Luther scrupled not to ascribe to Satan. And while trials for witchcraft form one of the most horrible and shameful records of Christianity, one of its ugliest features is the belief in the devil, and the degree in which this formidable caricature still rules people's minds or has been ejected thence, is a very fair measure of their civilization.

On the other hand, however, the removal of so essential a support is fraught with danger to the entire Christian edifice. Goëthe in his youth once remarked to Bahrdt, that this, if any, was a thoroughly biblical conception. If Christ, as St. John writes, appeared on earth in order to destroy the works of the devil, he might have been dispensed with if no devil had existed.

8.

But the serpent was not the only Hebrew symbol upon which a different construction was put by the Christian dogma. The author of the story wished to explain man's misery; the Christian interpretation made him first explain man's sinfulness. Again, he had actually understood physical death as that with which God punished the disobedience of our first parents; the Christian dogma understood it as signifying also spiritual death, *i.e.*, everlasting perdition. Through the fall of Adam and

Eve, sin, as well as damnation, is the inheritance of the whole human race.

This is the notorious doctrine of original sin, one of the pillars of Christendom. The Augsburg creed defines it thus : "After the fall of Adam all naturally begotten men (here a margin is left for the exceptional case of Christ) are born in sin, *i.e.*, without the fear of, or trust in, God, and with the propensity to evil; and further, this hereditary disease or fault constitutes in very deed a sin, even now bringing death everlasting to those not born again through baptism and the Holy Ghost."

On the plea of a corruption, therefore, of which the individual has not been himself the cause, of which neither is it given him to free himself of his own power, he is to be condemned, he and the entire progeny of a childish and inexperienced pair—not excepting even the innocent little ones who die unbaptized—to the everlasting torments of hell! It is astonishing how a conception equally revolting to man's reason and sense of justice, a conception which transforms God from an object of adoration and affection into a hideous and detestable being, could at any time, however barbarous, have been found acceptable, or how the casuistries by which people strove to modify its harshness could ever even have been listened to with common patience.

9.

But we shall be reminded here that Christ was sent into the world to cure the mischief caused by the devil, and thus are brought back to the Apostles' Creed, of which the second article, arising out of the first concerning God the Father, is as follows:

And I believe in Jesus Christ, His only Son our Lord; who was conceived by the Holy Ghost, born of the Virgin Mary, suffered under Pontius Pilate, was crucified, dead, and buried; He descended into hell; on the third day He rose again from the dead; He ascended into heaven, and sitteth at the right hand of God the Father Almighty; from thence He shall come again to judge the quick and the dead."

The singularity here is that of all the different points enumerated we at this day accord belief, nay, are only able to attach some sort of an idea to those which, as regards belief in the sense of dogma, have no specific value of their own, because they only predicate that of Christ which might equally apply to any man. What the only begotten Son of God the Father may be we no longer can tell. The " conceived of the Holy Ghost, born of the

Virgin Mary," savours of mythology, only that Greek incarnations appear to us more felicitously invented than this Christian one. The agony and crucifixion under Pontius Pilate, we, as before mentioned, have no desire to dispute, as not unlikely in itself, and having moreover the Roman historian's testimony in its support. All the more wonderful is that which now follows. The descent into hell is not attested by even one Evangelist. On the other hand, they all bear testimony to the resurrection, but not one of them was an eyewitness, and it is described in a different manner by all; in short, attested like any other event that we are compelled to regard as unhistorical. And what sort of an event? One so impossible, in such direct antagonism to every law of nature, that it would require a testimony of tenfold reliability to be as much as discussed, not scouted from the very first. Finally, comes the ascension into heaven, where we know the heavenly bodies, but no longer the throne of God at whose right hand it would be possible to sit; then the return to judgment on the day of doom, a thing which we can form no idea of, as we admit either no divine judgment, or only such as fulfils itself hour by hour and day by day.

These, however, are not the fantastic notions of a later creed, but, like the devil himself, emphatically the doctrines of the New Testament.

10.

The second article of the Apostles' Creed is termed by the abridged Lutheran Catechism that of the scheme of salvation, and it therefore comments upon it especially from this point of view. It speaks of Christ as Him " who has redeemed me, a lost and ruined man, and delivered me from all sin, from death and the power of Satan, not by silver and gold, but by His sacred precious blood and His sinless agony and death."

This is the only genuine ecclesiastical conception of a Redeemer and his redemption. We, by the fall of our first parents, as well as by our own sin, had deserved death and everlasting damnation, had already been delivered to the dominion of Satan, but Jesus came, took upon himself death in its most painful form, bore the Divine wrath in our stead, and in consequence delivered us—if only we will believe in him and the efficacy of his death—from the punishment which was our due, or at least from its principal feature, eternal damnation.

Luther contrasts this death, by means of which

Christ ransomed us, with gold and silver, which could have accomplished nothing. But these, although biblical expressions, no longer represent the original antithesis; this is to be found in the Epistle to the Hebrews: it says that, not by the blood of goats and calves, but by his own, had Christ achieved this deliverance. The Christian scheme of the atonement had its origin in the sacrificial rites of the ancient Jews. A pious sentiment is no doubt at the root of this extremely ancient usage of propitiatory offerings, but it is enveloped in a rough husk, and we can by no means regard the transmutation it has undergone by Christianity in the light of a purification. On the contrary, everybody knows that the sacrifices whereby rude nations fancied they could pacify the anger of their gods were originally sacrifices of human beings. It was therefore a progress towards refinement when they began to sacrifice animals in their stead. But now, once again, the human sacrifice was substituted for that of the animal. True, it was only by way of an allegory; there was no question of a victim offered up with formal sacrificial rites, on the contrary, the criminal condemnation and execution of the Messiah, the Son of God, who resigned himself meekly to his fate—decreed by a deluded people and its rulers—was

looked upon as an atoning sacrifice. But, as happens in such cases, the allegory was not suffered
to remain such. God himself had pre-ordained it
thus; and the condition on which he would or
could extend his pardon to men was that Jesus
should let himself be slaughtered for their sakes.

11.

If the life of an innocent person is taken at all,
whether by rude violence or an unjust sentence,—
and especially if this happen in consequence of a
truth he has enunciated, of a good cause by him
represented, and for which he suffers a martyr's
death,—an effect never fails to ensue, varying only
in kind and influence according to the position and
the importance of the murdered man. The execution of a Socrates and a Giordano Bruno, of a
Charles I. and a Louis XVI., of an Oldenbarne-
veldt and a Jean Calas, each produced an impression of a certain nature and within a certain
sphere. What these cases had in common, however,
was that their efficacy was of a moral nature, the
result of the impression they had wrought on
men's minds.

A like moral efficacy belonged to the death of
Jesus; the profound and moving impression it

made on the minds of his disciples, the change of
their views as to the mission of the Messiah and of
the nature of his kingdom which it produced in
them is matter of history. According to the church,
however, this was the most insignificant part of the
result. The chief efficacy of the death of Jesus,
and its especial object, was rather, so to speak, a
metaphysical one ; not mainly in the minds of men,
but above all in the relation of God to man something was to be changed, and actually was changed,
by this death ; it, as we have heard already, satisfied
the wrath, the severe justice of God, and enabled
him, in spite of their sins, again to bestow his
mercy upon mankind.

It can scarcely need to be pointed out that a perfect jumble of the crudest conceptions is comprised
in this one of an atoning death, of a propitiation by
proxy. To punish some one for another's transgression, to accept even the voluntary suffering of the
innocent and let the guilty escape scathless in consequence, this, everybody admits now, is a barbarous
action ; to consider it matter of indifference in regard to a moral or a pecuniary debt, whether it be
discharged by the debtor or by some one else in
his stead, is, everybody now admits, a barbarous
conception.

If the impossibility of such a transfer has once been acknowledged, then it no longer signifies whether the vicarious sufferer to be transferred is an ordinary man or the incarnate God. On this point, however, the Church notoriously laid especial stress. " If I believe," said Luther, " that by His human nature alone did Christ suffer for my sake, I should account Him but a sorry Saviour who needed a Saviour himself. True, the Godhead cannot suffer and die, but the Person that is very God doth suffer and dies ; it is right therefore to say, the Son of God has died for me."

This union of the two natures in the single person of Christ, and the interchange of their mutual properties, was still further developed into a system by the Church, the super-subtle doctrines of which must needs completely extinguish the historic human personality of Christ, while the relation which the heavenly Father bore to this atonement of the Son, inspired a Diderot with the sarcasm : " Il n'y a point de bon père qui voulût ressembler à notre père céleste."

12.

The Apostles' Creed concludes its scheme of the Christian faith by the third article, which reads as follows: "I believe in the Holy Ghost, the Holy Catholic Church, the communion of saints, the forgiveness of sins, the resurrection of the body, and the life everlasting."

The second person of the Godhead, in its union with human nature, has, as stated, obtained for us the remission of sins; but, in order that we may actually become partakers in this, the third person, the Holy Ghost, must also now emerge into activity and, so to speak, transmit it to us. This is effected by the Church and the means of grace which are especially presided over by this alleged third person of the Deity.

The Word of God is preached in the Church, and this in its essence is preaching the cross, *i.e.*, the doctrine of the remission of sins by the death of Christ, and that because of our faith in this effect of Jesus' death we shall be justified before God, without respect to works,——to the improvement of our lives, by which, indeed, a genuine faith must necessarily be attended, but which does not signify in the sight of God, who only regards us as righteous in so far as we shall by this faith have vicariously acquired Christ's righteousness. Thus spake Luther, in opposition to the Catholic practice of his days, which thought to obtain justification in the sight of God by outward works, fasting, pilgrimage, and the like. If in contrast to these trivial superficialities Luther had emphasized the moral disposition as the one thing needful, had he further proclaimed that God is satisfied to take account of earnestness and purity of heart, for, whatever man may accomplish, the fulfilment of the moral purpose must always remain very imperfect in him: then we must have awarded him the palm above the Catholic Church for the refinement and profundity of his conception of man's relations to God. But his doctrine of justifying faith, to which uprightness of intention was quite subordinate, was strained to excess on the one hand, and extremely perilous to morality on the other.

In addition to the Word, the Sacraments act in the Church as channels of the remission of sin. Of these the Eucharist, as everybody knows, has caused about the same amount of strife and warfare in the West as the doctrine of the Trinity in the East. And yet to us in our day the question, so violently debated in the time of the Reformation, as to whether and how something of the actual body of Christ were partaken of in the Communion, has become as indifferent and incomprehensible as that other, whether God the Son is of the

same or only of similar essence with the Father. In
the interdependence of the Christian system, however, the other principal sacrament, Baptism, plays
a still more important part. "He who believes
and is baptised shall be saved," Christ had said: he
therefore, who is not baptised, shall be damned.
But is it always man's own fault that he is not
baptised ? What of the little children, for example,
who die before baptism ? Or of those millions of
pagans who died ere baptism was instituted ? Or
of those millions of heathens who even **now** in
distant regions know scarcely anything of baptism
and Christianity ? The Augsburg Confession expressly says: "We condemn the Anabaptists, who
assert that unbaptised children can be saved."
Only the humanist Zwingli was humane enough to
translate virtuous pagans like Socrates and Aris-
tides to heaven, in spite of their unbaptised condition, without further ado.

13.

The conception of the resurrection of the body,
so acceptable to Jewish believers in the Messiah
and to Hebrew Christians, has in our own time
become a stumbling-block to orthodoxy itself. The
Jew was by no means inclined to lose his share

in the anticipated glories of the Messiah's day, even if it should find him in his grave; but this could only be his portion if his spirit, recalled by God or the Messiah from the shadowy realm where in the meanwhile it had dragged on a dismal existence, and reunited to the resuscitated body, should thus be rendered once more capable of life and enjoyment. And although the conception of the delights of the Messiah's kingdom gradually assumed a more refined character in Christendom, a certain materialism nevertheless continued to adhere to the Church (with which on our part we do not quarrel), in that she could not conceive of a true and complete life of the soul without corporeal essence. The difficulties inherent in the restoration of so many mouldered human frames—frames, more properly speaking, utterly annihilated—were naturally no trouble to the Church; to overcome them was the business of omnipotence. Our superior scientific knowledge renders us but a poor service in demonstrating the simple preposterousness of such a conception. And besides, it is precisely the most ardent believers in immortality who have now-a-days come to be such arrant spiritualists, that, although fully trusting in the possibility of preserving their precious souls to all eternity, they are yet at a loss to know what to do with their bodies, at least, after life has forsaken its earthly tabernacle.

The resuscitated enter upon eternal life, but by no means all, for there is a twofold resurrection, one unto life, the other unto judgment, *i.e.,* to everlasting perdition. And unfortunately it appears that the number of the reprobate infinitely exceeds that of the elect. Damned, in the first place, is the whole of the human race before Christ, excepting a few chosen souls, such as those of the Jewish patriarchs, who are liberated from hell by a special interposition; damned, again, the heathen of our own time, and Jews and Mohammedans, as well as the heretics and the godless in Christendom itself; and of these, the latter only because of their personal guilt, all the others solely on account of Adam's sin; their inaccessibility to Christianity, (with a few exceptions among those born after Christ's time) being no fault of theirs.

This is but an unsatisfactory winding up; and any expectation we might have entertained of being indemnified for so much that is revolting in the first principles of the ecclesiastical creed, notably the doctrines of the Fall and of Original Sin, proves to have been a bitter deception. " For the most part, nevertheless," says Reimarus, "men go to the devil, and hardly one in a thousand is saved." My pious and pensive grandfather, brooding over these things, was during the whole of his life tormented by this idea; even as in a hive there is but one queen to many thousand bees, even so, argued he, with men also there only was one soul saved, to thousands doomed to the flames of hell.

14.

Such was in outline the old belief of Christendom, and for the object we have in view, the diversity of confessions makes but little difference. Emerging in this shape from the age of the Reformation, it encountered the spirit of modern times, whose first stirrings were already perceptible in the seventeenth century, more especially in England and the Netherlands. Reason, fortified by historical and scientific research, developed apace, and as it increased in vigour found itself less disposed to accept the ecclesiastical tradition. This commotion of intellects first passed in the eighteenth century from England into France, already prepared for it by Bayle, then to Germany as well; so that in the process of attacking the old dogma we find a special part undertaken by each of these countries.

To England's share fell that of the first assault, and of the forging of the weapons, the work of the so-called free-thinkers or deists; Frenchmen then brought these weapons across the Channel, and knew how to wield them with briskness and adroitness in incessant light skirmishing; while in Germany it was chiefly one man who silently undertook the investment in form of the Zion of Orthodoxy. France and Germany especially seemed to divide between them the parts of seriousness and mockery; a Voltaire on the one side, a Hermann Samuel Reimarus on the other, fully typified the genius of their respective nations.

The result of the attentive scrutiny to which the latter had subjected the Bible and Christianity had proved thoroughly unfavourable to both. They fared no better at the hands of the grave Reimarus than with the scoffer Voltaire. In the whole course of biblical history Reimarus had not only failed to discover traces of the divine, but had found on the other hand much of what is human in the worst sense: the patriarchs he pronounced worldly, selfish, and crafty men; Moses an ambitious personage, unscrupulous enough to procure the enactment of an indifferent code by deceit and crime; and David, the "man after God's own heart," a cruel, voluptuous, and hypocritical despot. Even as regards Jesus, Reimarus found cause to regret that he had not confined himself to the conversion of mankind, instead of regarding it only as a preparation toward his ambitious scheme of founding the Messiah's kingdom on earth. This was his ruin, and his disciples then stole his corpse in order to declare him risen from the dead, and in consequence make this fraud the basis of their new religious system and of their spiritual power. Nor does the Christian system, according to Reimarus, belie its origin. Its axioms are false and full of contradictions, entirely opposed to all rational religious ideas, and decidedly unfavourable to the moral improvement of our race. The tenets of the early Church, which formed the justification of this judgment, have been given in the foregoing exposition.

But the more seriously this negative result presented itself to the German intellect, a result which the investigation of the old faith from an altered intellectual standpoint seemed to render inevitable, the more keenly did we feel the necessity of effecting a compromise. To turn to-day with loathing and contempt from what but yesterday was to us and the whole of society a sacred object of reverence, may be possible to him who can get over the glaring contradiction by raillery and ridicule, but he who is impressed by the gravity of the subject will soon find this contradiction unendurable. Therefore it was that Germany, and not France, became the cradle of Rationalism.

15.

Rationalism is a compromise between the tenets of the early Church and the distinctly negative result of its investigation by modern enlightened reason. It deems that although everything in biblical history took place naturally, yet in the main it took place honestly. The representative men of the Old Testament it judges to have been men even as we, but not worse than we, on the contrary, eminent in many respects; Jesus, it is true, was no Son of God as the Christian dogma has it, but neither was he ambitious, nor eager to thrust himself forward as an earthly Messiah, but rather one who was inspired by a genuine love for God and he fellow-men, who perished as a martyr in endeavouring to promulgate a purer moral and religious creed among his countrymen. The numerous stories of miracles in the Bible, especially in the Gospels, are founded not on fraud but on misconception, natural occurrences being sometimes considered miracles by eye-witnesses or historians, and the reader at other times putting a miraculous interpretation upon circumstances which the narrator did not intend to relate as prodigies.

The position which Rationalism occupies in relation to the ultra standpoint of a Reimarus shall be illustrated by two examples, one taken from the beginning of Holy Writ, the other from the end. The account of the Fall of man, which, indeed, he considered as fabulous, had chiefly been denounced as immoral by Reimarus because it made of God— from the fact of his having planted the seductive tree in sight of a primitive inexperienced pair, stimulated their desire by means of the arbitrary prohibition, and admitted the instigating serpent— the veritable author of the whole catastrophe. But then, questioned the rationalist Eichhorn, Who knows whether the prohibition to eat of the fruit was really arbitrary? The tree was probably a poisonous one, whose fruits were noxious to mankind. True, the prohibiting deity was as great a puzzle to Rationalism as the talking serpent; but perhaps primæval man had once observed that on partaking of the fruit a serpent had expired in convulsions, while at another time no harm had occurred to the reptile, and thus, in spite of these warning symptoms, had been emboldened to venture upon a gratification which, although not immediately fatal, yet by degrees brought death on himself, and banefully affected the physical and moral condition of his posterity.

The other example shall be the resurrection of Jesus. Here, as we know, our Reimarus considers nothing as more certain than that the Apostles had abstracted the corpse of their Master from the sepulchre, in order to proclaim his resuscitation, and be able thenceforth to make this the foundation of a new fanatical system of religion, which commended itself to their ambition and self-interest. Nothing of the sort! again interposes the rationalist The disciples were the farther from such baseness the less they stood in need of it. Jesus was not really dead, although supposed to be so, when taken down from the cross and laid with spices in the sepulchral vault; here he again recovered consciousness, and by his reappearance astonished his disciples, who thenceforth, as long as he still abode among them, in spite of all his efforts to convince them of the contrary, regarded him as a supernatural being.

This method of dealing with biblical history was also pursued by rationalism with respect to the doctrines of Christianity. It evaded the offence which the radicalism of the free-thinkers had conceived as postulates antagonistic to reason, or deductions perilous to morality, by breaking off or blunting its point. The Trinity in its eyes was a misunderstood phrase; mankind not corrupt and accursed on Adam's account, but certainly weak and sensual by natural constitution; Jesus not a Saviour by his atoning death, but nevertheless such by his teaching and example, which exercise an elevating, therefore a redeeming, influence upon us all; men are justified not through faith in another's righteousness, but by faithfulness to their own conviction,——by the earnest endeavour always to shape action by a recognised standard of duty.

16.

When F. C. Schlosser, fifty-six years ago, began the consecutive narrative of his "Universal History," he engaged the mystic T. F. von Meyer, of Frankfort, to insert his own version of Jewish history. He mentioned in his preface that he could not credit himself with the pious disposition of his learned friend, but it is easy to read between the lines. He neither wished to play the hypocrite, nor to place a stumbling-block at the threshold of his deeply-planned undertaking. But if now, on the other hand, we glance over one of the more recent text-books of ancient or Jewish history, not one written to the order of the Ministry of Worship, we shall find that the better the book the more will Jewish history be placed on exactly the same footing as that of Greece or Rome, the more will the criticism which is brought to bear on Herodotus and Livy be applied also to Genesis and the Book of Kings; that Moses will be appreciated no otherwise than Numa or Lycurgus, and especially will the miraculous stories of the Old Testament be treated exactly in the manner of those occurring in Greek and Roman historians. Thus the study of the Old Testament, regarded hitherto as a branch of theological science, has become the study of Jewish literature in the same secular sense as if it were the literature of Germany, France, and England.

The difficulty of applying the purely historical view and method of treatment is of course increased when we come to the primitive history of Christianity and the writings of the New Testament. A resolute beginning, however, is made, a solid foundation secured. No modern theologian, who is also a scholar, now considers any of the four Gospels to be the work of its pretended author, or in fact to be by an apostle or the colleague of an apostle. The first three Gospels, as well as the Acts, pass for doctrinal compilations of the beginning of the second century after Christ, the fourth, since Baur's epoch-making investigation, as a dogmatising composition of the middle of the same century. The drift of the first is decided by the different positions which their authors (and in the second place, their sources) had occupied in the disputes between Jewish Christianity and that of St. Paul; the dogma which the fourth Evangelist proposed to demonstrate in his narrative is the Judaico-Alexandrine conception of Jesus as the incarnate Logos. Foremost among the undisputed writings of the New Testament are the first four Epistles of the Apostle Paul; but the present readiness of critics to acknowledge the Revelation of St. John as genuine is almost unwelcome to modern orthodoxy. After the admission had once necessarily to be made that the two writings could not possibly be by the same author, it would gladly have got rid of that fantastic Judaico-zelotical book for the sake of more securely retaining the Gospel according to St. John in its place. And now a malicious criticism simply inverted the thing: reft the Evangelist of his Gospel and left him the Apocalypse: and noted in addition that

the entire prophecy turned upon the expectation of
the fallen Nero's return in the character of Antichrist,
and had therefore certainly not been inspired by the
Holy Spirit, but by a delusion incident to the author's
age and nation.

17.

Things had not as yet come to such a pass, but
it needed no extraordinary acumen to foresee that
they soon would do so, when Schleiermacher—gifted
with perhaps but too much acumen,—propounded
his system of theology. He resigned himself
from the first to the possible necessity of yielding the point of the genuineness of the greater
part of the biblical writings, after having of
his own accord surrendered that of the traditional conception of Jewish history, as well as
that of primitive Christianity. For him, no less
than for the Rationalists, the historical and dogmatic value of the biblical account of Creation and
the Fall of man was null, and like them also,
only with rather better taste, he knew how, on
purely rational grounds, to explain the miracles
recorded in the Gospels, not excluding the cardinal
one of the Resurrection of Christ. Neither did
he retain the original sense of any of the Chris-

tian dogmas ; the difference consisting only in the greater ingenuity, though sometimes also in the more artificial character, of his interpret ation.

Of one article of belief only did he keep firm hold, and that certainly the central dogma of Christianity; the doctrine regarding the person of Christ. In this instance the well-meaning, didactic, and itinerant rabbi of the Rationalists was almost too insignificant, I might say, too prosaic, for him. He believed himself able to prove that Christ had played a more important, a more exceptional part. But whence obtain those proofs if, after all, so little reliance could be placed on the Gospels ? One of these, as we shall see, he considered as more authentic than the rest; the real and certain proof, however, in his opinion, lay nearer than any document of Scripture. The early Christians had been fond of alluding to the witness of the Holy Spirit, as the first assurance of the truth of Scripture ; Schleiermacher appealed to the witness of the Christian consciousness as giving us complete certainty in regard to the Saviour. We, as members of the Christian community, become conscious of something within us which can only be explained as being the effect of such a cause. This is the advancement of our religious life, the increased facility we find in effecting a harmonious union between the lower and the higher elements of our characters. The union we always find to be impeded if we are left to our own unregenerate nature: our fellow-Christians, we are aware, are no better off in this respect than ourselves; whence, then, proceeds this stimulus of which we are actually conscious when members of the Christian church? It can only be derived from the founder of the community, Jesus himself; and if we find this furtherance of the religious life to proceed from him for ever, and from him alone, it follows that the religious life must in him have been absolute and perfect, that the lower and higher consciousness must have been entirely one in him.

Man's higher consciousness is the consciousness of God, which in us, on account of the manifold obstructions opposed to it, can only be called a feeble reflection; whereas in Jesus, where its operation was unimpeded, it interpenetrated his entire nature, as revealed in feeling, thought, and action, a perfect realization, a presence of God in the form of consciousness. Thus, in a fashion of his own, Schleiermacher again evolves the divine man, not in the least conceiving, however, as did the ecclesiastical dogma the union of the human nature with the divine, but rather representing to himself a mere human soul so imbued with the consciousness of divinity that this constitutes its sole actuating principle. Schleiermacher also expresses this in more modern phraseology: Christ, the historically unique, he says, was at the same time the originally typical, *i.e.*, on the one hand, the ideal type in him became completely historical, and on the other hand, the course of his earthly existence was wholly conditioned by the original typical idea. This necessarily involves his sinlessness, for although even in Jesus this higher consciousness was only gradually developed along with the lower, yet the relative strength of each always preserved the same proportion, insomuch that the higher maintained an invariable preponderance, and thus controlled the lower without wavering and without aberration.

The influence which redeems us in Jesus, therefore, is the imparting to us this sitmulus in the religious life by means of the church which he established. His crucifixion is of no particular importance, and if Schleiermacher turns the ecclesiastical expression " vicarious satisfaction " into " satisfactory substitution," it is easy to perceive that in reality he is only trifling with these primitive Christian conceptions.

18.

Schleiermacher looking at the first three Gospels found indeed but little to correspond with that conception of Christ which he had entirely constructed out of his supposed subjective experience ; it accordingly cost him little to concede the point of their apostolic origin, and to regard them as later compilations of very qualified authority. Not so with the fourth Gospel. There he seemed to be greeted by tones in happiest accordance with the image he himself had constructed of Christ. In such utterances of the Johannine Christ as : the Son can do nothing of himself, but only what he seeth the Father do; he˙ who hath seen me hath seen the Father ; all that is mine is thine also, and what is thine is also mine ; in such and similar expressions Schleiermacher recognized, so it appeared to him, a perfect resemblance to his own Redeemer, whose consciousness of God was in truth the very God in him. This entire Gospel, in fact, with its mystic profundity, yet dialectical acuteness, its peculiar strangeness of spirit, was so wholly to Schleiermacher's mind that he clung passionately to the belief in its genuineness, and resolutely shut his eyes even to all the evident reasons for distrust which, during his own life-time, Bretschneider marshalled against this Gospel in compact array.

But only a few years after Schleiermacher's death it came to pass that, in the first place, the New Testament bulwark of his Christology, the so-called Gospel of St. John, succumbed past recovery to a renewed onslaught of criticism. Nor did its internal basis, the inference deduced from the facts of Christian consciousness as to the nature of the founder of the Christian community, prove itself less vulnerable. It is an absolutely gratuitous supposition, and, properly speaking, a remnant of the doctrine of original sin, which Schleiermacher tried, in fact, to set up again after a fashion of his own, to assume that the hindrance of the religious life is exclusively due to ourselves, and that therefore any furtherance of this same life experienced by us must necessarily have a source external to us. On the contrary, in all of us there is an incessant warfare between the higher and the lower consciousness, between the promptings of reason and of sense ; our religious and ethical nature meets, from ourselves as well as from others, not with obstructions only but also with encouragement ; and even in the most favourable instances this has nevertheless always been but a relative kind of stimulus, we are not therefore obliged to seek an originator, in whom it should exist absolutely. But, granting even that such had been the case with Christ, that he as individual man had, at each moment of his life, personified within himself the pure typical image of mankind, that he in the course of his development had been free from fault or vacillation, error and sin, then he would have essentially differed from all other men : a conclusion indeed allowable to the Church, which regarded him as begotten by the Holy Ghost, but not to Schleiermacher, according to whom he came into the world in the ordinary course of nature.

19.

It may perhaps surprise us that the debate as to the truth of Christianity has at last narrowed itself into one as to the personality of its founder, that the decisive battle of Christian theology should take place on the field of Christ's life; but in reality this is but what might have been expected. The value of a scientific or artistic production in no way depends on our acquaintance with the private life of him who produced it. Not one tittle the less highly do we rate the author of Hamlet because we know so little of his life, nor is our assurance of the worth of his contemporary Bacon's reformation of science impaired by our cognisance of many unfavourable features in his character. Even in the domain of religious history it is indeed of importance to assure ourselves that Moses and Mohammed were no impostors; but in other respects the religions established by them must be judged according to their own deserts, irrespectively of the greater or less accuracy of our acquaintance with their founders' lives. The reason is obvious. They are only the founders, not at the same time the objects of the religions they instituted. While withdrawing the veil from the new revelation, they themselves modestly stand aside. They are indeed objects of reverence, but not of adoration.

This is notoriously otherwise with Christianity. Here the founder is at the same time the most prominent object of worship; the system based upon him loses its support as soon as he is shown to be lacking in the qualities appropriate to an object of religious worship. This, indeed has long been apparent; for an object of religious adoration must be a Divinity, and thinking men have long since ceased to regard the founder of Christianity as such. But it is said now that he himself never aspired to this, that his deification has only been a later importation into the Church, and that if we seriously look upon him as man, we shall occupy the standpoint which was also his own. But even admitting this to be the case, nevertheless the whole regulation of our churches, Protestant as well as Catholic, is accommodated to the former hypothesis; the Christian *cultus*, this garment cut out to fit an incarnate God, looks slovenly and shapeless when but a mere man is invested with its ample folds.

At least he must have been such a man as the man framed by Schleiermacher who thoroughly appreciates the needs of the Church; a man so fashioned that in Schleiermacher's view the constitution of our religious life is still, and must ever remain, dependent on him, and that we shall certainly have cause to keep him always present to our minds, to recall him to remembrance at our religious meetings, to repeat and carefully ponder his words, and incessantly to dwell upon the main factors of his life.

Schleiermacher's reasons for regarding Jesus as such a man have not convinced us; but then, who knows? after all, he may have been something similar; he it may be, after all, to whom mankind must look more than to any one else for the perfecting of its inner life.

Of this we shall only be able to judge by studying those records of his life which we still possess.

20.

How could Schleiermacher be so highly edified by the Jesus of the fourth Gospel? If he was in truth the incarnate word of God, this, of course, alters the case; but he was not so for Schleiermacher, for him he was mere man, but one whose religious and moral faculties were completely developed. Will such an one dare to use such tremendous words as: "I and the Father are one; who seeth me seeth the Father also"? And if he does use them shall we not be forced, for that very reason, to question his own religious feeling? The more pious the man, the more sedulously will his awe observe the line of demarcation which divides him from that which he esteems as divine. As we cannot believe Jesus a God, we should lose our faith in his excellence as a man if we were forced to believe that he uttered those words, and we should lose our faith in the soundness of his reason, if compelled to seriously believe that in prayer he had reminded God of the glory which he had shared with him before the world was. And moreover we should be ashamed now-a-days to make use of the perverting exegesis by means of which Schleiermacher strove to make utterances of such a nature acceptable.

Happily it is only the fourth Evangelist who attributes such phrases to Jesus, and he derived them not from historic information, but merely from the conception which in harmony with a philosophic scheme of his own he had formed of him a century later. The veritable Christ is only to be found, if at all, in the first three Gospels. There we have no figure tortured into accordance with Alexandrine speculation, we have reminiscences of the very man, gathered and garnered on the very spot. Not that here even there is an entire absence of effort to mould these after a particular pattern. For was not Jesus, according to his adherents, the Messiah, and what his attributes, and destinies were, had long been known, down to the minutest detail, by the devout and expectant Jewish people. It was of course self-evident to the faithful that everything which had been foretold as about to happen to and by the Messiah, actually had happened to and by the instrumentality of the Jesus they had known. These things came to pass that it might be fulfilled as it is written, is the invariable comment of our honest Matthew, whenever he has been relating something that never came to pass at all. Thus, for example, the name of Nazareth, Christ's native town, adhered to him even after his death ; but according to a passage in Micah, as then expounded, the Messiah, like to his ancestor David, would be born in Bethlehem; therefore of course it was obligatory that he should be born there, not in Nazareth, as sure as he was the Messiah. But, in order to be convinced that we have not here matter of actual history, but only concoctions with especial reference to the expectations entertained respecting the Messiah, we need only observe how diametrically opposed to each other are the manners in which Matthew and Luke set about proving the fulfilment of the prophecy, the one by removing Christ's parents after his birth from Bethlehem to Nazareth, the other by removing them before his birth from Nazareth to Bethlehem. No less obviously manufactured, and equally betraying their character by the discrepancy of their statements, are the two genealogies which are designed to prove that the supposed son of David actually was a descendant of his ; while in truth all they prove is, that at the time they were first promulgated, Christ still passed for the son of Joseph, and that therefore that other title of the Messiah, the term " Son of God," had not yet come to be applied to him in the coarsely literal sense. But the Messiah was also the second Moses and the chief of the prophets, and the events and actions in the lives of the lawgiver and of the foremost prophets must necessarily be repeated in that of the Messiah and of Jesus, if Messiah indeed were come. As Pharaoh had sought to slay the infant Moses, Herod must have made the like attempt on the infant Christ; at a later period he must have been tempted like Israel in the wilderness, only that he passed the *examen rigorosum* more creditably; then again he must be transfigured on a mountain, even as his prototype Moses had descended from his Mount Sinai with shining countenance. It was necessary that he should have raised the dead, that he should have multiplied insufficient food, else would he have lagged behind Elijah and Elisha. His whole career had to be one unbroken chain of miracles of healing. For had not Isaiah spoken in his prophecies of the advent of the Messiah as a time when the eyes of the blind, and the ears of the deaf should be opened, when the lame should leap, and the tongue of the dumb utter rejoicings?

21.

A large portion indeed of the actions and fortunes of Jesus, as narrated by the Evangelists, neces-

sarily vanishes when the tissue of marvels apper-
taining to his supposed Messianic character is again
disengaged from his life by criticism; but this is by
no means all, nor even half of that against which
criticism finds reason to object. Even as regards the
discourses in the Gospels grave doubts have arisen.
When Bretschneider first discerned Christ's speeches
in the fourth Gospel to be independent compositions
of the Evangelist he pointed to those contained
in the first three Gospels as samples of Christ's
actual manner of expressing himself. So firm was
the prevalent belief in their authenticity——generally speaking, and as compared to that of the
fourth Gospel, not without cause. Such had been
the style of teaching, such the range of his ideas,
such doubtless at times also the very words of
Christ.

But how strange! In that case he must often
have glaringly contradicted himself. When, at the
beginning of his career, he first sent his apostles
forth, he is stated to have prohibited them from
addressing themselves to the heathen and Samaritans; at a later period, however, while on his way
to Jerusalem, it is reported of him that he—as in
his parable of the good Samaritan, and the healing
of the ten lepers—had contrasted members of this

mongrel race with his compatriots, to the disadvantage of the latter; then, again, in his parables of the vineyard and of the royal marriage feast, in the temple at Jerusalem, he had predicted the rejection of the stubborn Jews and the election of the Gentiles in their stead; and lastly, when, after his alleged resurrection, he gave the disciples his parting directions, he is said to have distinctly bidden them preach the gospel to all, without distinction of race. This, of course, would not be incredible, for in the interval which must have elapsed between this prohibition and the prediction and injunction which came later, it would have been quite possible that his horizon should have become enlarged in consequence of a wider experience. But even previous to the above-mentioned prohibition, Jesus had unhesitatingly aided the centurion of Capernaum, a Gentile, and on occasion of the latter's faith had foretold the future reception of the Gentiles, instead of the unbelieving Jews, into the Messiah's kingdom; by the above-mentioned interdict, therefore, he would have prohibited his disciples from acting as he himself had done, and from preparing the way to the fulfilment of his prophecy; nay, in the still later case of the Canaanitish woman, he himself would have acted in a spirit entirely adverse to that

manifested towards the centurion, and, with the
utmost harshness of Hebrew exclusiveness, would
have allowed himself only to be softened at last by
the humble persistency of the woman.

This is more than we can make allowance for,
and is not sufficiently explained by the supposition
that the arrangement of the different narratives in
the first three Gospels is not chronological. For
in that case how shall we obtain any information whatever as to their proper chronological
order? But we are seasonably reminded that the
period in which our first three Gospels were in
process of formation was that of the most violent
conflict between the two parties into which the
infant Church had been sundered by the decided
action of the Apostle Paul. To judge by their pro-
ceedings, as disclosed by St. Paul's Epistle to the
Galatians, as well as by the Apocalypse, if genuine,
the first apostles seem only to have conceived of the
kingdom of their crucified Messiah as exclusively
intended for the posterity of Abraham, or for such
as by accepting the circumcision and the law should
be incorporated with the chosen people. St. Paul,
on the contrary, enunciated the principle, and made
it the guide of his apostolic mission, that the law
had been superseded by Christ's death, and that

only faith (implying baptism) was requisite in order to gain admission into his kingdom; that the Gentiles, therefore, were entitled to it fully as much as the Jews.

The national egotism of the Jewish proselytes to the new sect rebelled all the more passionately against this doctrine, as the successes of St. Paul amongst the Gentiles increased, and as, in consequence, the anticipated share in the glories of the Messiah's day (destined only for the true sons of Abraham) seemed in danger of being diminished by the numerous interlopers. The dissensions thence occasioned were carried on with much virulence for a considerable time after the death of the Apostle Paul; the stubborn Hebrew-Christians called him the malevolent, the lawless one, the false apostle, especially obnoxious because of his hostile behaviour towards Peter at Antioch; and it required the sheer force of facts, as manifested on the one hand, in the destruction of the Hebrew state, on the other, in the ever wider dissemination of Christianity among the Greeks and Romans, to bring about a reconciliation of parties, and render possible a peaceful juxtaposition of the two apostles, Peter and Paul. The origin and attempted pacification of these differences are related in the epistles of St. Paul, and also in the Acts, but in the spirit of conciliation, and of mitigation, and suppression.

Now, the battle-field of these conflicts, as they continued to exist even after the death of the apostle of the Gentiles and the destruction of the Hebrew commonwealth, lies before us in the first three Gospels. We observe in them the fluctuation of the strife, discover the spots where halts were made, tents pitched, and fortifications erected; but we note at the same time how, in cases of retreat or advance, these intrenchments were abandoned and new ones cast up in other places in their stead.

22.

Of course after the manner in which religious documents were produced at that time, or indeed, at any time, it followed naturally that what was considered as truth by a party or its leader must have been believed to be the doctrine of Jesus himself. If we were still in possession of a gospel written from a severely Hebrew-Christian standpoint, Christ's discourses would unquestionably wear a very different aspect. But such a gospel we no longer possess, nor have we one composed entirely from the point of view of St. Paul; for in every one of the first Gospels (the fourth not counting as an historical document) the two standpoints lie over and across each other, like the strata of a geological formation. In St. Matthew the Hebrew-Christian spirit is still the most apparent, being nevertheless much mitigated and alloyed by philo-Gentile elements; while in Luke, on the contrary, a bias towards St. Paul's views is unmistakable; but, as if to preserve the equilibrium, he has also inserted pieces of a peculiarly uncompromising Judaical character. If sometimes, therefore, we read in documents of this kind that Jesus forbade his disciples to preach the Gospel to heathens and Samaritans, because (the passage of the Sermon on the Mount refers unquestionably to the same subject) this was giving holy things to dogs and casting pearls before swine; while, on the other hand, we are told that he bade them bear the glad tidings to all nations; we, in point of fact, only learn what, at different times and in different circles, were the convictions of earliest Christianity on this head; while the standpoint occupied by Jesus himself remains doubtful. Thus, in the narrative of the Canaanitish woman we discern the disposition of a time which, although it could no longer prevent the admission of the Gentiles, had yet given way with the utmost reluctance; while that of the Centurion of Capernaum either dates from a later period, or proceeds from a more liberal circle, by which Gentile believers were made welcome without demur. It is possible that the former passages make Jesus appear more narrow-minded than he really was, but it is also possible that the latter make him out to be more liberal-minded; and when we consider the position which after his death his foremost apostles occupied in relation to St. Paul's undertaking, we shall be inclined to judge the latter hypothesis the more probable.

I cannot here enter on a closer investigation; I have only wished to throw out a hint as to the uncertainty of everything on this head, how we cannot make sure of the sayings and teachings of Christ on any one point, whether we really have his own words and thoughts before us, or only such as later times found it convenient to ascribe to him.

23.

If a recent delineator of Buddhism finds its significance to have consisted in its "having found a Brahminism grown decrepid in mythology and theology, scholasticism and speculation, ceremonies and outward observances of every sort, meretricious works and hypocrisy, sacerdotal and philosophical pride; and opposed it by placing the essence of sanctity in

the heart, in purity of life and conversation, in benevolence, compassion, philanthropy and unbounded
alacrity of self-sacrifice; and its having consistently
appealed from wild, dreary traditions and priestly
formulas, oppressive to the mind and heart, from
abstruse scholastic sophistry, and high-flying speculation, to the natural feeling and the common sense of
mankind as the highest tribunal in religious matters:" we cannot fail to recognize the similarity of
position and of activity between the Indian sage of
the times of Darius and Xerxes and the Jewish sage
of the period of Augustus and Tiberius.

The Hindu's rigid system of caste had now for
counterpart the invidious line of demarcation between Jews, Gentiles, and Samaritans; not to
mention later proselytes to Christianity. A kind
of mythology and speculative philosophy had been
gradually formed among the Jews, at least, among
the sect of the Essenes, whilst a species of subtle
scholasticism obtained among the scribes of the
other two sects. Ecclesiastical formulæ, cere-
monial observances, meritorious works, and hypocrisy were equally rampant in either religion;
and in both instances the new teacher sought to
convince his disciples of the importance of substi-

tuting an inward for an outward life, a change of heart for mere external observances; and inculcated humility, charity, and tolerance instead of pride, self-seeking, and hatred. The way of life traced out by Sakhyamuni is called by the Buddhists simply "the way," precisely the same expression as that applied to the new Messianic faith by the Acts; the same reason held good in both cases, Buddhism as well as Christianity being originally more practical than theoretic, more of a compendious doctrine of salvation than of a voluminous system of belief.

It would appear nevertheless as though Sakhyamuni had effected a more complete rupture with the established religion of Brahma than Jesus with Mosaism. The former not only abolished the Brahminical organization of caste but its whole body of ritual also, with its sacrificial observances and penances, nay, its very heaven, with its deities. The saying of Buddha, "My law is a law of mercy for all," which was specially addressed by him against the vile system of caste, has at the same time a certain Christian savour, only that, as above mentioned, we know not for certain whether such largeheartedness, extending beyond the limits of the chosen people, was actually reduced to practice by Jesus, or only in the first instance by St. Paul. That other saying of the Indian reformer comes home to us with as Christian a sound, " To honour your father and mother is better than to serve the gods of heaven and earth," a saying which with him however had a still more extensive signification. Recent researches on Buddhism have established the paradox that originally it was a religion without a god or gods, that its founder, in fact, was an Atheist. He does not exactly deny the existence of gods, but he simply ignores them, thrusts them aside, as in the utterance we have quoted. Jesus, on the other hand, not only imported its one God from the religion of his people into his own, but even its law.

But just as his interpretation of the law was more spiritual, and as he wished to see it purified from traditional appendages, so also, availing himself of isolated expressions in the Old Testament, he transformed the conception of God from that of a stern master to that of a loving father, and thus imbued the religious life of man with a freedom and cheerfulness before unknown.

24.

Both reformers had in common, however, an enthusiastic world-renouncing tendency, although its root was not the same in both. Sakhyamuni was a Nihilist, Jesus a Dualist. The first, recognizing in life and its accompanying suffering the consequences of appetites and the love of existence, endeavoured by destroying this love to re-enter the Nirvana, the painless void ; the second exhorted his disciples to strive above all things after the kingdom of God, to lay up imperishable treasures in heaven rather than perishable ones on earth; he pronounced those happy who are now poor and heavy-laden, because of the great recompense which awaited them in heaven.

Schopenhauer has called Christianity a pessimist religion, and finds in its avowal of the utter misery of mankind the strength which enabled it to overcome the optimist creed of Jew and Pagan. But this Pessimism, the rejection of that which it designates as "this world," is only one side of Christianity, and without its other side as a complement, that of the glory of the heavenly world to come, which it proclaimed as near at hand, it would have had but inconsiderable success. As Schopenhauer declines the latter for himself, and holds fast for his own part by the Buddhist Nirvana, he is in sympathy with only that side of Christianity which it has in

common with Buddhism, which, as regards the
value of this life, may also be called pessimist. In
fact, as concerns the theory of human life and the
regulation of its various relations, Christian Dualism
produces essentially the same consequences as
Buddhist Nihilism. No incentive to, nor any object
of, human activity possesses any actual value; all
man's endeavour and striving in pursuit of such is
not only mere vanity, but actually prejudicial to
the attainment of his true destiny, whether this be
called heaven or Nirvana. The surest means of
attaining to the goal is to maintain as passive a
disposition of mind as possible, saving the efforts
required to soothe the sufferings of others, or to
disseminate the redeeming doctrine, the teaching of
Buddha or of Christ.

Pernicious above all is the pursuit after worldly
goods, nay, even the possession of such, in so far as
one is not willing to relinquish them. The rich
man in Scripture is certain to go to hell, on the
sole ground, so far as appears, of his faring sump-
tuously every day. Jesus has no better advice to
give to the wealthy youth who would do something
more beyond the mere fulfilling of the ordinary
commandments, than to sell everything he has and
give it to the poor. Christianity in common with

Buddhism teaches a thorough cult of poverty and mendicity. The mendicant monks of the middle ages, as well as the still flourishing mendicancy at Rome, are genuinely Christian institutions, which have only been restricted in Protestant countries by a culture proceeding from quite another source. "We are perpetually reminded of the evils produced by wealth and the sinful love of money," says Buckle, "and yet assuredly no other passion, except the love of knowledge, has been productive of equal benefit to mankind; to it we owe all commerce and industry; industrial undertakings and trade have made us acquainted with the productions of many countries, have aroused our curiosity, enlarged the field of our vision, by bringing us in contact with nations of various ideas, customs, and languages, accustomed us to vast undertakings, to foresight and prudence, taught us besides many useful technical crafts, and, lastly, endowed us with invaluable means for the preservation of life and the alleviation of suffering. All this we owe to the love of money. Could theology succeed in extirpating it, all these influences would cease, and we should in a measure relapse into barbarism." That leisure could not exist without wealth, nor art and science without leisure, has been shown to demonstration by Buckle in his well-known work.

It does not therefore follow that the love of acquisition should not, like every other impulse, be kept within reasonable bounds, and subordinated to higher aims, but in the teaching of Jesus it is ignored from the very first, and its effectiveness in promoting culture and humanitarian tendencies is misunderstood, Christianity in this respect manifesting itself as a principle directly antagonistic to culture. It only prolongs its existence among the enlightened and commercial nations of our time by the emendations which a cultivated but profane reason has made in it, and yet this Reason, so magnanimous, or perhaps so weak and hypocritical, as to impute the good effects not to itself but to Christianity, to whose spirit it is nevertheless entirely opposed.

In his celebrated letter addressed to me during the last war, Ernest Rénan remarked with perfect justice, only unfortunately somewhat too late, how neither in the Beatitudes of the Sermon on the Mount, nor anywhere else in the Gospel, is any promise of heaven made to military valour. But neither does it contain a word in favour of pacific political virtue, of patriotism and the efficient discharge of civic obligations. The sentence, "Give unto Cæsar the things that are Cæsar's," etc., is, after all, but an evasive answer. Nay, even in regard to the virtues of private and family life, the efficacy of the example and teaching of Jesus is diminished by his own exemption from domestic ties. We possess various utterances of his on the subject, depreciating natural bonds in comparison with the spiritual, not indeed wholly devoid of justice, yet liable, by reason of their abrupt austerity, to misconstruction. We learn, besides, that while he looked upon celibacy as the higher state for persons destined to higher things, he entertained rigorous notions as to the indissolubility of marriage, and also that he was a lover of children.

It will, however, be equitable to take into account the then state of the people to which Jesus belonged. It may be said to have resembled the present condition of Poland under Russia; the political independence of the Jewish nation had ceased to exist, the Jews were incorporated into the enormous empire of Rome, they could no longer make war publicly on their own account, only hatch conspiracies and raise rebellions which could but plunge the people, as had already been sufficiently proved, into ever deepening misery. Even the peaceful vocations of the citizen had only the very narrowest sphere of action allowed to them under the administration of Roman pro-consuls and the system of extortion practised by Roman tax-gatherers; every higher aspiration unavoidably turned either to conspiracy or to reform, which, however, being debarred from every practical outlet, necessarily assumed a character of fanaticism.

Still less, under such circumstances, was there any prospect of a higher culture, a refinement of manners, and embellishment of life, by means of science and art. The Jews, in the first place, had less natural capacity for these, not only than the Greeks and Romans, but less even than many other oriental nations; in the second place, the nation in Jesus' time, on the verge of its political dissolution, had, especially in its native country, declined to the lowest point of prosperity and culture. It is impossible to realize to the full the squalor and penury which were rife at that time in the villages and small towns of Galilee. How could any conception of art or science, or any impulse toward them, spring from such a source? As it was believed that the truth could only be found in Scripture, in the sacred books of Moses and the prophets, science was entirely made to consist in a specially pitiful and arbitrary art of interpretation, of which we possess but too many samples in the New Testament. In a word, the world and existence therein had grown to be so unbearable to the oppressed and degenerate race which then dragged on its days by the banks of the Jordan and the Sea of Tiberias, that precisely the noblest and the loftiest spirits among them would have nothing more to do with it, did not consider it worth the pains of trying to improve it, but preferred to abandon it to the prince of this world, the devil, while, with the concentrated powers of longing and imagination, they themselves turned towards the deliverance which, according to ancient prophecies and more modern glosses, was presently to come from above.

25.

The only thing needful was to hasten its advent. But the people, so it seemed, must, ere it came, be worthy of it. John, therefore, preached repentance, because the kingdom of heaven was at hand, and administered the regenerating rite of baptism to those who acknowledged their sins. If reliance is to be placed on the accounts in the Gospel, he did not proclaim himself as being the bearer of this deliverance, the Messiah. This was first done by Jesus.

But how did Jesus propose to bring this deliverance? At first, he followed in the footprints of the Baptist, and likewise preached repentance in view of the approaching kingdom of heaven. But what next? When at his passover he rode into Jerusalem he willingly suffered himself to be greeted by the people as the Son of David, the expected Messianic King. It has been hence inferred that he expected a *coup de main* on the part of his adherents, a popular insurrection which should place him at the head of the Jewish commonwealth. But then, did not he ride intentionally into Jerusalem seated on a peaceable beast? and had he taken the slightest pains to prepare any violent uprising? When subsequently, at his imprisonment, one of his disciples unsheathed his sword, he not only declared himself opposed on principle to the use of the sword, but assured him that even now he need only express the wish, and God his father would send more than twelve legions of angels to his assistance.

Jesus may or may not have uttered these words at that moment; in my judgment they accurately convey the essential foundation of his ideas. The actual advent of the heavenly kingdom was to be effected not in any way by a political, or in fact natural, but by a supernatural machinery. But

neither was this to be of a purely moral nature—
the moral part always remaining merely prepara-
tory—but it was rather of a transcendent, or one
might say magical, character.

Jesus having given an affirmative answer to the
question of the high priest as to whether he were
the Messiah, had added that he would forthwith be
seen sitting at the right hand of the heavenly Power,
and descending in the clouds of heaven. At that
time, when, a captive under heavy accusations, he
foresaw his execution, this might signify that, resuscitated by God after his death, he should return in
that Messianic character indicated by Daniel; but
had it pleased God to send him his legions of
angels, death might have been spared him, the
heavenly hosts might (as was afterwards expected in
regard to the Christians surviving at the resurrection) have borne him up to the clouds with a sudden
transfiguration of his earthly frame, and there
have seated him on his Messianic throne. The
Gospels, of course, represent the case entirely as if
Jesus, with supernatural foresight, had always been
cognizant of his violent death; with us it can only
be a question as to whether he was more or less
taken by surprise at the unfortunate catastrophe of
his mission, and at what period of his career he

applied himself to the task of reconstructing his hopes in the anticipated prodigies.

26.

After he—to the surprise of his disciples, at all events—had expired on the cross as a condemned malefactor, the whole issue now hung upon these disciples' strength of soul. If they allowed their belief in him as the Messiah to be shaken by his violent death amid the wreck of his undertaking, his cause was lost; then, although the memory of him and of many of his pregnant sayings might possibly be preserved for awhile in Judæa, yet its impression must soon be effaced, like the circles on the surface of a pool into which some one has cast a stone. But if, in defiance of his unhappy end, they would hold fast by the belief in him as the Messiah, then it behoved them to solve the contradiction which seemed to exist between the two; it behoved them especially to knit together his natural existence, thus violently interrupted, with the supernatural part which, according to his repeated prediction, he would at no distant date perform, as the Son of man appearing in the clouds of heaven. According to man's common lot, he, since his death on the cross, had devolved to the

realm of shades; but once identified with them
the thread was snapped, his part played out; no
faith, no hope could henceforth be founded upon him.
This, then, was the point which required to be made
secure: he must not have died, or rather, as the
whole country-side knew him to be dead, he must
not have continued so; recourse was had to Scripture—a great gain to begin with. For with the
facility of the time in exegesis, everything that
might be desirable could with certainty be found
there. The author of the sixteenth Psalm, whether
David or another, had, as may be imagined, not
dreamt of speaking in the name of the Messiah, but
merely given vent to his own joyful trust in God;
and if he expressed this by saying that God would
not leave his soul in hell, nor suffer his holy one
to see corruption, he only meant that with God's
help he would emerge happily from every trial and
danger. "But David," argued a disciple of Jesus,
seeking to prop his vacillating faith, "David is dead
and mouldered to dust; consequently he cannot in
this passage have spoken of himself, but rather he
spoke prophetically of his great scion, the Messiah—
and this of course was Jesus—who, accordingly,
cannot have remained in the grave, cannot have
succumbed to the nether powers." In the Acts St.

Peter certainly only recites this model interpretation on the day of Pentecost, after the resurrection
of Jesus; but we see here, on the contrary, one of the
processes of thought by which the disciples gradually
wrought themselves up to the production of the
idea of the resuscitation of their martyred Lord.
The passage in Isaiah about the lamb which is led
to the shambles produced a similar effect, and
Philip the Evangelist is said to have interpreted
it to the Ethiopian eunuch as referring to Christ;
and if we read that at the time of the resurrection,
Christ, appearing to his disciples journeying to
Emmaus, had explained to them all the passages
referring to himself, *i.e.*, to his death and resurrection, this, taken historically, can only mean that it
was chiefly from Scripture that the disciples succeeded in extracting comfort and hope in those
days of sorrow.

Consternation at the execution of their master
had scared them far from the dangerous metropolis,
to their native Galilee; here they may have held
secret meetings in honour of his memory, they may
have found strength in their faith in him, have
searched Scripture through and through, and strained
every nerve to reach unto light and certainty;
these were spiritual conflicts which, in Oriental

and especially female natures of an unbalanced religious and fantastical development, easily turned into ecstasies and visions. As soon as it seemed once patent that he could not have remained in the grave, being the Messiah, the step was not great to the tidings—we have seen him who hath risen from the dead, he hath met us, spoken with us; we did not know him at first, but afterwards, when he had departed, the scales fell from our eyes, we saw that it could have been none other than he, etc. And in successive narratives the manifestations grew even more palpable: he had eaten with the disciples, had shown them his hands and feet, and bidden them place their fingers in his wounds.

Thus the disciples, by elaborating the conception of the resurrection of their slain master, had rescued his work ; and, moreover, it was their honest conviction that they had actually beheld and conversed with the risen Lord. It was no case of pious deception, but all the more of self-deception; embellishment and legend, of course, although possibly still in good faith, soon became intermingled with it.

But looking at it historically, as an outward event, the resurrection of Jesus had not the very slightest foundation. Rarely has an incredible fact been worse attested, or one so ill-attested been more incredible in itself. In my "Life of Jesus" I have devoted a full investigation to this subject, which I will not repeat here. But the result I consider it my duty as well as my right to express here without any reserve. Taken historically, *i.e.*, comparing the immense effect of this belief with its absolute baselessness, the story of the resurrection of Jesus can only be called a world-wide deception. It may be humiliating to human pride, but nevertheless the fact remains: Jesus might still have taught and embodied in his life all that is true and good, as well as what is one-sided and harsh— the latter after all always producing the strongest impression on the masses; nevertheless, his teachings would have been blown away and scattered like solitary leaves by the wind, had these leaves not been held together and thus preserved, as if with a stout tangible binding, by an illusory belief in his resurrection.

27.

Jesus is not to be held to account for this belief in his resurrection except indirectly and for a reason very honorable to him, viz., that the very fact of its existence proves what a strong and lasting impression

he must have made on his disciples. This impression, certainly arose not only from what was
rational and moral in his genius and ideas, but in
at least as great a degree from that which was
irrational and fantastic. A Socrates, with his
purely reasonable method of teaching, would not
have fascinated the Galilean mind at that time;
neither would Jesus have been able to effect this
by merely preaching purity of heart, love of God
and your neighbour, and by declaring the poor and
oppressed as destined to blessedness; or rather he
could not have declared them blessed if he had not
been able to promise them an indemnification in
the kingdom of God, in which he himself expected
ere long to commence his reign as Messiah. The
expectation of this terrestrial heaven—which we
must not imagine as representing the present
idealized conception of a future world, but rather the
sensuous descriptions in the Revelation of St. John
—had already, during Christ's lifetime, exercised
the utmost influence; and the belief produced in
his resurrection was chiefly valuable as rehabilita-
ting an expectation shaken by his death.

But with Jesus himself this conception forms
the basis upon which the general system of his
ideas and precepts rests, and the point to which

everything else refers. The rejection of the world and all material interests has only a meaning as implying the reverse proposition—that the true interests, the abiding satisfaction, may only be found in the approaching kingdom of heaven. Jesus himself, it was alleged, had described the prospect of his arrival or return at the head of this kingdom as so nigh, that a portion of those who listened to him should live to see it; and the Apostle Paul tells us expressly that he himself still hoped to witness it.

Christianity, as we know, has during the last eighteen centuries found itself perpetually deceived in this expectation, and has therefore hit upon the expedient of putting a gloss upon Christ's words, postponing his return to some incalculable distance of time, and in compensation antedating each person's entrance into heaven or hell as an event to occur immediately upon the close of his earthly existence.

Not only has the first expectation, however, after a gradual decay, at present become virtually extinct, but the other also—the hope of a future recompense—has been shaken to its foundations. And why? Of the cause anon; at present, I only claim the concession of the fact.

If we open our eyes, and are honest enough to avow what they show us, we must acknowledge that the entire activity and aspiration of the civi- lized nations of our time is based on views of life which run directly counter to those entertained by Christ. The ratio of value between the here and the hereafter is exactly reversed. And this is by no means the result of the merely luxurious and so- called materialistic tendencies of our age, nor even of its marvellous progress in technical and industrial improvements; but it is equally due to its discoveries in science, its astronomy, chemistry and physiology, as well as its political aims and national combinations, nay, even its productions in poetry and the sister arts. All that is best and happiest which has been achieved by us has been attainable only on the basis of a con- ception which regarded this present world as by no means despicable, but rather as man's proper field of labour, as the sum total of the aims to which his efforts should be directed. If from the force of habit, a certain proportion of workers in this field still carry the belief in an hereafter along with them, it is nev- ertheless a mere shadow which attends their footsteps, without exercising any determining influence on their actions.

28.

Let us now bethink ourselves what it was that we really set out to discover. We had quite given up the ecclesiastical conception of Jesus as the Saviour and Son of God, and had found Schleiermacher's "God in Christ" to be a mere phrase. But we asked whether as an historical personage he might not have been one on whom our religious life still continues to be dependent on whom more than to any other great man it must look for moral perfection. This question we are now in a position to answer.

To begin with, we shall be obliged to state that our authentic information respecting Jesus is far too scanty for this purpose. The evangelists have overlaid the picture of his life with so thick a coat of supernatural colouring, have confused it by so many cross lights of contradictory doctrine, that the natural colours cannot now be restored. If one may not with impunity walk among palms, still less so among gods. He who has once been deified has irretrievably lost his manhood. It is an idle notion that by any kind of operation we could restore a natural and harmonious picture of a life and a human being from sources of information which, like the Gospels, have been adapted to suit a supernatural being, and distorted, moreover, by parties whose conceptions and interests conflicted with each other's. To check these, we ought to possess information concerning the same life, compiled from a purely natural and common-sense point of view; and in this case we are not in possession of such. However grandiloquently the most recent delineators of the life of Jesus may have come forward, and pretended to be enabled by our actual sources of information to depict a human development, a natural germination and growth of insight, a gradual expansion of Jesus' horizon; their essays have been shown to be apologetic artifices, devoid of all historical value, from the absence of all proof in the record (with the exception of that vague phrase in Luke's history of the Infancy) and by the necessity of most gratuitously transposing the various accounts.

But not only does the manner of Jesus' development remain enveloped in impenetrable obscurity; it is by no means very apparent into what he developed, and ultimately became. To mention only one more fact, after all we have said; we cannot even be certain whether at the last he did not lose his faith in himself and his mission. If he spoke the famous words on the cross, "My God, my God, why hast thou forsaken me ?" then he did. It is possible, and I myself have pointed out the possibility, of the exclamation only being attributed to him in order that a psalm, considered by the earliest Christianity as the programme of the Messianic agony, might at its very commencement be applicable to him; but it certainly is equally probable that he may really have uttered the significant words. If he rose afterwards, *i.e.*, if he was the incarnate suffering deity, then it is nowise prejudicial to him ; then it only marks the lowest degree of this agony, is the cry of anguish wrung from weak mortality, which is compensated for by the strength of his divine nature as immediately manifested in his resuscitation. If, however, he is regarded as purely a human hero, the words, if he uttered them, give rise to grave misgivings. If so, then he had not calculated upon his death, then he had to the very end nursed the illusion respecting the angelic hosts, and at last, as still they came not, as they suffered him to hang languishing to death on the cross and to perish, then he had died with blasted hope and broken heart. And however much, even then, we should commiserate him on account of the excellence of his heart and his aspirations, however much we might deprecate the punishment awarded him as cruel and unjust, nevertheless we could not fail to acknowledge that so enthusiastic an expectation but receives its deserts when it is mocked by miscarriage.

As we have said, nothing is firmly established, save the objection that so many and such essential facts in the life of Jesus are *not* firmly established that we neither are clearly cognizant of his aims, nor the mode and degree in which he hoped for their realization. Perhaps these things may be ascertained; but the necessity of first ascertaining them, and the prospect of at best only attaining probability as the result of far-reaching critical investigations, instead of the intuitive assurance of faith, gives a rather discouraging aspect to the matter.   Above all, I must have a distinct, definite conception of him in whom I am to believe, whom I am to imitate as an exemplar of moral excellence.   A being of which I can only catch fitful glimpses, which remains obscure to me in essential respects, may, it is true, interest me as a problem for scientific investigation, but it must remain ineffectual as regards practical influence on my life.   But a being with distinct features, capable of affording a definite conception, is only to be found in the Christ of faith, of legend, and there, of course, only by the votary who is willing to take into the bargain all the impossibilities, all the contradictions contained in the picture : the Jesus of history, of science, is only a problem; but a problem cannot be an object of worship, or a pattern by which to shape our lives.

29.

And among the things which, comparatively speaking, we still know most positively of Jesus, there is unfortunately something which we must mention as the second and decisive reason why, if science is to assert her rights in his case, he, as the religious leader, must come to be daily more and more estranged from mankind, as mankind has developed under the influence of the civilizing momenta of modern times.

Whether he designed his kingdom for Jews, or Gentiles as well; whether he attached much or little importance to the Mosaic law and the services of the Temple; whether he assigned to himself and his disciples a greater or less amount of actual authority; whether he foresaw his death, or was surprised by it : either there is no historical basis to be found anywhere in the Gospels, or Jesus expected promptly to reappear enthroned on the clouds of heaven, in order to inaugurate the kingdom of the Messiah as foretold by him. Now, if he was the Son of God, or otherwise a being of supernatural dignity, all we have to say is that the event did not occur, and that therefore he who predicted it could not have been a divinity. But if he was not such— if he was a mere man, and yet nourished such an expectation—then there is no help for it: according to our conceptions he was an enthusiast. The word has long since ceased to be a term of opprobrium and obloquy, as it was in the last century. We know there have been noble enthusiasts—enthusiasts of genius; the influence of an enthusiast can rouse, exalt, and occasion prolonged historic effects; but we shall not be desirous to choose him as the guide of our life. He will be sure to mislead us, if we do not subject his influence to the control of our reason.

But this latter precaution was neglected by Christendom during the Middle Ages. Not only did it suffer itself to be seduced by Christ's utter disdain for the world ; it even outdid him. He at least continued to abide in the world, were it only to convince men of its worthlessness; if hermits and monks at a later period shunned all intercourse with it, they indeed outstripped him, but only on the path along which he led them himself. As concerned renunciation of worldly goods, indeed, they were at no loss for a subterfuge : the individual, it was true, could own nothing, but the community, the monastery, the church, and its heads, so much the more. Thus, too, the precept of turning the other cheek to the smiter has always found its corrective in the sound common sense of mankind; some personages of especial sanctity excepted, the pious Middle Ages were as contentious and bellicose as any other era in the history of the world. Its sturdy goodmen and housewives, moreover, took good thought for the morrow, in spite of the precept of their Saviour; but the performance of their worldly duties weighed on the conscience of these excellent people; at least, made them appear low and common in their own eyes. For had not Jesus told the wealthy youth, that if he would be perfect he must sell all his possessions and give the price to the poor ? and at another time he had likewise said that all, indeed, could not receive this saying, but that there were those who had made themselves eunuchs for the sake of God's kingdom.

The Reformation first went to work on a systematic principle, in order to place this ascetic, fanatical side of Christianity under the due control of reason. Luther's dicta concerning the value of the performance of duty in all the relations of life, whether matrimonial, domestic, or civil—on the useful activity

of housewives, mothers, maid or man-servants, as
compared with the profitless macerations, senseless
babble, and drone-like laziness of monks and nuns,
are inspired by a thoroughly healthy humanity.
But this was supposed to militate against the degeneracy of the Catholic Church, not against Christianity itself. The earth continued a vale of tears ;
man's gaze was still to remain fixed on the celestial
glories to come. " If heaven is our home," asked
Calvin, " what is the earth but a place of exile ?
Only because God has placed us in this world, and
appointed us our functions therein, must it also
be our endeavour to fulfil the same ; it is solely the
divine commandment which imparts a true value
to our earthly vocations, which are in themselves
devoid of such." This is clearly a miserable compromise : if our earthly occupations are valueless in
themselves, this value cannot be imparted to them
from without ; but if they do possess such value, it
can consist in nothing but the moral relations which
are implied by them. Man's earthly existence bears
its own law, its rule of guidance, its aims and ends
included in itself.

30.

But, we are told, he whom you call an enthusiast was at the same time he who, not to mention many other moral precepts of the highest value, first implanted in mankind, both by precept and example, the principles of charity, of compassion,—nay, of the love of foes, and fraternal feelings for all men ; and even he who should only profess these principles professes thereby his belief in Christ and in Christianity. They certainly remain its fairest attribute, we reply, and are the highest glory of its founder; but they neither exclusively appertain to him, nor are they annulled without him.

Five centuries before the Christian era Buddhism had already inculcated gentleness and compassion, not only towards men, but towards all living creatures. Among the Jews themselves, the Rabbi Hillel had already taught, a generation before Christ, that the commandment of loving one's neighbour as one's self constituted the very essence of the law. To assist even our enemies was a maxim of the Stoics in Jesus' time. And but one generation later, although without doubt independently of him, and strictly in keeping with the principles of the Stoic school, Epictetus called all men brothers, inasmuch as all were the children of God. The recognition of this truth is so obviously involved in the development of humanity, that it must inevitably occur at certain stages of the process, and not to one individual alone. At that very time this perception had been brought home to the nobler minds of Greece and Rome by the abolition of barriers between nation and nation in the Roman Empire, to the Jews by their dispersal into all lands. In exile among the Gentiles, a close band of fellowship, a readiness to help and support each other, was developed and organized, and rendered still more intimate by the additional element of Christian faith in the recent manifestation and speedy return of the Messiah. The two centuries of oppression and persecution which Christianity had still to pass through—a time to which on the whole it owes all that is best in its development —were a continuous training in those very virtues.

It must be admitted that compatriots and fellow-believers were the first to benefit by this active charity. Jesus himself, it is true, had proposed to his disciples the example of their heavenly Father, who caused the sun to shine equally on the evil and the good, and sent his rain upon the just and the unjust. Nevertheless, he had prohibited his disciples, on their first mission, from suffering the sunshine and fertilizing rain of his saving doctrine to fall also on Gentiles and Samaritans; thus, at least, we are informed by Matthew the Evangelist. No wonder that the Christian Church yielded more and more to the temptation of limiting its charity to the circle of the faithful,—nay, even within the confines of this circle, to the professors of the pretended true Christianity, *i.e.*, the members of that Church which each respectively considered orthodox. Christianity as such never rose above crusades and persecutions of heretics; it has never even attained to tolerance, which yet is merely the negative side of universal benevolence. Their assiduity in works of philanthropy, their zeal and ability in the organization of charitable labours and institutions, are qualities of the " unco gude " among us, the glory of which shall not be diminished, excepting in so far as they diminish it themselves, by the *arrière pensée* of hierarchy or proselytism. Christianity indeed emphasized the idea of humanity; but the task of elaborating it into a pure and complete form, of stating it as a principle, was reserved for the philosophico-secular civilization of the sceptical eighteenth century. The belief that Christ died for all men is not only a transcendental

ground for the love of all mankind, the true reason
of which lies much closer at hand ; it also runs the
danger of confining this love to those who believe
in the atonement, at least to those who do not
wittingly disbelieve it.

The same holds good of all the other Christian
precepts; Christianity did not bring them to the
world, nor will they disappear from the world along
with it. We shall retain all that was really achieved
by Christianity as we have retained what was accomplished by Greece and Rome, without the form of
religion in which that kernel ripened as in its
husk. Thus only shall we succeed in discard-
ing at the same time the narrowness and the
partiality which throughout adhered to the doctrines of Christianity.

31.

But why, we shall perhaps be asked, separate
what after all might be capable of union ? In its
present development Christianity is not likely to
circumscribe our philanthropy, rather to vivify it;
and such quickening will be by no means amiss in
this age of materialistic interests, of unfettered
egotism. Why not, then, in this case also, try to

come up to the precept, "This ought ye to have done, and not to have left the other undone?"

Because, we answer, this absolutely will not do. Why it will not do has been sufficiently elucidated in the foregoing pages; we cannot make a prop of our action out of a faith which we no longer possess, a community from whose persuasions and temper we are estranged. We will make a trial of it, but it shall be the last. The old creed was our starting-point, and as step by step we traced its development and transformation, we found that in none of its forms was it any longer acceptable by us. Let us now, to conclude, take it in its latest, mildest, most modern and at the same time concrete form, as it reveals itself in worship; let us assist in thought at the Christian festivals in a Protestant church, the minister of which is versed in the scientific modes of thought, and see whether we can still be sincerely and naturally edified thereby. How will this man —or we, if we put ourselves in his place—set to work, and what must the chain of his reasoning necessarily be, even if he does not care to give formal expression to everything?

At Christmas he will tell himself, and perhaps also hint to the intelligent among his audience, that the miraculous birth and the virgin mother are utterly out of the question. Further, that **the** whole story as to the journey of Jesus' parents to Bethlehem because of the tax imposed under Cyrenius, is an awkward fiction, as the tax was not imposed until Jesus had already reached boyhood. That the child presumably came quite peaceably into the world in the bosom of its Nazarene family. That the shepherds vanish with the manger, and the angels with the shepherds. That with this child not peace alone came on earth, but enough and to spare of warfare and contention. In short, that although on that day we certainly celebrate the birthday of a remarkable personage, destined to great influence on the history of mankind, we nevertheless only celebrate that of one worker among many in the cause of human progress.

Such a minister would again have to make a clearance at the Epiphany, *i.e.*, to eliminate the gospel narrative as a Messianic myth. He would remind himself, and if he were courageous enough, his congregation also, how the errant star was none other than that star which, according to the narrative in Numbers, the heathen seer Balaam had foretold should come out of Jacob, only, however, using it as an emblem of a triumphant Jewish king; how the wise men of the East had only been invented to suit the star, while their gifts were modelled after a passage of the pseudo-Isaiah, where, of the light which had risen over Jerusalem—*i.e.*, the light of divine favour again vouchsafed to the Jews at the end of their exile—it is said, that the Gentiles shall come to this light, and all they from Sheba shall bring gold and incense. The infant Jesus, this clergyman must admit, had undoubtedly at that time lain as unheeded by the wide world—and moreover, not in Bethlehem, but probably in Nazareth—as children of plain citizens usually do.

As at Christmas the virgin's son, so on Good Friday our clergyman would have to set aside the sacrificial death—the idea of the Redeemer altogether. The more honestly he should do this, the more would he offend the staunch believers; the more discreetly, the less satisfied would be the more advanced among his audience, who, in fact, would be justified in accusing him of equivocation, should he still wish to hold fast by the conception of salvation and a Saviour in any nonnatural sense.

His task would become more critical still as regards Easter. In this case it is hardly possible to call the thing by its correct name in a Christian

Church, and if this be not done, then all speech concerning it is mere phrase.

Lastly, on Ascension-day it becomes difficult to refrain from satire. To speak of this event as one of actual occurrence is simply to affront educated people at this time of day. Therefore it must be treated symbolically; as has already been done with the resurrection, and must likewise be done with the miracles, the healing of the sick, the raising from the dead, the casting out of devils— themes which repeatedly furnish texts for sermons on ordinary Sundays, and which all admit of a moral application. But why take such a roundabout way? why beat the bush after things for which we have no use, in order at last to reach some desired point, which we might have attained in much simpler and at the same time more decided fashion by going straight at it?

On all these festivals, as well as on ordinary Sundays, our clergyman begins his discourse with prayer, not only to God but to Christ as well, after which he reads verses or sections from Holy Writ as a text. Very well; but now, as to the first point, whence does he derive the right of praying to a mere man? for as such he regards Christ. Habit alone makes us overlook the enormity of such a usage, which has been imported from quite another standpoint; or is the fact to be looked at in the light of rhetorical licence, as it may be allowable to address a mountain, a river? then it must be objected that the church, where everything is and should be seriously treated, is not the place for such a licence. But as regards the texts of Scripture—has the minister arrived at an understanding with his audience as to what they possess in the so-called Holy Scripture? Has he told them the men of the Reformation have conquered for us the right of free inquiry in Scripture, but modern science has conquered for itself that of free inquiry *about* Scripture? And has he clearly shown them what this implies? That reason which institutes inquiries about Scripture — *i.e.*, not in order to comprehend its contents, but also to ascertain its origin, the measure of its credibility and its worth — necessarily stands above Scripture? that Scripture has ceased, therefore, to be the highest source of religious knowledge? We can count the theologians who have hitherto honestly spoken out on this point. Progress, it is pretended, has taken place in gradual ascent along easy ground, from the standpoint of the reformers to the liberal theology of our time, while the fact of the displacement of Scripture as a supreme authority involves a step higher and more dangerous even than that other one which had to be scaled from the Catholic standpoint by the Reformers.

But let us still for a moment remain in our modern Protestant church, and assist at the administration of the sacraments. Deducting all mere formalism, we here get the impression that the rite of baptism might not have been without a sufficient meaning at a time when it was necessary to gather in the new Messianic community from the world of Jew and Gentile, and to unite it by a common consecration. To-day, in the midst of a Christian world, there is no longer any meaning in this; but as the later ecclesiastical relation of baptism to original sin and the devil is even more out of the question, baptisms in the modern church, in the service of which we are mentally participating, must necessarily appear as a ceremony without any real significance, nay, with a meaning which is repugnant to us. We will leave it to the Jews to stamp their infant sons as something special by a permanent physical mark; we would not have even a transient one, for we would not have our children something special, we would only have them men, and to be men we will bring them up.

As baptism, along with its relations to the world of Jew and Gentile, and further, to original sin and the devil, has lost its real meaning, thus also has it fared with the Lord's Supper in regard to the atonement, nothing remaining now but the repulsive oriental metaphor of drinking the blood and eating of the body of a man. In the next place, the imbecile and yet fateful quarrels about it, as to whether the thing should not be taken literally—whether it were not the actual flesh and blood—are painful to remember. We might be well pleased by a fraternal feast of humanity, with a common draught from a single cup; but blood would be the very last beverage we should dream of putting into the latter.

On the altar of our modern Protestant church, in so far as it stands on Lutheran ground, we shall find the image of the crucified Christ, the so-called crucifix. This old chief symbol of Christianity the Catholic church, as is known, is extravagantly fond of placing up and down the country-side; the Protestant church, in so far as it did not put it on one side with other images, has, at least, with a kind of shame, removed it to the interior of churches and houses, besides allowing the empty cross to stand on cemeteries, steeples, and the like. It was possibly on his Italian journey, or in some other Catholic country, that Goethe, vexed by its obtrusiveness, took the dislike which impelled him, in the notorious verse of his Venetian epigram, to put the cross side by side with garlic and vermin. Nothing but the mere form of this sign—the stiff little piece of wood placed crosswise on another little piece of wood, as he expresses it in the "West-Eastern Divan,"—was unpleasant to him, and it would certainly have cheered him had he known that in this he agreed with that staunch Elizabeth Charlotte, Princess of the Palatinate and Duchess of Orleans, who likewise confessed "to not at all liking to see the cross," because its form did not please her. Perhaps even half-unconsciously in her case, and certainly in Goethe's, there was something over and above the mere form, over and above a simple æsthetic dislike, which repelled him in the cross. It was "the image of sorrow on the tree," which, according to the passage referred to in the "Divan," ought not to be "made a god." The crucifix is, on the one hand, the visible and tangible pledge of the remission of sins to the faithful; on the other, however, the deification of sorrow generally; it is humanity in its saddest plight, broken and shattered in all its limbs, so to speak, and in a certain sense rejoicing thereat; it is the most one-sided, rigid embodiment of Christian world-renunciation and passiveness. In a symbol of this kind, mankind rejoicing in life and action can now no longer find the expression of its religious consciousness; and the continued regard accorded it in the modern Protestant Church is, after all, but one more of those compromises and untruths which make it a thing of such feeble vitality.

And now, I think we have reached the end. And the result? Our answer to the question with which we have headed this section of our account? Shall I still give a distinct statement, and place the sum of all we have said in round numbers under the account? Most unnecessary, I should say; but I would not, on any consideration, appear to shirk even the most unpalatable word. My conviction, therefore, is, if we would not evade difficulties or put forced constructions upon them, if we would have our yea yea, and our nay nay,—in short, if we would speak as honest, upright men, we must acknowledge we are no longer Christians.

In saying this we have not, however, as already remarked at the beginning, altogether renounced religion; we might still be religious, even if we were so no longer in the form of Christianity. We therefore put our second question thus:

II.

32.

WE shall be all the less inclined to reply in the negative, without further examination, as we are in the habit of regarding the capacity for religion as a prerogative of human nature, nay, as its most illustrious pre-eminence. One thing, at all events, is certain: that the brute, destitute of what we term reason, is devoid of this capacity also. The tribes which have left travellers in doubt of their possessing a religion have always been found to be in other respects, the most miserable and brutal. As we ascend in history, the higher development of religion goes hand in hand with the progress of culture among nations. Let us, first of all, therefore, cast a glance at the origin and earliest development of religion among mankind.

Hume is undoubtedly correct in his assertion that mankind have originally been led to religion, not by the disinterested desire of knowledge and truth, but by the selfish craving for material welfare; and that pain has contributed more potently than allurement to the propagation of religion. The Epicurean derivation of piety from fear has, incontestably, a good deal of truth in it. For if man had all he wished, if his needs were always satisfied, if his plans never miscarried, if no painful lessons of experience constrained him to regard the future with apprehension, the notion of a higher power would hardly have arisen within his breast. He would have thought that thus it must be, and accordingly have accepted his lot with stolid indifference.

As things are, however, his first perception in regard to Nature is that of his being confronted by a weird, sinister power. True, Nature has a side which may appear friendly to man. The sun which gives him warmth, the air he breathes, the fountain that slakes his thirst, the tree affording him grateful shade, the flocks and herds that yield him milk and wool, appear to exist for the welfare of man, to have been the gift of a beneficent power. Up to a certain limit Nature likewise allows man to exercise a determining influence upon her; he ploughs his field, tames and makes use of domestic animals, hunts and kills the wild, constructs his bark for river or lake, and prepares his hut, his scanty clothing, as a protection against the inclemency of the weather. But terrible indeed is the reverse side of this kindly countenance. Beside and behind the narrow border-land on which Nature gives him free play, she reserves to herself an enormous predominance, which, bursting forth unexpectedly, makes cruel sport of every human effort. The hurricane overwhelms the boat and the boatman; lightning consumes the hut, or inundation sweeps it away; a murrain ravages the flock; heat parches or hail annihilates the produce of the fields; while man himself knows he is exposed, without permanent protection, to chance and calamity, disease and death.

This indifference of Nature to him, his constant dealing with a power which is alien to him, and to which he himself is alien, and with which, in a word, nothing can be done,—this it is that man finds unbearable, against which his inmost being rises in resistance. The only deliverance from Nature is to invest her with the attributes of which he is conscious in himself. She is only then not inhuman when she becomes a power in the image of man. Even the destructive natural forces are then no longer as pernicious as they seemed. The simoom of the desert, the pestilence which stalks through the land—if they are only conceived of as blind impersonal powers, then man, in regard to them, is a helpless cypher. Conceived of as persons, as higher beings, as dæmons or divinities, although still evil, nevertheless much has been gained—a hold upon them. Are there not also wicked, cruel, and malignant men, and such, moreover, as, like those natural forces, are at the same time so powerful as to be irresistible? and nevertheless there are means to come to an arrangement with such—at least, to escape their clutches with but passable damage. Let submission be duly made, be not chary of flattery and gifts, and behold, they show themselves more tractable than one dared to hope. So it comes to pass with those destructive natural forces, as soon as it is settled that they are endowed with reason and will—beings, in short, resembling man. Now people go forth to meet Typhon with prayers and sacrifice; they offer up appropriate gifts to the god of the plague; they are comforted by the reflection that, from a human point of view, they may hope to have influenced these beings in their favour, to have appeased their wrath by such means.

Neither, by any means, are all the forces of Nature so utterly evil as those we have adduced:

Kindly from heaven's cloud the rain
Streams on the plain ;
Blindly from the cloud of heaven
Leaps forth the levin.

Rain and lightning are only the various manifestations of the same power, the deity of the upper
air ; the Zeus of the Hellenic conception, who, now
merciful, now terrible, sometimes sends fertilizing
rain to the plain, and sometimes, not so blindly, however, as the modern poet imagines, his destructive
thunderbolts.   Such a power, in spite of the pernicious forces at its disposal, may nevertheless be good
in itself, and benevolently inclined to man, and only
cause those evil effects when man has exasperated it,
and kindled its wrath against him.   All the easier,
therefore, will it be for man to appease the excited
passion of an inherently beneficent being, by proofs
of his submission and devotion.

But if such a manifestation of Nature, or an
aggregate of natural phenomena, especially such as
those on which the weal or woe of the entire popu-
lation of a country is dependent in an extraordinary
degree—as, for example, in Egypt, the Nile on the
one hand, the blast of the desert on the other—be
once personified in this fashion, the process will soon
traverse the whole circumference of nature and

human existence. To heaven as Uranos or Zeus we shall have confronted the earth as Gaia or Demeter, the sea as Poseidon; the breeding of cattle, and agriculture, corn, and the vine, have each their presiding deities; as well as music and medicine, commerce and war. The imagination of the various nations proceeds, as to this, with the utmost freedom and carelessness : the same departments are sometimes distributed among different deities, sometimes, again, assigned to one and the same god, as especial aspects or manifestations of his nature. Apollo, besides being the god of music and prophecy, is also that of medicine, which yet he has transferred to his son Æsculapius as its presiding genius; Mars is the god of war, but Minerva also is a warlike goddess : in the former, war is personified as a rude inhuman pursuit; in the latter, so to speak, as the regular military art. And what a multitude of functions and names,— from Stator to Pistor and Stercutius, from Regina to Pronuba and Lucina,—were not heaped on Jupiter and Juno, to be taken away again in manifold changes by the inferior deities !

For the further a nation advances in civilization, the more importance will it attach to human life and its various relations, as well as to the terrors and blessings of inanimate nature. And the more insecurity and hazard in mortal life, the more things dependent on circumstances which elude human calculation and are yet more beyond the control of human power, the more pressing will grow man's need to postulate powers akin to his own nature, accessible to his wishes and prayers. At the same time, man's moral constitution now comes into play as a co-operating agent : not only against others, but against his own sensuality and capriciousness as well, would he protect himself by placing in reserve behind the dictates of his conscience, a commanding God.

How helpless is the stranger in a foreign country amid a foreign people, and how easy is it to take advantage of his defenceless situation; but there is a Ζεύς ξένιος who protects the guest.   How unsafe is it to rely on the promises—even the oaths—of men, and how pressing the temptation under certain circumstances to seek to evade them ; but there rules a Ζεύς ὅρκιος who punishes perjury.   Not always is bloody murder discovered by men ; but the sleepless Eumenides dog the step of the fugitive assassin. One of the most important relations of life among civilized nations has always been the marriage bond; but how hazardous is it not ? what manifold possibilities of unhappy results, how much temptation to transgression does it not involve ?   To counteract these, the pious Greek and Roman sought a security in the celestial marriage of Zeus and Hera.   It certainly is no model wedlock, in the ideal sense, rather an emblem of the frailty of human unions, besides being depicted by the Greeks with all the moral levity of that people; nevertheless, Jupiter and Juno make and protect matrimonial alliances; Juno especially leads the bride to her husband, conducts her to his house, unbinds her zone, as later on she unravels the misunderstandings between them, and at last, without imperilling the mother, ushers the yearned-for fruits of marriage to the light of day.

33.

Hence it follows that polytheism was the original, and in some respects the natural form of religion. A multiplicity of phenomena presented themselves to man, a multiplicity of forces pressed in upon him, from which he either wished himself protected, or of whose favour he desired to be assured; then also a variety of relations which he craved to have sanctified and securely established ; thus naturally arose, also, a multiplicity of divinities. This conclusion is confirmed by the observation, that all those tribes of the earth which are still to a certain extent in a state of nature, continue now, as formerly, to be polytheists. Monotheism appears everywhere in history, the Jewish not excepted, as something secondary, as something educed in the lapse of time out of a more primitive polytheism. How was this transition effected?

Is is said, certainly, that a more exact observation of Nature must have led man to perceive the connexion of all her phenomena, the unity of design in which all her laws converge. And in like manner the development of man's powers of reflection must have rendered it evident that a plurality of deities must mutually limit each other, and in consequence deprive each other of the very attributes of divinity, so that the deity, in the true and complete sense of that word, could only be a unit. Insight of this kind, it is argued, came to a few highly-gifted individuals of antiquity, and these became in consequence the founders of monotheism.

We know full well the highly-gifted individuals who acquired insight in this manner: they were the Greek philosophers; but they became founders, not of a religion, but of philosophical systems and schools. Of a like nature is the oscillating monotheism of the Indian religion: it is an esoteric, mystical doctrine, the presentiment of a few, developed from the popular polytheism.

Monotheism first occurs among the Jews in the firm serried form of a popular religion. And here also we can clearly apprehend its origin. Hebrew monotheism was certainly not produced by a deeper observation of nature; the Hebrews for a long while caring only for nature in its relation to their own wants. Neither did it arise from philosophical speculation; for before the impulse communicated to them by the Greeks, the Jews did not speculate, at least not in the philosophical sense. Monotheism (the fact becomes evident in that of the Jews, and is further confirmed by Islamism) is originally and essentially the religion of a wandering clan. The requirements of such a nomadic band are very simple, as are also its social arrangements; and although at first (as may also here be assumed to have been the primitive idea) these may have been presided over by distinct Fetishes, Dæmons, or deities, nevertheless this distinction disappeared in proportion as the horde concentrated itself (as did, for example, the Israelites in their invasion of Canaan) and receded more and more, as in course of warfare with hordes like themselves, or with tribes and nations of different institutions, the contrast to

these latter gained prominence. As it was but a
single enthusiasm which inspired the clan, which
strengthened it in its conflict with others, gave it
hope in victory, and even in defeat the trust in
future triumph; even thus it was only one god
whom it served, from whom it expected all things;
or, rather even this god was, in fact, only its deified
popular spirit.   True, at first the gods of other
tribes and nations were conceived as antagonistic to
the one god of the clan—the gods of the Canaanites
to the god of Israel; but as the weaker, the inferior,
destined to be overcome by the god of the clan—vain
gods, who at last must actually vanish into nothing,
leaving the one true God alone.

It is only an ancient Christian-Hebrew prejudice
to consider monotheism in itself, as contrasted with
polytheism, the higher form of religion.   There is a
monotheism which is superior to polytheism; but
also one which is the reverse.   He who should have
expected the Greeks of the centuries between
Homer and Æschylus to exchange their Olympian
circle of gods for the one god of Sinai, would have
demanded from them the surrender of their rich
and complete existence, putting forth in all directions the boughs and blossoms of a most beautiful
humanity, for the poverty and one-sidedness of the

Jewish nature. In Schiller's "Gods of Greece," there still echoes the lament over the impoverishment of life by the triumph of monotheism; and yet the one god of his conception is already far removed from the ancient Hebrew divinity.

One advantage monotheism attains, so to speak, adventitiously, which at a later period produces the most important results. The plurality of gods, agreeably to the law of their origin, however they may be transferred to the domain of ethics, must ever remain bound to the individual forces and aspects of nature, and in consequence, as we observe in the case of the Grecian gods, something sensuous adheres to their essence. The distinction of sex inseparable from polytheism is, of itself, a sufficient proof of this. The one God, however, merely because he is the one, while nature consists of a multiplicity of forces and manifestations, must necessarily rise above nature. This exaltation was accomplished only gradually, and with a certain repugnance by the Jewish people, but nevertheless, with the greater strictness at last, as the neighbouring tribes, with whom it had to contend, declined in their worship of rude physical deities. These were detestable to the Jew, even in their very images; therefore at last he interdicted himself any image of his God. The worship of these deities, which diverged sometimes into the excess of the terrible, sometimes into that of the sensual, must have appeared unclean to the worshipper of the one God throned above nature; the service rendered by him to his God was, indeed, far from spiritual, but nevertheless, such as it was, purity formed one of its principal requisites. But out of this external purity grew the inward, in consequence of a gradually deepening conception ; the one God developed into the severe Law-giver, monotheism into the nursery of discipline and morality.

It was further limited, however, among the Jewish people by an innate spirit of provincialism. The precepts which Jehovah gave his people were chiefly framed to isolate it from all the rest. The one God was the Maker of all, yet not the God of all nations in the same sense : properly he was the God only of the little tribe of his worshippers, in comparison to whom he treated the other nations as step-children. From this proceeded something harsh, rigid, personally irascible in the whole character of this God. In this respect the Jewish conception of God awaited its completion at the hands of Hellenism. It was in Alexandria that the tribal national god of Israel intermingled and soon became

one with the God of the world and of mankind, who had been evolved by Greek philosophers from the multitude of Olympian deities in their national religion.

34.

Our modern monotheistic conception of God has two sides, that of the absolute, and that of the personal, which, although united in him, are so in the same manner as that in which two qualities are sometimes found in one person, one of which can be traced to the father's side, the other to the mother's. The one element is the Hebrew-Christian, the other the Græco-philosophical contribution to our conception of God. We may say that we inherit from the Old Testament the Lord-God, from the New the God-Father, but from Greek philosophy the God-head, or the Absolute.

Undoubtedly the Jew also conceived his Jehovah as absolute, in so far as he possessed the capacity of such a conception; *i.e.,* as at least unlimited in power and duration; above all, however, his God was a being which asserted itself as a personality. Not only that in remotest times he walks in the garden and converses with Adam; that later he in human guise allows himself to be regaled by the patriarch under the tree by his hut; that he confers with the law-giver on the mountain, and himself hands him the two tables; but his whole demeanour, as an angry and jealous God, who repents having made men, and prepares to destroy them, who regards the transgressions of his chosen people as personal injuries, and avenges them accordingly, is altogether that of a personal being. The transformation accomplished by Christianity of the Lord-God into the God-Father, did not affect the element of personality; on the contrary, it rather intensified it. The more tender the form which intercourse of the pious with his God may assume, the more certainly will the latter appear to him as a person, for a tender relation can only subsist towards a person, at the least a fictitious one.

Philosophy, however, has always, in the first instance, laid the emphasis in regard to the conception of God on the other side—that of the absolute. It required a Supreme Being, from whom the existence and ordering of the world might be deduced. In this, however, it found several of the personal attributes which Judaism and Christianity had intermingled with their conception of God, inconvenient and offensive. Not only could it make nothing of a repenting and wrathful deity, but just as little of one from whom something might be obtained by human prayers. It lay not in its intention to deprive God of personality, but such was practically its tendency; for it required an illimitable deity, and personality is a limit.

Copernicus is sometimes represented as the man who has, so to speak, withdrawn the seat from under the body of the ancient Hebrew and Christian Deity by means of his system of the universe. This is an error, not only from a personal point of view, inasmuch as Copernicus, like Kepler and Newton, did not cease to be a devout Christian, but also in regard to his theory. It initiated a reformation only within the limits of the solar system; beyond this it suffered the sphere of the fixed stars, the expanded firmament of Scripture, to remain untouched, as a firm, crystalline, spherical shell, enclosing our solar and planetary worlds like a walnut-shell, so that beyond it there was room and to spare for a properly furnished heaven, with its throne of God, etc. It was not until, in consequence of continued observation and calculation, the fixed stars were recognized to be bodies similar to our sun, and surrounded presumably by analogous planetary systems–until the universe resolved itself into an infinity of heavenly bodies, and heaven itself into an optical illusion, that the ancient personal God was, as it were, dispossessed of his habitation.

No matter, it is said; we know well that God is omnipresent, and not in need of any particular residence. Certainly people know this, but then they also forget it again. Reason may conceive of God as omnipresent, but imagination, nevertheless, cannot rid itself of the endeavour to represent Him as limited by space. Formerly she could do this unhindered, when she still disposed of a convenient area. Now she finds this more difficult, as she knows that such an area is nowhere to be found. For this knowledge must unavoidably penetrate from the reasoning faculty to the imaginative. He who has a clear cosmical conception, in harmony with the present standpoint of astronomy, can no longer represent to himself a Deity throned in heaven, and surrounded by angelic hosts.

The retinue of angels is necessary, however, to the idea of a personal God. A person must needs have society—a ruler his court. But with our present cosmical conception, which knows inhabitants of the heavenly bodies, not any longer a divine court, the angels disappear likewise. With heaven, therefore, no more his palace; with no angels assembled round his throne; with neither thunder and light-

ning for his missiles, nor war, famine, and pestilence,
for his scourges ;—with all these but effects of
natural causes, how, since he has thus lost every
attribute of personal existence and action, how can
we still continue to conceive of a personality of
God ?

35.

Many a book of travels has told us what a
terrifying impression the unforeseen eclipses of the
sun and moon continually produce on savage
tribes; how by screams and clamour of all sorts,
they attempt to lend assistance to the luminous
power, and drive far from him the huge toad, or
whatever other shape they may ascribe to the ob-
scuring principle. This is but natural; and it is
also but natural that these phenomena, which,
according to the calculations of astronomy, have
been announced to us in the almanack, should no
longer affect us religiously; that even the most
ignorant boor should no longer say an Ave Maria
or a Pater Noster to render them harmless.

But what shall we say to the fact that, as late as
the year 1866, English peers reproached Lord Russell
with not having ordered a general fast against the
murrain which had broken out? shall we in this case

ascribe it to ecclesiastical stupidity, or miserable hypocrisy? If in a profoundly Catholic country, when rain is too long deferred, and continuous drought threatens ruin to the crops, then we can imagine the peasants expecting their priest to make a procession around the fields, and draw down rain from heaven by his entreaties. If we meet such a procession, we shall exclaim in regard to the peasants, *O sancta simplicitas!* in regard to the priest we shall leave it open for the present whether he has rather yielded to the urgency of pious simplicity, or has encouraged it in the interest of the hierarchy; but at any rate we shall be confirmed in our wish, that by an improved education even the rustic may also be brought to see that these are manifestations of nature subject to laws as stringent as the eclipses of the sun and the moon, although they have not as yet been investigated as completely as the latter.

It is not quite the same thing if plague or cholera have invaded a country, or broken out in a city, claiming victims in every street, every dwelling; or if, as with us in the past year, the majority of the sons of a people have gone to the wars, and are opposed in combat to the enemy. In both instances public prayers arise spontaneously; in the one case

from people still in health, in the other from those
left behind—the masses expecting the granting of
their petitions, *i.e.*, an objective effect which is to
be produced in favour of those in danger, while the
reflecting portion is content to achieve for itself,
by collective prayer, a subjective furtherance of
its end, through serenity and exaltation of spirit—
the only thing, in fact, which is gained by the
rest. Feuerbach justly remarks, however, that a
real genuine prayer is only that by means of which
the suppliant hopes to effect something which
could not have been effected without it. Luther
was such a suppliant. He was thoroughly convinced that he had saved the life of the dying
Melancthon by the prayers and reproaches he addressed to God, in case he should just at that time
snatch his indispensable colleague from his side.
Schleiermacher was no longer such a suppliant.
He saw but too clearly that every assumption of a
desire or a right to influence the divine decision by
even the purest and most reasonable of human
wishes was as foolish as it was impious. Nevertheless, he still continued to pray; only that he no
longer placed the real importance of prayer in bringing about an objective result, but in its subjective
influence on the soul of the suppliant himself. That

in individual cases this may possibly remain the only effect of prayer, *i.e.*, that God may perhaps not grant the prayer—this is a contingency which must enter into the calculation of even the sincerest believer. But nevertheless, he always looks upon the granting of his prayer, *i.e.*, its objective effectiveness, as possible in general and probable in his particular case. If, on the other hand, I entreat, for example, the preservation of a life precious to me, while, nevertheless, I clearly perceive that my prayer cannot produce the smallest objective result—that, supposing even the subject of it to recover, my supplication has had no more influence on the course of the malady than the lifting of my finger on the course of the moon,—if with this conviction, and in spite of it, I still go on praying, I am playing a game with myself, excusable indeed, in view of its momentary effect, but neither consistent with dignity nor devoid of danger.

In Schleiermacher's case especially, prayer was the expression of a conscious illusion, partly the result of early habit, partly in view of the congregation which surrounded him ; and he intentionally avoided lifting himself above it by his critical consciousness.

Kant was no longer a suppliant, but all the more honest to himself and to others. He is shocked,

quite irrespectively of the supposed efficacy of prayer
by the pure position which the supplicant assumes.
"Let us picture," he says, " a pious and well-meaning man, but narrow-minded as regards a purified
conception of religion, who should be taken unawares
not saying his prayers, but only making the gestures
appropriate to the act. I need not say that he will
naturally be expected to grow embarrassed and
confused, just as if he had been in a situation of
which he must needs be ashamed. But why so ?
A person found speaking to himself is at first
sight suspected of temporary insanity ; and he is
not quite unjustly judged somewhat similarly, if,
being alone, his occupation or gesticulation is such
as can only be used by him who has some other
person before his eyes, which, nevertheless, is not
so in the case supposed." Thus Kant in his "Religion within the limits of mere Reason:" still more
incisively does he express himself in an essay in
his posthumous works : " To ascribe to prayer
other effects than natural (subjective-psychological)
ones, is foolish," he remarks here, " and requires
no refutation ; we can only enquire, Should the
prayer be retained on account of its natural results?
to which the answer is, that in any case it can be
recommended only according to circumstances ; for

he who can attain the vaunted advantages of prayer by other means will stand in no need of it."

That Kant has here, with his wonted simplicity and precision, candidly stated the convictions of modern times in regard to prayer, can be as little disputed as that one of the most essential attributes of the personal God has perished with the belief in the efficacy of prayer.

36.

Now at last, it seems, we must draw up the heavy, somewhat old-fashioned, scientific artillery of the so-called proofs of the existence of God, all of them seeking to demonstrate, according to the intention of those who originated them, a God in the peculiar sense of the word, who, after all, can only be a personal one.

In the first place, then, according to the law that everything must have a sufficient cause, the so-called cosmological argument infers from the existence of the world the necessary existence of a personal God. Of all the various things which we perceive in the world, not one is self-existent, each owing its origin to something else, which, however is in the like predicament of owing its origin to some other thing; thus reflection is ever sent on from one

thing to another, and never rests till it has reached
the thought of the One Being, the cause of whose
existence rests not with another, but in himself, who
is no longer a contingent, but a necessary existence.

In the first place, however, the personality of
this necessary Being would by no means have been
established, for we should merely have proved a first
Cause, not an intelligent Creator of the world. But
in the second place, we have not even demonstrated
a Cause. A cause is other than its effect; the cause
of the universe would be something else than the universe; our conclusion would therefore land us beyond
the limits of the Cosmos. But is this result reached
by fair means? If we invariably arrive at the
conclusion, in regard to every individual existence
or phenomenon in the world, examine as many as
we please, that each has the ground of its existence
in some other, which again stands in the same
predicament as regards something else, then we
justly conclude that the same law obtains with
regard to all individual existences and phenomena,
even those which we have not especially examined.
But are we, then, justified in concluding the totality
of these individual existences and phenomena to
be caused by a Being not similarly conditioned
which has not, like these, the source of its existence

in something else, but in itself ? This is a conclusion devoid of all coherence, all logic. By any method of logical reasoning we shall not get beyond the universe. If everything in the universe has been caused by something else, and so on, *ad infinitum*, what we finally reach is not the conception of a Cause of which the Cosmos is the effect, but of a Substance of which individual cosmical phenomena are but the accidents. We reach not a deity, but a self-centred Cosmos, unchangeable amid the eternal change of things.

But we shall be reminded that the cosmological proof is not to be taken by itself; that it must, to gain its proper weight, be united to the teleological or physico-theological demonstration. This latter takes for a starting-point not only the bare fact of the derivative and contingent existence of all things, but also their distinctive character, their judicious adaptation as a whole and in their parts. Whichever way we look in the world — in the infinitely little or great, in the order of the solar system as well as in the structure and nutrition of the tiniest insect—we see means employed by which certain ends are attained ; we may define the world as a whole of infinitely judicious contrivance. The contemplation of ends, however, and the employment of means to attain them, are exclusively the functions of consciousness, of intelligence. We are therefore constrained by the physico-theological proof to define the first Cause, in the cosmological argument, as an intelligent personal Creator.

But how if the cosmological argument, as shown above, has not furnished us a transcendental first Cause, but only a Substance immanent in the universe? Certainly in that case the Primal Substance will have received one predicate the more: we shall conceive of it as of an entity manifesting itself in endless variety, not only causatively, but also in the adaptation and co-ordination of phenomena. In so doing we must, however, beware of mistaking one for the other. We being men, are only capable of producing a work the parts of which shall harmonize for the attainment of a certain result, by means of the conscious conception of an end and an equally conscious selection of means, but we must not therefore conclude that natural works of a like description can only have been produced by the corresponding agency of an intelligent Creator. This by no means follows, and Nature herself proves the fallacy of the assumption that adaptation can only be the work of conscious intelligence. Kant already, in regard to this, pointed to the artistic instincts of

several animals, and Schopenhauer justly remarks
that the instinct of animals generally is the best exposition of the teleology of nature. Just as instinct
is an activity apparently displayed in obedience to a
conscious aim, and yet acting without any such aim,
so is it with the operations of Nature. The method
of her procedure, however, must be reserved for
another place.

Of the remaining so-called proofs for the existence
of God, the only one we need still advert to is the
moral one. The argument is twofold: I. that the
absolute stringency with which the moral law manifests itself in our conscience, proves its origin from
an absolute Being; and II. that the necessity under
which we lie of proposing to ourselves the furtherance of the highest good in the world—of morality,
with corresponding happiness—points to the existence
of a Being which shall be able to realize in a future
life the just balance between the two sides, which is
never attained in this.

But, as regards the first form of this presumptive
proof, we possess nothing but the contrivance of
our reasoning instincts, to ascribe to heaven, as long
as their origin is unrecognized, the moral precepts
which have necessarily been educed from the nature
of man, or the wants of society. We fasten them to

Heaven, as it were, in order to place them out of the reach of the violence or subtlety of our passions.

But in the second form, devised by Kant, this proof is, so to speak, the spare room in which God, reduced to passivity in the rest of his system, may still be decently housed and employed. The conformity between morality and happiness, *i.e.*, action and feeling, which this argument takes for its starting-point, exists in one respect spontaneously in the inner consciousness. That these may be realized in the outward life, also, is a natural wish and righteous endeavour, but its gratification, at best imperfect, is only attainable by an accurate conception of life and happiness, not by the postulate of a *deus ex machinâ*.

37.

Kant, we have said, after his criticism had dissipated the other arguments for the existence of God, as, according to the precedents of older philosophers and theologians, they had been formulated in the systems of Wolff and Leibnitz, and after he had worked out his own system (I allude to the later one, based upon his Critique of Pure Reason, of which the cosmogonic essay, to be soon discussed more fully, does not form a part), without reference to the conception of a personal deity, was loth, nevertheless, entirely to miss the God of his youth and his nurture, and accordingly assigned him at least an auxiliary part at a vacant place in his system.

Fichte set to work after a more radical fashion during the first and systematic period of his philosophic activity. He defined God as the moral order of the universe; a definition partial indeed, like his whole system, in which nature is not adequately recognized; but at the same time he repelled the conception of a personal God with arguments which will remain irrefutable for all time. " You attribute personality and consciousness to God," he said, when accused of Atheism on account of his conception of God; "but what, then, do you call personality and consciousness ? That, no doubt, which you have found in yourselves, become cognizant of in yourselves, and distinguished by that name. But if you will only give the slightest attention to the nature of your conception, you will see that you do not and cannot conceive of this without limitation and finality. By attributing that predicate to this Being, you in consequence make of it a finite one, a creature like yourselves;

you have not, as was your wish, conceived God, but merely the multiplied representation of yourselves." In his later period of mysticism, Fichte spoke much of the Deity and the divine, but never so as to convey an intelligible conception of his doctrine of the Deity.

The absolute identity of the real and the ideal, the leading conception of Schelling's original system, occupied the same standpoint, as far as we are concerned, as the Substance of Spinoza, with its two attributes of extension and thought—*i.e.*, it afforded no possibility of conceiving a personal supernatural God. Schelling's later philosophy, again, endeavoured to demonstrate this conception, but in such fashion that no scientific value is accorded it.

Lastly, Hegel, with his proposition that everything depended as to whether the substance were conceived as subject or spirit, has bequeathed a riddle to his expounders and a subterfuge to his adherents. One party discerned in it simply the acknowledgment of a personal God, while another proved from the more distinct utterances of the philosopher, as well as from the whole spirit of his system, that all that was intended to be postulated by it was that Becoming and Development were the essential momenta of the Absolute, and further, that thought, that the consciousness of the divine in man, were the ideal existence of God, opposed to Nature as the real existence.

Schleiermacher has expressed himself more clearly and frankly than the last-named philosophers in regard to this question—a fact which may surprise us —but he has only recourse to the patching-up system when he treats of Christianity. In his discourses on Christianity, he attached little importance to the conception of the Being on whom we are absolutely dependent, as personal or impersonal; and even the suggestive remarks of his work " On Religious Doctrine" were not of a nature to dispel the pantheistic haze enveloping his thought. In his posthumous work on dialectics he has expressed himself on this question with all possible clearness. "The two ideas, God and the universe," he remarks in this work, "are, on the one hand, not identical. For in conceiving God we postulate a unity *minus* plurality, in conceiving the universe, a plurality *minus* unity ; in other words, the universe is the sum-total of all opposites, the deity, the negation of all opposites. On the other hand, however, neither of these ideas can be conceived without the other. As soon, especially, as we endeavour to conceive

God as existing before or without the world, we become conscious at once that all we have left is an unsubstantial phantasy. We are not warranted in postulating any other relation between God and the world than that of their co-existence. They are not identical, nevertheless they are ' only two values for the same thing.' At the same time, both ideas are only empty thoughts—mere formulæ, and no sooner do we endeavour to fill them in and quicken them, than we necessarily draw them down into the realm of the finite; as, for example, when we conceive of God as a conscious absolute Ego."

Thus far Schleiermacher; and we may add that in these propositions is summed up the total result of modern philosophy in regard to the conception of God. The basis of this view is, that in conceiving of the Esse, to retain Schleiermacher's formula, the element of unity is separated from that of plurality, the one being defined as the determining cause of the many, and by reason of the manifestation of the latter as an orderly series of phenomena, conscious intelligence being attributed to the former. But as the first conception of the Esse can only be that by which it is conceived as unity in plurality, and *vice-versâ*, the idea of the Cosmos alone remains ultimate and supreme. And it follows that everything which shall be recognized as motive power and life, as order and law, throughout the range of the physical and moral world, both can and must contribute to the completion and enrichment of this conception, but never shall we find it possible to get beyond it; and if nevertheless we endeavour to conceive of a Creator, of the Cosmos as an absolute personality, the arguments just presented ought to convince us that we are merely dealing with an idle phantasy.

But here we must recur to a branch of our enquiry which may be appropriately subjoined to the so-called moral argument for the existence of God, in the form ultimately given it by Kant. This argument, as we have seen, was obliged, in order to attain its goal, to proceed a good way beyond it, into the domain of a future life. With this domain of the so-called immortality of the soul we must still occupy ourselves for a moment, as, next to the belief in God, that in immortality is usually considered the most essential part of religion.

Man sees all living creatures around him, his fellow-creatures included, succumb to death; he knows that, sooner or later, the same fate awaits himself also : how happens it that, for himself and

his kind, at least, he does not acknowledge death
to be complete annihilation? In the first place,
assuredly, because the survivor retains the conception of the deceased. The image of the departed
husband or child, of the friend and companion, but
of the troublesome enemy as well, continues vividly
present with the surviving one, hovers round him in
his hours of solitude, and meets him with delusive
reality in his dreams. The primitive nature of this
belief in immortality corresponds to its origin. As
it is but a phantasm of the deceased which hovers
round the survivor, and which, even when apparently most tangible, reveals itself as an evanescent
delusion as soon as the sleeper awakes from his
dreams; so in Homer, Hades is nothing but
an assemblage of shades who must quaff the
blood of victims ere they can gather strength sufficient for recollection and speech, and who, like the
image of a dream, elude the hands of the living
outstretched towards them with longing love. In
this earliest conception of a future life, the leading
features of which are the same in the Old Testament,
the reality lies entirely on the side of the present
life. Man's true self is his body, which after death
has been consumed by the flames of the funeral
pyre, or has mouldered in the grave, or has been

devoured by dogs and birds of prey; the soul which survives it is but an empty phantom. It follows from this that the existence after death was so little prized that, as we know, the soul of Achilles would rather have been the most miserable hind on earth than the monarch of the universal dead; and one must needs have been as plagued as Job to wish to be in the world below. In an existence of this kind there could be no question of intrinsic distinctions,—of what we call retribution; for unfortunately the dead are no longer alive; and although doubtless, on the one hand, we meet with Tityos and his vultures, and Sisyphus rolling his stone, and on the other hand, although the shade of Hercules is likewise in Hades, he himself is nevertheless among the circle of immortals,—these are only the gigantic creations of ancient legend, and form no exception to the common lot of man.

But as the moral sentiment acquired intensity among mankind, the distinction between good and evil which was observed in life necessarily affected the conception of man's condition after death. The existence of rewards and punishments in a future world was taught by Socrates among the Greeks, and among the Jews by the Pharisees and Essenes, as well as by the latest books of the Old

Testament. And by reason of that spiritualism which had its source in the far East, and which, chiefly by means of Plato, penetrated into Greek philosophy and the later Judaism, and soon afterwards into the Christian church, up to a recent period dominating even modern modes of thought, the relation between this life and the next was so completely reversed, that, as we have already observed in treating of the Christian religion, the future life appeared as the essentially true and real one, the present serving merely as its precursive shadowy semblance—earth as a miserable ante-room to heaven.

The Homeric and Old Testament belief in a realm of shades was too much the product of the spontaneous activity of human phantasy to require proof, and too little a source of consolation to deserve it; whereas the doctrine that the just man who is oppressed and miserable here shall be rewarded and exalted hereafter, while the evil-doer who feasts and revels now shall then be duly punished, was a doctrine of retribution which needed to be firmly secured against possible doubts. Nay, the comprehensive question must sooner or later present itself, by what right we dispute the reality of the apparent dissolution of the entire individuality in

death, and assume the continued existence of a
portion, of whose existence our perceptions afford
us no evidence ? This supposition is, in fact, an
assumption on a colossal scale, and if we enquire
after its proofs, all we shall meet with will be a
wish. Man would not perish when he dies, therefore he believes that he shall not perish. This,
undoubtedly, is but a sorry reason, and that is why
it is bedizened in every possible way. Here, above
all, the idea of recompense is invoked : we have
not only the wish, but in so far as we have been
pious and just, the right also, to prolong our existence after death. To fulfil the divine commandments we not only have here below denied ourselves
many pleasures, but have also taken upon ourselves
much labour and pain, and undergone much hostility
and persecution : shall not a just God requite us
for this in a happier hereafter ? And, on the other
hand, the tyrants, the tormentors, the wicked and
vicious of all kinds, who escaped all punishment
here, who succeeded in all they undertook,—shall
they for ever go scathless ? shall they not be called
to account in a future existence? Even the Apostle
Paul, as we know, believed, or fancied he believed
—for I deem him better than his speech—that if
the dead rose not, then he and men like unto him

must be fools, if they would not rather eat and
drink instead of endangering themselves for the
sake of their convictions. An argument of this
sort might appear respectable at a certain period;
but only in one which stood still very low in the
deeper moral conception of life. "He who still
cares to assert," I have remarked already in my
Glaubenslehre, "that the good are so often afflicted
in this life, while the wicked prosper, that therefore
an adjustment is requisite in a future state, only
shows thereby that he has not yet learnt to distinguish between the external and internal, between
appearances and reality. He, likewise, who still
needs the expectation of a future recompense as a
spring of action, stands in the outer court of morality,
and let him take heed lest he fall. For supposing
that in the course of his life this belief is over-
thrown by doubt, what then becomes of his morality?
Nay, how will it fare with the latter, even in the
case of the former remaining unshaken? He who
does good in view of future beatitude, acts, after
all, only from selfish motives." "It is the notion
of the vulgar herd," says Spinoza, "to regard the
service of the desires as freedom, and life according
to reason as entitling the pious bondsman, on his
release, to an anodyne of future bliss. Beatitude is

not a reward distinct from virtue, but virtue herself; it is not the consequence of our empire over our desires; rather is this empire itself a fruit of the beatitude we enjoy in the knowledge and the love of God."

38.

Goethe observed to Eckermann three years before his death, "The conviction of continuous existence suggests itself to me from the conception of activity; for if I am unceasingly active to my very end, nature is bound to assign to me another form of being, if the present one is no longer capable of fulfilling the requirements of my spirit." Doubtless a grand and a beautiful utterance, as pregnant with the force of subjective truth on the lips of the hoar old poet, indefatigably active to his dying day, as it is entirely devoid of all objective cogency. " Nature is bound "—what is the meaning of that ? Goethe, if any one, knew that Nature acknowledges no duties —only laws; but that man rather, even the most gifted and energetic, has the duty of humbly sub-mitting to them. What Nature did owe him for his restless activity, that is, what ensued from it according to the laws of Nature, Goethe had fully enjoyed during his lifetime, in the healthy sense of

his power, in the delight of progress and self-per-
fection, in the recognition and reverence accorded to
him by all the noble spirits among his contemporaries.
To demand more than this was a weakness of old
age, and its character as such was revealed by the
care with which, during those latter years, he
avoided all mention of death. For if he felt certain
that, in case of his death, Nature would fulfil her
duties towards him, then why this shrinking from
the name?

Goethe's argument in favour of immortality
is moreover only a special, I might say the heroic,
form of one frequently proposed in another shape.
The destiny of man, it is argued, is the development
of all his faculties; but this is attained by none in
the present life; which, therefore, must be followed
by another existence admitting of it. Of course we
naturally enquire how this alleged destiny of man has
been ascertained. Do we, then, on the whole, observe
that Nature is contrived to afford full development
to every faculty, every germ? He who would say
so can never in the summer have walked in an
orchard, where the whole ground is often strewn
with small apples and pears, fallen ere they were
ripe, yet each of them containing the possibility of
more than one tree; can never have read in a book

of natural history, that if the spawn invariably
attained full growth, all the rivers and seas would
no longer suffice to lodge the swarming shoals.
Experience, therefore, teaches the exact opposite in
regard to Nature : that she lavishly scatters germs
and capacities, leaving it to their inherent soundness
how many of them, in the struggle with each other
and surrounding circumstances, shall attain development and maturity.   Neither, as may be supposed,
are those reasoners anxious about Nature in general;
they would only provide for man, *i.e.*, for themselves.   To this end, they must prove that Nature
makes an exception with man in regard to his
capacities.   But even here experience fails to render
them the smallest service.   We cannot even assert
that it militates against our experience for a man to
attain to the full development of his capacities in
this life.   We shall be forced to acknowledge that
most of the old people known to us are complete;
that they have yielded up all they had to bestow.
Nay, even of a Goethe we must concede that, in
spite of his activity up to the last, in his eighty-
two years he had lived out his life.   Schiller, it is
true, had not done so in the forty-five years allotted
him; he died in the midst of the grandest projects,
which, had a longer life enabled him to execute

them, would have enriched the roll of the creations of his genius. Thus we should even arrive at the conclusion that an existence after death must be demanded for Schiller which would have to be renounced in the case of Goethe; or in more general terms, that only he who should happen to die in the full flower of this life would be entitled to claim a life hereafter—not by any means a life extending interminably, but only to the extent of affording each individual an opportunity of developing his capacities to the full.

This distinction, as well as this indefiniteness of duration, too clearly characterize the gratuitous and visionary nature of the speculation, which surpasses itself by asserting that the capacity inherent in every human soul is infinite and inexhaustible, and only to be completely realized in eternity. Such an assertion is obviously incapable of proof: it is a mere vaunt, which is confuted by the consciousness of every modest, candid mind. He who does not inflate himself is well aware of the humble measure of his capacities, and while grateful for the time allowed him for their development, makes no claim for its prolongation beyond the duration of this earthly life; nay, its eternal persistence would fill him with dismay.

But now the belief in immortality withdraws to its central citadel, and while putting the expectation of retribution or complete development on one side, it lays its full stress on the essence of the human soul. No matter to what end the soul may exist after death, exist it must, because it cannot die. Man's body is material, extended, and composite—susceptible, in consequence, of dissolution and destruction. But the soul is immaterial and simple—exempt, therefore, from dissolution and death. This was the ancient psychology, already exploded by Kant. All those alleged properties of the soul, whence its immortality is deduced, are most arbitrarily attributed to it. We have learnt, from closer observations in the domain of physiology and psychology, that the body and soul, even if we continue to distinguish between them as two separate essences, are nevertheless so nearly united, the so-called soul so entirely conditioned by the nature and circumstances of its material organ, the brain, that its continuance is unimaginable without it. The so-called spiritual functions develope, grow, and gain strength along with the body, especially with their distinctive organ, the brain, decline in sympathy with it in old age, and suffer corresponding disorders in case of cerebral affections—in such wise, moreover, that the derangement of certain mental functions corresponds to that of certain parts of the brain. But a thing so closely and completely bound to a physical organism can as little exist after the latter's destruction as the centre of a circle after the dissolution of the circumference.

When it comes to a question of the existence of living beings, and, moreover, of many thousand millions of such beings, it is indispensable to enquire after the place where such beings—we allude to the souls of the departed—are to be disposed of. Ancient Christianity was at no loss how to answer such a question, having abundant space at its command for the elect in heaven beyond the starry firmament—for the damned in hell deep under the earth. For us, as we have seen already, that heavenly space has vanished from around the throne of God; while the space in the interior of our globe is so completely filled with terrestrial matter of various kinds, that for hell also we have no locality to spare. But the persistent faith in immortality has striven to gain a new advantage from our modern Cosmic conception. If we no longer possess a Christian heaven, we have in its stead an innumerable multitude of stars; and on these surely there is space and to spare for more multitudinous hosts of departed spirits than our earth is able to furnish. These heavenly bodies are also apparently of such various formations, the circumstances of their material constitution, the modes by which light and heat are imparted to them, are so manifold, that some of them may plausibly be regarded as paradises, others as hells. But then, if the conditions requisite to the existence of rational beings are fulfilled on other heavenly bodies, they will arise there as they have arisen on our earth; our colonies of souls, therefore, arriving there as emigrants from this world, would find the ground already occupied. Of course we shall and must be reminded that immaterial essences are in question, whose existence after death is demonstrated by the very fact of their incomposite constitution and inability to occupy space, and that therefore they will not be circumscribed by the indigenous inhabitants of other heavenly bodies. But in that case they might as well have remained on the earth; or rather, they stand in no relation whatever to space, are everywhere and nowhere, in short, not real, but imaginary beings. For in that respect the remark of a somewhat crazy but all the more ingenious father of the church has become the principle of modern science : "Naught is immaterial but what is naught."

39.

If the preceding consideration has conducted us to the conclusion that we can no longer either hold the idea of a personal God, or of life after death, then it would seem that the question with which we have prefaced this section—if we still have a religion?—must be answered in the negative. For religion, according to the accepted idea, consists in the recognition and veneration of God, and the belief in a future life, a purified residuum of the older Christian faith in the resurrection, which, since the era of rationalism, has taken its place next to the belief in God, as an essential attribute of it. But this very conception of the idea of religion has in our time, and not without cause, been judged inadequate. We know that there is no religion which has not the conception and worship of divine beings (for even in the originally godless Buddhism they soon got in by the back door); but we wish also to know how religion came by this conception. The right definition is only that by which we do not merely get at the thing, but behind it.

It was Schleiermacher, as we know, who sought to satisfy this requirement in respect of religion. " That," he said, "which the most varying expressions of piety have in common: the essence of religion, in consequence, consists in our consciousness of absolute dependence, and the Whereon of this dependence— *i.e.*, that on which we feel ourselves to be dependent in this manner—we call God. The reason why, in the earlier stages of religion, there appear many instead of this single Whereon, a plurality of gods instead of the one, is explained in this deduction of religion, from the fact that the various forces of nature, or relations of life, which inspire man with the sentiment of unqualified dependence, still act upon him in the commencement with the full force of their distinctive characteristics; that he has not as yet become conscious how, in regard to his unmitigated dependence upon them, there is no distinction between them, and that therefore the Whereon of this dependence, or the Being to which it conducts in the last instance, can only be one."

If we compare this explanation with what it is meant to explain, with the phenomena of religion in its various stages, we must at first accord it our assent. Man worships the sun, the spring, the stream, because he feels his whole existence dependent on the light and the warmth which proceed from the first, on the freshness and fertility caused by the latter. Upon a being like Zeus, who, besides thunder and lightning and rain, governs the state and its institutions, the law and its maxims, man feels a twofold, a moral as well as a physical, dependence. Even upon an evil being, like fever, if he strives to mollify it by religious worship, he feels himself thoroughly dependent, inasmuch as he is persuaded that he cannot resist it unless it will desist of its own accord. But then, to persuade it to desist of itself, and generally to gain an influence on the Powers upon which he knows himself to be dependent, is the motive of worship, nay, is, as we have already seen, the secret motive of man's representing those Powers as personal, as beings similar to himself.

To this extent, Feuerbach is right when he declares the origin, nay, the true essence of religion, to be the wish. Had man no wish he would have no god. What man would have liked to be, but was not, he made his god; what he would like to have, but could not get for himself, his god was to get for him. It is therefore not merely the dependence in which man finds himself, but at the same time the need to react against it, to regain his freedom in regard to it, whence man draws his religion. Absolute, unmitigated dependence would crush, annihilate him; he must be able to defend himself against it,—must, under the weight which presses on him seek to win for himself both air and elbow-room.

40.

The normal way which is prescribed to man as that which shall liberate him in respect to Nature, on whom he in the first instance finds himself dependent, is that of work, of culture, of invention. A real, thorough satisfaction here greets his wishes: many of the attributes which man in former times ascribed to his gods—I will only mention as an example our rapid mode of locomotion—he himself has now acquired in consequence of his rational sway over Nature. But it has been a long, a fatiguing way, the goal of which could not even be foreshadowed by man thousands of years back. Ere he had learnt to master disease by natural means, he was forced either to resign himself helplessly to it, or to seek to subdue it by the aid of a Fetish, a Dæmon, or a god. And a remnant yet subsists: even at the goal of our rational route we cannot strike the balance of our sum. However numerous the maladies which medicine will heal, some nevertheless resist all appliances; and no herb will cure death. However great the triumphs of agriculture in respect to Nature may be, it must still acknowledge itself defenceless against frost and hail, excess of rain, or drought. Here is space and to spare for wishes, processions, masses. Or, take we a step higher in religion: notwithstanding all his efforts, all his struggles with the sensuousness and selfishness of his nature, man never suffices to his own ethical aspirations; he longs for a purity, a perfection, which he is at a loss to procure for himself, which he may hope to attain only through the blood of the Redeemer, by the vicarious transfer of another's righteousness to himself by means of faith.

If we regard the matter thus, it certainly cannot be disguised that the rational, secular, or (as far as man's efforts concern his own nature) the moral way, is the only one which will lead him to the desired goal; while the religious way, on the other hand, is but a pleasant delusion. Herein lies the contrast between Feuerbach's and Schleiermacher's views of religion, although both proceed from the same starting-point. With the latter, religion is the sentiment of unmitigated dependence; and as this is an undeniably correct sentiment of man's position in the universe, religion must also be a truth. Feuerbach also recognizes this sentiment of dependence as the original source of religion ; but, in order to actually call it forth, the wish must be superadded, to give to this dependence, by the shortest cut, a turn favourable to man. This wish, this endeavour, is also thoroughly justifiable ; but the delusion lies in this shortest cut by which it would reach the goal—by prayer, sacrifice, faith, etc., etc. ; and because this shortest cut is the distinctive feature of every religion hitherto, religion itself must from this point of view appear as a delusion, to abolish which ought to be the endeavour of every man whose eyes are open to the truth.

At this point the estimate of religion, with which we started at the beginning of this section, turns to its precise opposite. Instead of a prerogative of human nature, it appears as a weakness, which adhered to mankind chiefly during the period of childhood, but which mankind must outgrow on attaining maturity. The Middle Ages were more religious than ours in proportion to their greater ignorance and barbarism ; and at present the same difference exists, for example, between Spain and Germany, or in Germany between Tyrol and Saxony. Religion and civilization accordingly occupy not an equal but an inverted position in regard to each other, so that with the progress of the latter the former retreats.

Two objections may be opposed here. In the first a distinction is made between true and false religion, between superstition and true piety; and in like manner we may distinguish between true and false culture or enlightenment. In this respect we may say the Middle Ages were more superstitious, not more truly pious, than our era; and if culture in our era has really damaged piety, then it must have been a false superficial culture.

But this explanation is not sufficient. In order to treat the matter more accurately, we must distinguish between religion and religiousness, or between religion in the senses of extension and of intensity. Thus it may be said the Middle Ages believed more, had richer materials of belief than our era; but were not, on that account, more intensely pious. Admitting this for a moment, the Middle Ages possessed not only a greater number of articles of belief, but also more of the religious momenta in the life of man, in regard to society and the individual; in the daily life of a mediæval Christian, the religious element—such as prayer, making the sign of the cross, going to mass, etc.—manifested itself much more frequently and uninterruptedly than in the life of a modern Christian. And this, after all, is hand in hand with that other element of piety, the intensive. Now-a-days we find neither so many virtuosos in piety, such as were then more especially resident in convents, nor such exalted individual masters as a. St. Bernard, or St. Francis, and, at a later period, even a Luther. Beside these, our Schleiermachers, our Neanders, make a very worldly figure.

The reason of this, in the first place, lies in the fact that, as we have seen, a multiplicity of phenomena which stirred the religious sentiment of man on lower stages of civilization, are now understood in their orderly natural sequence, and therefore no longer immediately appeal to the pious sentiment, but only continue doing so mediately and feebly. The other and the principal reason of the retrogression of religion in our time, we have already discovered in the present enquiry. It lies in the circumstance that we are no longer able to form so lively a conception of the personality of the absolute Being as did our predecessors. It cannot be otherwise; although up to a certain point religion and civilization may go hand in hand, this nevertheless happens only so long as the civilization of nations manifests itself in the shape of imagination; as soon as it comes to be a culture of the reasoning faculties, and more especially as soon it is manifested through observation of Nature and her laws, an opposition gradually develops itself which circumscribes religion more and more. The religious domain in the human soul resembles the domain of the Red Indians in America, which, however much we may deplore or deprecate it, is, year after year, reduced into constantly narrowing limits by their white neighbours.

41.

But limitation—even transmutation—is still by no means annihilation. Religion with us is no longer what it was with our fathers; but it does not follow that it is extinct in us.

At all events we have retained the essential ingredient of all religion—the sentiment of unconditional dependence. Whether we say God or Cosmos, we feel our relation to the one, as to the other, to be one of absolute dependence. Even as regards the latter, we know ourselves as "part of a part," our might as nought in comparison to the almightiness of Nature, our thought only capable of slowly and laboriously comprehending the least part of that which the universe offers to our contemplation as the object of knowledge.

But this very knowledge, however restricted it be, leads us to yet another result. We perceive a perpetual change in the world; soon, however, we discover in this change something unchanging— order, and law. We perceive in Nature tremendous contrasts, awful struggles; but we discover that these do not disturb the stability and harmony of the whole—that they, on the contrary, preserve it. We further perceive a gradation, a development of the higher from the lower, of the refined from the coarse, of the gentle from the rude. And in ourselves we make the experience that we are advanced in our personal as well as our social life, just so far as we succeed in regulating the element of capricious change within and around us, and in developing the higher from the lower, the delicate from the rugged.

This, when we meet with it within the circle of human life, we call good and reasonable. What is analogous to it in the world around us, we cannot avoid calling so likewise. And moreover, as we feel ourselves absolutely dependent on this world, as we can only deduce our existence and the adjustment of our nature from it, we are compelled to conceive of it in its fullest sense, or as Cosmos, as being also the primary source of all that is reason-

able and good. The argument of the old religion was,
that as the reasonable and good in mankind proceeded from consciousness and will, that therefore
what on a large scale corresponds to this in the
world must likewise proceed from an author endowed
with intelligent volition. We have given up this
mode of inference; we no longer regard the Cosmos
as the work of a reasonable and good creator, but
rather as the laboratory of the reasonable and good.
We consider it not as planned by the highest
reason, but planned for the highest reason. Of course,
in this case, we must place in the cause what lies in
the effect; that which comes out must have been in.
But it is only the limitation of our human faculty
of representation which forces us to make these
distinctions: the Cosmos is simultaneously both
cause and effect, the outward and the inward
together.

We stand here at the limits of our knowledge;
we gaze into an abyss we can fathom no farther.
But this much at least is certain,—that the personal
image which meets our gaze, there is but a reflection of the wondering spectator himself. If we
always bore this in mind, there would be as little
objection to the expression—" God," as to that of
the rising and the setting of the sun, where we

are all the time quite conscious of the actual circumstances. But this condition is not fulfilled. Even the conception of the Absolute, to which our modern philosophy is so partial, easily tends again to assume some kind of personality. We, in consequence, prefer the designation of the All, or the Cosmos, not overlooking, however, that this again runs the danger of leading us to think of the sumtotal of phenomena instead of the one essence of forces and laws which manifest and fulfil themselves. But we would rather say too little than too much.

At any rate, that on which we feel ourselves entirely dependent, is by no means merely a rude power to which we bow in mute resignation, but is at the same time both order and law, reason and goodness, to which we surrender ourselves in loving trust. More than this : as we perceive in ourselves the same disposition to the reasonable and the good which we seem to recognize in the Cosmos, and find ourselves to be the beings by whom it is felt and recognized, in whom it is to become personified, we also feel ourselves related in our inmost nature to that on which we are dependent, we discover ourselves at the same time to be free in this dependence ; and pride and humility, joy and submission, intermingle in our feeling for the Cosmos.

True, a feeling of this kind will hardly produce a form of worship, hardly manifest itself in a series of festivals. Nevertheless, it will not fail of moral influence, as we shall find in its due place. And why no longer a form of worship? Because we have freed ourselves from that other constituent of religion, ignoble and untrue in comparison with the sentiment of dependence—the desire and expectation of obtaining something from God by our worship. We need but take the expression "divine service," and realize the low anthropopathism which it involves, in order to perceive the why and wherefore of nothing of this kind being any longer possible from our point of view.

But what we have found to remain to us will not be suffered to pass as religion. If we would know whether there be still any life in an organism which appears dead to us, we are wont to test it by some violent or even painful shock, as by stabbing it for instance. Let us try this experiment in regard to our feeling for the Cosmos. We need only turn over the leaves of Arthur Schopenhauer's works (although we shall on many other accounts do well not only to glance over but to study them), in order to come upon the proposition, variously expressed, that the Cosmos is something which had much

better not have existed. Or, as the author of the
"Philosophy of the Unconscious" (E. von Hartmann)
has expressed it in his manner, with a still finer point,
that although in the existing universe everything
be ordained as well as was possible, that it nevertheless is "miserable throughout, and "—the opposite
of that which we are wont to say jocularly about
the weather—"worse than no universe at all." According to Schopenhauer, therefore, the fundamental
distinction between all religions and systems of
philosophy consists in their optimist or pessimist
character; and, moreover, he regards Optimism
throughout as the standpoint of dulness and trivi-
ality, while all the more profound and distinguished
spirits occupy, like himself, the standpoint of Pessimism. After an especially vehement outburst of this
kind (that it would be better if no life had arisen
on the earth any more than on the moon—that her
surface had remained equally rigid and crystalline),
Schopenhauer adds that now he would probably again
have to hear of the melancholy of his philosophy.
Certainly, if we may take it in the sense that its
author, in formulating such propositions, was
melancholy-mad. In truth, they involve the most
glaring contradiction. If the universe is a thing
which had better not have existed, then surely the

speculation of the philosopher, as forming part of this universe, is a speculation which had better not have speculated. The pessimist philosopher fails to perceive how he, above all, declares his own thought, which declares the world to be bad, as bad also; but if the thought which declares the world to be bad is a bad thought, then it follows naturally that the world is good. As a rule, Optimism may take things too easily. Schopenhauer's references to the colossal part which sorrow and evil play in the world are quite in their right place as a counterpoise; but every true philosophy is necessarily optimistic, as otherwise she hews down the branch on which she herself is sitting.

But this was a digression; for we wished to discover whether our standpoint, whose highest idea is the law-governed Cosmos, full of life and reason, can still be called a religious one; and to this end we opened Schopenhauer, who takes every occasion to scout this our idea. Sallies of this kind, as we remarked, impress our intelligence as absurd, but our feeling as blasphemous. We consider it arrogant and profane on the part of a single individual to oppose himself with such audacious levity to the Cosmos, whence he springs, from which, also, he derives that spark of reason which he misuses. We recognize in this a repudiation of the sentiment of dependence which we expect from every man. We demand the same piety for our Cosmos that the devout man of old demanded for his God. If wounded, our feeling for the Cosmos simply reacts in a religious manner. Finally, therefore, if we are asked whether we still have a religion, our answer will not be as roundly negative as in the former case, but we shall say Yes or No, according to the spirit of the enquiry.

By our previous investigations we have severed ourselves from the Cosmic conception of ancient Christianity, inasmuch as that part of religion to which we still prefer a claim rests on a basis essentially different from the traditional religious ideas. Now the question is, what do we propose to put in the vacant place? Let us therefore turn to the other part of our task, and endeavour to give an answer to the question:—

III.

WHAT IS OUR CONCEPTION OF THE UNIVERSE?

42.

IN the investigation regarding our relations to religion we finally arrived at the idea of the Cosmos. After the plurality of gods in the various religions had resolved themselves into the one personal God, he in like manner resolved himself into the impersonal but person-shaping All. This same idea forms likewise the ultimate point of departure —from whichever point of view one regards it—of our Cosmic conception.

Experience, as we know, offers us immediately a variety of impressions and subjective states which are conditioned by it: that we should regard external objects as causes of these impressions, and in consequence arrive at the conception of a world confronting us, has indeed long ago become a second nature, yet is nevertheless the result of a process of syllogistic reasoning. In this world thus conceived by us, we distinguish the hypothetical causes of impressions we receive, or the external objects, from that side of our own being by which we receive these impressions, *i. e.*, our physical organization; as we distinguish in our own being between this external side and that which receives its impressions through it, our Ego or Self.

We cannot here further elucidate how, in our physical organization, we distinguish between its various states of impressibility and between the several senses; and how, on the other side, the objective causes of impressions tend more and more to separate themselves into groups, which range themselves either side by side, or above and below one another, according to the degree of their diversity and affinity, substance and compass, till at last is matured this whole complex, orderly system of our present conception of Nature and the Cosmos. We proceed from the isolated circles of phenomena around us, from the secure basis of elemental forces, to vegetable and animal life, to the universal vital principle of the earth, thence to that of our solar system, and ever on and on, till at last we comprehend all that exists in one single conception, and this conception is that of the Cosmos.

But as these smaller circles, from and by which

we ascended to that highest idea, by no means
represent mere aggregations of externally co-ordi-
nated objects, but are intrinsically united by
forces and laws: so we shall have to conceive
of the Cosmos as being the sum not only of all
phenomena, but of all forces and all laws.
Whether we define this as the totality of the
impelled matter, or of the impelling forces, of
motion according to laws, or laws of motion, it is
always the same thing, only viewed from different
sides.

The unity of the All is obviously but a conclusion
deduced from analysis; the same seems to hold good
in respect to its infinity, as regards both duration
and extent. The All being the All, nothing can
exist outside of it; it seems even to exclude the
idea of a void beyond. Nevertheless, the infinitude
or finiteness of the Cosmos has at all times been
a subject of controversy. And here it lay in the
interest of theology to affirm its finite nature, so
that infinity might be reserved to the world-creating
Deity; the bias of independent philosophy was
towards the opposite side.

Kant, as we know, has here adduced a so-called
antinomy, *i. e.*, he has apparently contrived to
establish proposition and counter-proposition by

equally cogent arguments, believing himself to have
at last discovered the solution of the contradiction,
in the perception that our reason has exceeded her
privilege in seeking to determine anything in
respect to a domain so far removed from all experience. To myself this antinomy has always appeared
as one not only admitting but demanding an objective solution. It is already thirty years since I
expressed myself as follows in my work on Dogmatic
Divinity, in speaking of the Christian doctrine of
the end of the world :—" As we are competent to
geologically trace the gradual formation of our
earth, it follows with metaphysical necessity that
she must likewise perish ; as a something having a
beginning and not likewise an end would add to
the sum of being in the universe, and in consequence
annul its infinity. It can only remain a constant
and absolute whole in virtue of a perpetual alter-
nation of birth and dissolution among its individual
component parts. A gradation in respect of their
comparative maturity is unquestionably observable
among the members of our solar system; thus even
may the mighty whole of the Cosmos resemble one
of those tropical trees on which, simultaneously, here
a blossom bursts into flower, there a ripe fruit
drops from the bough."

In other words, we must make this distinction between the world or universe in the absolute, and the world in the relative sense of the term, when it admits of a plural; that indeed every world in the latter sense, even to the most comprehensive of its constituents, has a limit in space, as well as a beginning and end in time, yet that the universe diffuses itself in boundless yet coherent extension throughout all space and all time. Not only our earth, but the solar system as well, has been what it is not at present—had at one time no existence as a system and will one day cease to exist as such. Time has been when our earth was not yet inhabited by a rational creature, and yet farther back, not even by a living creature; nay, a time when she was not as yet compacted to a solid body, when she was not as yet separated from the sun and the other planets. But if we contemplate the universe as a whole, there never has been a time when it did not exist, when there did not exist in it a distinction between the heavenly bodies, life, and reason; for all this, if not as yet existing in one part of the Cosmos, already existed in another, while in a third it had already ceased to exist: here it was in the act of blooming, yonder in full flower, at a third place already in decline; but the Cosmos itself—the sum-

total of infinite worlds in all stages of growth and
decay—abode eternally unchanged, in the constancy
of its absolute energy, amid the everlasting revolution and mutation of things.

43.

On this subject no one has given expression to
thoughts more sublime, although not fully elaborated, than Kant himself, in his " General History
and Theory of the Heavens," published in 1755, a
work which has always appeared to me as being
not less important than his later " Critique of Pure
Reason." If in the latter we admire the depth of
insight, the breadth of observation strikes us in the
former. If in the latter we can trace the old man's
anxiety to hold fast to even a limited possession
of knowledge, so it be but on a firm basis, in the
former we encounter the mature man, full of
the daring of the discoverer and conqueror in the
realm of thought. And by the one work he is as
much the founder of modern cosmogony, as of
modern philosophy by the other.

He here calls the world " a phœnix, which but
consumes itself in order to rise rejuvenated from
its ashes." Just as on our earth, decay in one
place is compensated by new growth in another,

"in the same manner worlds and systems of worlds perish, and are engulfed in the abyss of eternity: meanwhile, creation is ever active to erect new structures in other regions of the heavens" (he means, in other parts of infinite Cosmic space), " and to replace the loss with profit; and if a system of worlds has, in the course of its duration, exhausted every variety of life of which its constitution will allow, if it has become a superfluous link in the chain of being, then nothing can be more fit than that it should now play its last part in the drama of the successive transformations of the universe—a part which is but the due of every finite phenomenon— that of rendering its tribute to mutability.   Creation is so infinite that we may unhesitatingly regard a world, or a galaxy of worlds, in comparison to it, as we would a flower or an insect as compared to the earth."

Neither, as already hinted, is any destruction final.   Even as the order of Nature, such as it now exists, has evolved itself out of Chaos, so likewise can it again evolve itself out of the new Chaos occasioned by its destruction; especially as Kant conceives the destruction as taking place by combustion, by which the same conditions must again be produced as those whence, according to him,

our planetary system was primarily evolved. "We
shall not hesitate," he says, "to admit this (*i.e.*
the possibility of a new formation), when it is
considered that as soon as the planets and comets
have attained the last degree of exhaustion induced
by their circling motion in space, they will all be
precipitated on the sun, and thus add immeasurably
to his heat. This fire, violently increased by the
added fuel, will, unquestionably, not only resolve all
things again into their minutest elements, but will
likewise, with an expansive power commensurate
to its heat, again diffuse and distribute them over
the same ample spaces which they had occupied
before the first formation of Nature. Then the
vehemence of the central fire having abated, from
the almost complete destruction of its mass, it
will regularly repeat the ancient procreations and
systematically-connected motions, by a combination
of the forces of attraction and repulsion, and thus
once more produce a new macrocosm."

All this could not possibly be better expressed;
nevertheless, Kant has only realized the idea of the
perpetual mutation in the growth and decay of
the parts; not to the same extent that of the
immutable infinity of the whole. True, as regards
space, the universe is limitless in his eyes, and on

this subject he certainly has the most exalted views. It was the Englishman Wright, of Durham, who supplied him with the conception of the Milky Way as a system of innumerable fixed stars or suns, grouped in a lenticular form; and he recognized the so-called nebulæ as similar systems, which only appear small or indistinct to us from their immeasurable distance. But now, as regards time, although to Kant the creation is never complete, yet it once had a beginning. This very expression—the creation—will suffice to show us whence his thought had come by this limit. He would not lose the act of creation, and this he can only conceive as a beginning. This leads him to the singular conception of God having commenced the organization and vivification of Chaos at a definite point in space, probably in the centre—which he further conceives of as a huge primal mass, the centre of gravity— and proceeding thence towards its periphery. The exterior sphere is still Chaos, and order is only gradually communicated to it from the centre. He adds, further, that this theory "of a consecutive perfection of creation" fills the human mind with sublime amazement. But what of these contradictions: a centre of infinite space, a beginning of infinite time?

44.

In regard, however, to the finite space of our
solar system, which he undertook to explain as
having originated according to purely mechanical
principles—to the exclusion of a Creator acting
with determinate aims — Kant became, in the
above-mentioned work, the founder of a theory
which is still accepted at the present day. He does
not, that is, exclude the Creator in the sense of
denying his existence ; what he denies is any intervention of God in the cosmogonical process : the
Creator, at the beginning, has endowed matter with
such forces and laws as, without further action on
his part, must develop into the well-ordered Cosmos.

Whence   arise   sun   and   planets ? whence   the
revolutions of the latter, all following that of
the sun round its own axis, and also much on the
same plane ? The pious Newton sought the explanation in the finger of God; Buffon in a comet.
One of these, he surmised, having been precipitated
on the sun, detached thence a torrent of fiery
matter, which at various distances concentrated itself into spheres, and gradually became opaque and
solid through refrigeration. " I assume," says Kant,
on the other hand, " that all the matter of which

the globes, planets, and comets which belong to our solar system, consist, was once, in the beginning of things, resolved into its elemental primal essence, and filled the universal space where these highly-developed heavenly bodies now revolve." The same idea was at a later period expressed, not more felicitously, by Laplace, who was unacquainted with his precursor, the German philosopher. He says that, in observing the revolutions of the planets, we are led to the supposition that the solar atmosphere, in consequence of its enormous heat, had originally extended beyond all the planetary orbits, and had only very gradually contracted to its present limits. Both, however, as we shall see, explain the formation of the heavenly bodies, as well as their motions, by this original dissipation of elementary matter.

If Kant, in so doing, speaks of the beginning of all things, we may take this quite seriously according to his theory; as, however, he admits that in the future also, after the destruction of our solar system, an exactly similar condition will result from the dissolution of its parts, he cannot determine whether in the first instance also this condition was not the result of a preceding destruction. Much less can we, who recognize a beginning of the Cosmos as little as an end, regard the matter in a different light; while at the same time we leave it an open question whether the dissolution and transformation concerned our solar system alone, or the whole galaxy of which it forms but a single province.

At bottom this was the Cosmic conception of the Stoics; only they extended this view to the whole Cosmos, and conceived of it in harmony with their pantheism. The Primal Being secretes the world as its body, but gradually absorbs it again, so that at last this produces a universal conflagration, which reduces all things to their primal condition, *i.e.*, resolves them in the divine primordial fire. But the great year of the world having thus elapsed, the formation of a new world begins, in which, according to a whimsical Stoic notion, the former one was exactly reproduced, down to particular events and persons (Socrates and Xanthippe). Kant, in combating this whim, remarks, with deep insight, which on other occasions also serves him in good stead, that there can be no question of absolute precision in the arrangement of Nature, "because," as he expresses it, "the multiplicity of circumstances which participate in every natural process preclude precise regularity." According to Buddhism, also, there never has been a time when worlds and beings have not been evolved in endless revolutions of birth and decay: every world has arisen from a former ruined world; infinite time is divided into the great and lesser Kalpas, *i.e.*, into more or less extensive periods of destruction and renovation, caused by the elemental forces of water, wind, or fire.

These auguries of religion and philosophy have in recent times gained scientific probability, owing to two discoveries in physics. From the gradual diminution of the orbit of Encke's comet has been inferred the existence in space of matter, which, even though attenuated to the last degree, by the resistance it opposes to the revolving bodies must gradually, at however distant a period, narrow the orbits of the planets, and produce finally their collision with the sun. The other discovery is that of the conservation of energy. If it be a Cosmic law that impeded motion is transformed to heat, and heat again begotten by motion—that, in fact, the force of nature, as soon as it has disappeared in one form, reappears in another—the possibility surely here dawns upon us that in this retardation of Cosmic motion, Nature may possess the means of summoning new life out of death.

45.

Although we allow the mass of diffused matter which, with Kant and Laplace, we assume to have constituted the primal matter of our planetary system, to have been evolved from a preceding pro · cess of combustion, we must regard it as now completely refrigerated, in consequence of the extreme dispersion of its parts. Only when, in virtue of the law of gravitation, the dispersed atoms gradually approached each other, and subsequently assumed the form of an enormous sphere of nebulous matter, would they again have acquired light and heat on the one hand, on the other the rotating motion which is naturally inherent in the sphere; just as the form itself belongs to masses consisting of gaseous or fluid substances. The matter comprised within the circumference of the globe would gradually have settled towards the centre, while the radiation of heat from its surface would have produced further contraction. At the same time, the rapidity of the nebulous globe's rotation on its axis would have become accelerated in the ratio of the diminution of its volume. The speed of the rotation would be greatest at the equator of the globe, which we, in consequence, must picture to ourselves as prodigiously inflated at the central zone, while it is flattened at the poles.

But the concurring diminution of the sphere's volume and acceleration of its rotation will now occasion portions to separate themselves from the refluent mass in the region where rotation is most rapid, and to revolve, at first, perhaps, in an annular shape, along with, and in the same direction as, the contracting nebulous globe. Astronomy was led to this conjecture of the separations from the primal mass having first taken place in the shape of rings, by the observation of the ring of Saturn. For as astronomers consider themselves justified in regarding the origin of the satellites which spin round the different planets as a repetition on a small scale of the origin of the planets themselves, and as they further opine that the ring of Saturn consists, so to speak, of one or more of the innermost satellites of the Saturnian system arrested in the process of formation; they readily assume the same annular form in their speculations respecting the origin of the planetary system. The ring, it is further asserted, then burst, and condensed itself into a globe, which henceforth continued to revolve in the direction of the rotation of the primal mass, first round it, then in the same direction round its own axis. If we explain

the origin of the planets from such a process of dis-
integration, this process must have repeated itself
several times, so that the planet most remote from
the sun would be its firstborn, that nearest it the
youngling of the planetary band.

That the orbits of the planets form, not circles, but
ellipses, that they do not exactly, but only approxi-
mately, lie within the plane of the sun's equator,
and that they rotate on their axes at angles of
various degrees of inclination towards the plane of
their orbits,—these belong to those irregularities in
the incidents of Nature of which we have just heard
Kant speak, and may have their origin in general
or particular circumstances connected with the
separation and formation of these bodies. Thus
the circumstance that the planets most remote from
the sun are in general the larger, and the more
abundantly furnished with satellites, but at the
same time the less dense, may be explained from
the abundant existence but imperfect concentration
of matter at the period of the original separation;
although here also chance, *i.e.*, the combined action
of hitherto undiscovered causes, must have had a
considerable share, as not the outermost but the
innermost of this more remote group—*viz.*, Jupiter
—is the largest, while Neptune's density again

exceeds that of Saturn and Uranus. Again—it has
as yet not been possible to formulate the law of the
increase, or, more correctly speaking, the decrease,
of the distances of the planets from one another and
from the sun. That is to say, every planetary orbit
in the order of its remoteness from the sun (the
orbit of the asteroids being counted as one) is
between one-and-a-half times and twice as distant from it as the preceding one. Schopenhauer
sought to explain this by the hypothesis of a contraction consequent upon a succession of shocks
ensuing in the central body, and contracting it on
each occasion to one-half of its former dimensions,
and the spaces between the planets formed by
these shocks regularly diminishing in proportion.

The globes thus separating from and revolving
around the central body contracted in like manner,
and while the larger members of the system
repeated their own process of formation in the
casting off of satellites, they cooled down at the
same time, and acquired opacity and density. Here,
however, two causes acted in opposite directions.
The contraction of the spheres, and the closer
pressure of their parts upon each other, increased
the temperature; but then again its radiation
into the cold space around diminished it. And

as the latter cause necessarily predominated the more, the smaller the body was, the lesser planets became cool and firm sooner than the larger; as Jupiter especially will probably be found to be even now less cool and solid at his surface than the earth, and to have in consequence retained something of innate luminosity. The fire in the enormous central body continues as before, and supports itself, as physicists conjecture, partly by further although imperceptible contraction, partly by the perpetual crashing down on its mass of small cosmic bodies analogous to our meteorites. The manner in which our whole solar system, however, is governed and maintained by those great laws of the relations of distance and motion which Kepler discovered, and Newton traced back to the effect of one law of gravity, need not be further elucidated here.

46.

Together with the general cosmogonic idea of Kant, modern astronomy has confirmed and further developed his conception of the galaxy as a lens-shaped aggregation of countless suns, and of the nebulæ as similar groups, whose apparent smallness is merely the effect of their enormous distance. In the place of his supposition of a central body for our Milky Way (which he supposed to be Sirius) the generally accepted view is now that of an equal mutual attraction and corresponding motion of all the stars in the same group—a republic instead of a monarchy, as it were.

The discovery of double stars has also imparted unexpected variety to our conception of the system of the universe. Once the so-called fixed stars were conceived of as analogous to our sun, each environed by a number of planets; but later, two suns were every now and then observed to revolve round each other, or their common centre of gravity. Although this by no means excludes the supposition that each of these may be surrounded by a number of planetary bodies, it nevertheless engenders very peculiar combinations as to the conditions of light and motion to which they are subject. The recent discovery of such double stars, where one of the pair is not a sun, but an opaque body, was still more surprising. We find that amongst others the resplendent Sirius is mated with such an obscure companion. It would seem, therefore, that we have here a case differing materially from the formation of our solar system—that the planetary mass does not constitute a plurality of smaller bodies revolving round the sun, but a single body, closely approximating, however, to the sun in bulk and weight.

Many of the so-called nebulæ have, like the galaxy, been resolved by the telescope into clusters of stars ; and after several, which had formerly been considered irresolvable, had failed to resist the power of keener telescopes, the idea began to be entertained that all the nebulæ were probably, in reality, groups of suns similar to our Milky Way. Kirchhoff's marvellous discovery of spectrum analysis unexpectedly brought about a decision which could not be given by the telescope. In the spectroscope some of the nebulæ manifest the same lines as the fixed stars ; others, however, are recognizable, by the lines of their spectra, as glowing gaseous masses. The importance of this discovery for our cosmogonic theory is self-evident. It actually proves the truth of our previous assumption—that boundless space contains not only completed worlds, but also such as are only in process of formation, or just developing out of a gaseous state. And if, on the other side, we think of those stars which were once invisible, or barely visible, but which suddenly flaming up, rose to be stars of the first or second magnitude, in order to disappear again after a longer or shorter interval,—we are perforce led to regard these as worlds which, while blazing into ruin, were preparing for a fresh evolution.

Kant thinks it precipitate to infer, from the fact of the earth's being a planet inhabited by living, and in part intelligent, beings, that therefore, all planets are inhabited; and that it would, on the other hand, be absurd to deny this in the case of all, or even of the greater part of them. Similar circumstances acting as causes lead to the conjecture of similar effects; but we must carefully investigate the circumstances before we are justified in drawing conclusions from them. The fact of being lighted and heated by the sun, of revolution on their axes, and consequent alternations of day and night,—these and other similarities in planets may be modified to such a degree, by differences in the distance from the sun, by size and density, that the inference from analogy is invalidated.

Here also Kant perceived the true state of the case. " Perhaps," he says, "all the heavenly bodies are not yet completely developed; hundreds, nay, thousands (we may safely add several cyphers) of years are necessary for the matter of one of the larger globes to attain firm consistency. Jupiter still seems to be unsolidified. We may, however, rest contented in the supposition that, although he should be uninhabited as yet, he nevertheless will have inhabitants when the period of his development is completed." But granted even that he never should attain a habitable condition, this, according to Kant, ought as little to disturb us as we are disturbed by the existence of uninhabitable wildernesses on our earth.

Our moon, which of course is an infinitely smaller sphere, we must resign ourselves, it seems, to conceive of as a barren rock ; for we are unable to perceive any atmosphere, even of the rarest kind, on the side which is visible to us, and the arguments lately adduced to prove its possibility on the side continually averted from the earth are still subject to considerable doubt. As regards the sun the case is different, inasmuch as he, although unable to shelter organic life on his burning surface, is nevertheless mediately, by reason of the heat he radiates, the cause of all life throughout the realm over which he reigns. As to the vagrant race of comets there can, of course, be no question of inhabitants. Kant endeavoured, by his hypothesis of the existence

of other planets beyond Saturn, with constantly
increasing eccentricity of orbit, to establish a steady
transition from planets to comets. Modern astronomy, however, has long recognized the radically
different nature of these two kinds of heavenly
bodies, and now inclines to look upon the comets as
intermundane bodies, which, domiciled outside of our
solar system, only pass through it from time to time,
when some few, retained by the forces of attraction,
take up their abode among us for better or worse.

Once fairly launched into speculation concerning
the inhabitants of the planets, Kant raises the
question as to the relations of rank which may
possibly exist among them. On the one hand, it
seems natural to infer that the inhabitants of the
planets must be the more perfect in the degree of
their vicinity to the sun, the source of all light and
life. Thus the inhabitants of Mercury would be
more perfect than those of Venus, these latter than
those of our earth, while, lastly, the inhabitants of
Uranus and Neptune, if such there be, would be, so
to speak, the Lapps and Samoyeds of our system.
Kant takes exactly the opposite view. As distance
from the sun increases, the heat of the planets no
doubt grows less, but so too does their density and
the grossness of the matter of which they consist.

Thence, Kant believes, he may deduce the law, "that the perfection of the spiritual as well as of the material world on the planets, from Mercury to Saturn, and perhaps beyond him (Uranus had not as yet been discovered), increases in direct proportion to their distance from the sun."

According to this arrangement, man, the inhabitant of the third planet from within outwards—of the fourth, according to the science of that time, if counting from without inwards — appears, so to speak, as the average creature. The vacillation of his moral nature between evil and good, animal and angel, may possibly be caused by this mean position. Perhaps, Kant suspects, the inhabitants of the two lowest planets are of too animal a constitution to be capable of sin, while those of the upper are too ethereal. "In this case the earth, and perhaps Mars (that the poor comfort of having companions in misfortune may not be wanting us), would alone be in that middle position," where sin disports itself.

We shall take good care not to carry quite so far as this our conjectures concerning the inhabitants of the planets ; but is it not amusing that we must be on our guard lest we be led into extravagant fancies by him who was destined to write the Critique of Pure Reason ?

47.

If henceforth we confine ourselves to the earth, we shall find that what we meet with upon and beneath her surface harmonizes most beautifully with the conclusions we have hitherto drawn. According to our preceding exposition, we have to imagine the earth in her primal condition, as a smaller vaporous sphere, which has severed itself from the larger one, and contracts itself towards its centre by reason of the law of gravity, and which, in spite of the increase of temperature caused thereby, gradually cools, by reason of the preponderant radiation of heat. This refrigeration begins on the surface of the globe, where the radiation takes place: we must conceive the gaseous matter as here passing into iquid fire, and finally assuming consistence. The earth's crust, in process of formation, will first assume the shape of a smooth ball or spheroid; but the contraction of the cooling globe continuing, the crust will show wrinkled inequalities, and sometimes chasms will result, whence, beneath the pressure exercised by the collapsing crust, parts of the still liquid fire or gaseous stuff of the interior, bursting forth, bubble-like, will issue, and thus the mountains and valleys of the earth will be formed.

One of the chief epochs in the formation of the earth occurs at the time when the cooling process is so far advanced that the ascending vapours, being condensed to clouds, descend again as rain. Water now begins to play its part, by washing matter ashore and carrying off, dissolving and mixing it, and this first makes organic life possible. The enormous evaporation of the gradually cooling earth sets huge masses of clouds and rain in motion : the earth is covered by a tepid ocean, whence only the highest mountains tower like islands. Even at this point reactions of the glowing interior of the earth, as well as atmospheric action, may from time to time have produced colossal revolutions on the surface ; but in this department of science imagination has been too active, and Geology, especially since the strictures of Sir Charles Lyell, is more inclined to conceive the process as a much more orderly one—as more analogous to what we still see taking place in nature. The assumption of older naturalists, especially,—that the first rudiments of vegetable and animal organism on the earth were repeatedly overwhelmed and destroyed by those revolutions, in consequence of which their subsequent creation was each time requisite —has now been given up, the supposed general revolutions of the earth having been proved to have been very partial ones, and the uninterrupted continuance and development of organic life from its beginnings satisfactorily established.

48.

The most ancient strata of the earth's crust show no traces of living beings; later strata contain such traces; *i.e.*, in them we find petrifactions of vegetable and animal bodies: now whence did this life suddenly come ? People have been loth to admit this original deficiency of life; they have called attention to the fact that those oldest strata have experienced all kinds of metamorphoses, by which the remains formerly contained in them might have been destroyed. It may be so; but that does not alter the result. The temperature of the earth, at all events, was at one time so high that living organisms could not exist on it : there was once no organic life on the earth; at a later period there was; it must, consequently, have had a beginning and the question is, how ?

Faith here intervenes, with its miracle. God said, Let the earth bring forth grass, and the herb yielding seed; let her bring forth the living creature after his kind. This was still accepted by the older science of Nature; according to Linnæus, all the various kinds of animals and plants were created from a single pair, or from a hermaphroditical individual. Kant judged likewise that it might well be said, "Give me matter, and I will explain the origin of a world;" but not, "Give me matter, and I will explain the production of a caterpillar." However, if the problem is insoluble in this form, it is because of the inaccurate manner in which it is stated. Whether I say a caterpillar, or the elephant, or even man—each time I already presuppose an organism so artificially compacted that it evidently could not have proceeded immediately out of inorganic matter. In order to bridge this chasm, we must take organic matter in its simplest form, which, as we know, is the cell. Could not an organic cell (not a caterpillar) be naturally produced from inorganic matter, which was previously the sole existing thing? Even in this form Darwin himself has not yet ventured to answer the question in the affirmative, but has considered it necessary, at this first point, at least, to call miracle to his assistance. At the beginning of things—this, at least, was the doctrine of his first and principal work—the Creator formed several, or perhaps even only one primal cell, and inspired it with life, whence in the course of time the whole variety of organic life on the earth expanded itself. His French precursor, Lamarck, had been bolder, attributing the origin of the lowest and simplest organisms, both at the beginning and subsequently, to spontaneous generation.

This question as to the *generatio œquivoca* or *spontanea—i.e.*, as to whether it be possible for an organic individual, of however imperfect a nature, to be produced otherwise than by its kind, that is to say, through chemical or morphological processes not taking place in the egg or womb, but in matter of a different description, organic or inorganic liquids — this question, already eagerly discussed in the last century, has again of late engaged the attention of science. But by reason of the difficulty of instituting conclusive experiments, the discussion has not led to any generally accepted decision. But even if the occurrence of such spontaneous generation could not be proved in regard to our present terrestrial period, this would establish nothing with respect to a primæval period, under totally dissimilar conditions. "All known facts," says Virchow, "are opposed to the theory that spontaneous generation now takes place. But as, nevertheless, we see life at some time making its appearance for the first time in the course of the earth's development, what must our conclusion be, if not that, under quite unusual circumstances, at the time of vast terrestrial revolutions, the miracle," or first appearance of life—of course in its most rudimentary form—has " actually come to pass ? " The existence of this crudest form has since been actually demonstrated. Huxley has discovered the Bathybius, a slimy heap of jelly on the sea-bottom; Häckel what he has called the Moneres, structureless clots of an albuminous carbon, which, although inorganic in their constitution, yet are capable of nutrition and accretion. By these the chasm may be said to be bridged, and the transition effected from the inorganic to the organic.

To regard this transition as a natural one, is rendered easier to Natural Science at present, not only by the more exact statement of the problem, but also by the rectified conception of life and its manifestations. As long as the contrast between nature, inorganic and organic, lifeless and living, was understood as an absolute one, as long as the conception of a specific vital force was retained, there was no possibility of spanning the chasm without the aid of a miracle. Natural Science, however, now teaches, that " the separation between so-called organic and inorganic nature is altogether arbitrary; vital force, as commonly conceived, a chimera " (Du Bois Reymond). Matter, the vehicle of life, is nothing special; " no fundamental ingredient is to be found in organic bodies which is not already present in inorganic Nature; that which is special to it is the motion of matter." But even this " does not form a diametrical dualistic contrast to the general modes of motion in Nature; life is only a special, namely, the most complicated, kind of mechanics; a part of the sum-total of matter emerges from time to time out of the usual course of its motions into special chemico-organic combinations, and, after having for a time continued therein, it returns again to the general modes of motion " (Virchow). There was no question, properly speaking, therefore, of a new creation, but only that the matter and force already in existence should be brought into another kind of combination and motion; an adequate cause for which might exist in the conditions, the temperature, the atmospheric combinations of primæval times, so utterly different from ours.

49.

All we have thus far obtained, however, is but a number of the very lowest organic existences, while the problem before us comprises the whole variety of the terrestrial flora and fauna, a widely-ramified line or up-growth of organisms. The higher we ascend the more we are astonished as we note the artificial adaptation manifest in their construction, the marvellous mobility of their energies, their instincts, and ingenuity, culminating at last in human intelligence. All this must be explained in its origin; and we are not much assisted even if, peradventure, we can conceive the development of a cell or of a Monere from inorganic matter. Must we assume that Nature continued to proceed after the same fashion, and that, having evolved the most imperfect forms of life from lifeless matter, she, by ever stronger impulsion, knew how to evoke from it a perpetually ascending series of higher organisms? But this would land us amid the old difficulties—the problem of the caterpillar or the elephant.

The only outlet here would lie in the supposition that Nature, having once produced an organic structure, instead of continually recurring to the

inorganic, availed herself of her advantage, held
fast by the progress towards organism she had once
secured, and constructed a second more complex
organism from that first simplest form, a third from
the second, and so from the complex organism
thus constructed, another, and again another one.
This is better expressed by the supposition that
living things possess the impulse as well as the
capacity of developing themselves from the simplest beginnings to a variety of forms, partly by
progressive ascent, partly by lateral extension.

Such a supposition, it is true, seems most
decidedly at variance with all that we perceive
and observe around us. We see that in organic
nature like always proceeds from like, never unlike
from unlike; the differences of the generated from
the generating subordinating themselves as unes-
sential in comparison with the essential similarity.
Although no oak ever resembles another in every
respect, yet no acorn ever produces a beech or a fir;
the fish always reproduces a fish, never a bird or
a reptile; the sheep always a sheep, never a bull or
a goat. On this account natural science, till quite
recently, up to Cuvier and Agassiz, observed the
different species of organic beings as inviolable
limits admitting perforce the development of

varieties and domestic breeds, but declaring the evolution of one species into a really new and different one simply impossible. If this is so, then unquestionably we must take refuge in the conception of creation and of miracles; then God in the beginning must have created grass, and herbs, and trees, as well as the animals each after its kind.

Against this still essentially theological doctrine an opposition has since arisen: Natural Science has long endeavoured to substitute the evolutionary theory in place of the conception of creation, so alien to her spirit; but it was Charles Darwin who made the first truly scientific attempt to deal seriously with this conception, and trace it throughout the organic world.

50.

Nothing is easier than to ridicule the Darwinian theory, nothing cheaper than those sarcastic invectives against the descent of man from the ape, in which even the better class of reviews and newspapers are still so fond of indulging. But a theory whose very peculiarity is the interpolation of intermediate members, thus linking the seemingly remote in an unbroken chain of development, and indicating the levers by means of which Nature achieved the progressive ascension in this process of evolution—this theory surely no one can suppose himself to have refuted by bringing two formations of such utterly different calibre as ape and man in their present condition into immediate contact with each other, and utterly ignoring those intermediate gradations which the theory partly proves, partly assumes.

That the orthodox, the believers in Revelation and in miracles, should brandish their repugnance and its accompanying weapon, ridicule, against Darwin's theory, is perfectly intelligible. They know what they are about, and have good reason, too, in combating to the uttermost a principle so inimical to them. But those sarcastic newspaper writers, on the other hand—do they, then, belong to the faithful? Certainly not, as regards the vast majority; they swim with the stream of the times, and have nothing to say to miracles, or to the intervention of a Creator in the course of Nature. Very well; how, then, do they explain the origin of man, the evolution of the organic from the inorganic, if they find Darwin's explanation so ludicrous? Do they intend evolving primæval man a human organism, however rude and unformed he be, immediately from the inorganic:

the sea, the mud of the Nile, etc.? They are hardly so daring; but do they realize that the choice only lies between the miracle—the divine artificer—and Darwin?

Darwin was not the first author of the theory which is now usually called by his name; its rudiments are to be met with in the last century; and at the commencement of the present one it was propounded as a completed theory by the Frenchman Lamarck. Essential constituents were, however, wanting to its vitality; Lamarck only worked out the proposition that the species in nature are not fixed, but have been developed by transmutation, especially the higher from the lower. But to the question of the Catechism,— "How does this happen?" he sought a satisfactory answer, indeed, but could not find one. At this point Darwin came to the theory's assistance, and raised it from a scientific paradox to an influential system, a widely disseminated Cosmic conception.

The theory is unquestionably still very imperfect; it leaves an infinity of things unexplained, and moreover, not only details, but leading and cardinal questions; it rather indicates possible future solutions than gives them already itself.

But be this as it may, it contains something which exerts an irresistible attraction over spirits athirst for truth and freedom. It resembles a railway whose track is just marked out. What abysses will still require to be filled in or bridged over, what mountains to be tunnelled, how many a year will elapse ere the train full of eager travellers will swiftly and comfortably be borne along and onwards! Nevertheless, we can see the direction it will take: thither it shall and must go, where the flags are fluttering joyfully in the breeze. Yes, joyfully, in the purest, most exalted, spiritual delight. Vainly did we philosophers and critical theologians over and over again decree the extermination of miracles; our ineffectual sentence died away, because we could neither dispense with miraculous agency, nor point to any natural force able to supply it, where it had hitherto seemed most indispensable. Darwin has demonstrated this force, this process of Nature; he has opened the door by which a happier coming race will finally cast out miracles. Every one who knows what miracles imply will praise him as one of the greatest benefactors of the human race.

51.

I have elsewhere remarked that no greater joy could have been experienced by Goethe than to have lived to see the development of the Darwinian theory. For did not the question as to Lamarck's successor and the dispute between Geoffroy St. Hilaire and Cuvier in the French Academy, appear to him more important than the contemporaneous revolution of July, and inspire him with a detailed essay on the subject, which was only completed in the month of his death? "I have exerted myself," he said at the time to Soret, "for fifty years in this great affair; at first I stood alone, was then supported by others, and at last, to my great joy, I found myself surpassed by kindred spirits."

His discovery of the intermaxillary bone of the human upper jaw, which attested the continuity of the organic development between animals and man, his ideas concerning the metamorphosis of plants, as well as (subsequently) of animals, are generally known. In the entire organic world it seemed to him he observed a general archetype, an abiding form, on the one hand; on the other an infinite mutability and changeableness of form, an

eternal versatility and variability of the archetype.
The chief determining cause of these changes he
considered as being "the necessary relations
of organisms to the external world"—to dry or
humid, warm or cold conditions; to earth, air, or
water. "The animal is formed by circumstances
for circumstances. Thus the eagle is formed by
the air for the air, the mole for the loose soil of
earth, the seal for the water." Even within the
limits of single species of animals Goethe endeavours to prove this transmutation as effected by
elemental influences. "In attentively considering,"
he remarks somewhere, "the rodent species, I see,
that although it is generically fixed and held fast
from within, yet externally it disports itself in
unbridled freedom, specifically manifesting itself
by mutation and transmutation, and is thus
changed into every variety. If we look for the
creature in the waters, we shall find it hog-like in
the morass, then a beaver constructing its habitation near running water, still in need of humidity;
we shall next discover it burrowing in the earth,
or at least preferring hidden places; then, when
at last it emerges to the surface, it develops a
fondness for hopping and leaping, so that it now
shows itself in an erect posture, and, almost a

biped, moves hither and thither with marvellous rapidity."

But not only the distinct vegetable or animal species by themselves—the two arch-forms of organic life—but the vegetable and animal kingdom as a whole, were scrutinized by Goethe with a view to the possibility of comprehending them as the two divergent branches of one mighty tree of life. " If we observe plants and animals in their most imperfect state," he says, "they are scarcely distinguishable. One life-centre, rigid, moveable, or half moveable, is something scarcely perceptible to our senses. Whether these beginnings, determinable in both directions, may be evolved into the plant by the agency of light, into the animal by darkness, we do not feel sufficiently confident to decide, although there is no want of observations and analogies on the matter. Thus much we may say, however,—that the creatures which, as plants and animals, gradually develop out of a common, scarcely distinguishable stock, now go on improving in two opposite directions : thus in the tree the plant at last becomes durable and rigid, while in man the animal achieves the glory of the utmost mobility and freedom."

Concerning the origin of animal life, Eckermann

has preserved a remarkable expression of Goethe's. He was speaking of the various races of men with the naturalist Von Martius of Munich, who had paid him a visit. The orthodox naturalist strove to confirm the descent of man from a single primarily-created pair by the maxim that Nature always proceeds with the utmost economy in her productions. " I must contradict this view," replied Goethe, and straightway proved himself superior to the professor of the natural sciences. " I assert, on the contrary, that Nature always shows herself lavish, nay, extravagant, and that we shall judge far more correctly of her, in assuming that instead of a single sorry pair, she at once produced men by the dozen, nay, by the hundred. For as soon as the earth had attained a certain degree of maturity, when the waters had been gathered together, the epoch of man's formation had arrived, and by the power of God men originated everywhere where the soil admitted it— perhaps first on the table-lands. To assume that it occurred thus, I consider reasonable ; but to speculate how it came to pass I consider a useless effort, which we may leave to those who are fond of busying themselves with insoluble problems, and who have nothing better to do."

The veil which Goethe wishes to leave on this process, is only a remnant of that indefiniteness which continued to tinge his whole conception of these relations. It is nowhere very apparent how Goethe conceived the transmutation and progressive development of organisms to have taken place: whether by the different species gradually varying of their own accord, changing themselves from aquatic to lacustrine, and at last to land animals; or whether Nature merely tried experiments, first in one, then in another organization, shaping each of these, however, afresh, not from preceding formations. If Goethe inclined to the latter hypothesis, and deemed that man, instead of developing out of some higher species of animal, had simply, so to speak, started from the blank soil,—this unquestionably is a conception of so monstrous a nature that it is advisable to throw a veil over it.

52.

There is still another German thinker whom we have to note as among the precursors of Darwin: the same whom we have encountered already, as a predecessor of Laplace, in regard to the entire structure of the universe—the philosopher of Königsberg. And although the naturalistic im-

pulse and insight, as well as the fundamental outlines of his Cosmic conception, had been Goethe's
before the appearance of Kant's Critique of Pure
Reason, nevertheless the influence of this epochal
work can scarcely fail to be recognized in those
more definite results which we have just detailed.

Kant maintains an entirely critical reserve,
holding himself aloof from either the assumption
of a world-creating deity, acting according to conscious aims, or that of an unconscious adaptation
of formative Nature—a teleology, so to speak,
immanent in her mechanism.—He wished only to
establish that man, by reason of the nature of his
faculties of intuition and perception, can only
grasp the organic forms of Nature by calling to
his aid the conception of design. But he nevertheless could not entirely resist the temptation to
overstep, if only for one moment, the line he
had so carefully drawn, in order to " venture on an
experiment of the understanding." " The resemblance of so many species of animals conform-
ably to a certain general scheme," he says,
" which seems to underlie not only the structure
of their skeletons, but the arrangement of their
other parts as well, and where the admirable
simplicity of the outline has been capable of pro-

ducing so great a variety of species, by the diminution of some and the expansion of other parts, by the folding up or unfolding of others, admits at least one ray of hope, if only a feeble one, that here something may possibly be attained to by the principle of Nature's mechanism." For he is of opinion that this analogy of the forms of Nature strengthens the supposition that they may naturally be allied to each other by descent, and justifies the assumption of a gradual development of organic beings, from man down to the zoophyte, from this even to the mosses and lichen, and thus at last to the lowest degree of Nature by us perceptible—mere matter, whence, as well as from the mechanical laws by which she forms crystals, the whole mechanism of Nature (which is so incomprehensible to us in organic beings, that we deem ourselves obliged to have recourse to another principle) seems to be derived."

Specially remarkable in its application to man is an observation of Kant, in a note towards the conclusion of his Anthropology. He mentions the fact that of all animals, new-born man alone announces his entrance on existence by cries. This, although not signifying much in the present condition of civilization, which even among savages ensures a certain protection by the family, in the preceding rude state of nature would have acted as a signal attracting wild beasts, and thus have endangered the preservation of the species. In the primæval condition, therefore, this crying of the new-born could not have taken place, but could only have occurred in the second period, when no longer dangerous. "This observation," Kant adds, "leads us far— for example, to the thought as to whether this second period may not be followed, in the rear of great revolutions of Nature, by a still third period, when an orang utang or a chimpanzee might be enabled to develop his various organs into the human structure, his brain into an organ of thought, which might then gradually be further developed by social culture."

53.

The external outlines of the theory of Lamarck and Darwin are thus already indicated, and several of the springs inserted by which its internal motion is regulated. As the animal, according to Goethe, is formed by circumstances for circumstances, thus, according to Lamarck, the eyes of the mole are stunted by its residence in the earth, while the swan has acquired its webbed feet through the necessity of rowing, and its long flexible neck by dint of searching for its food at the bottom of the water. The world shook its head at such explanations; and Darwin also, although convinced of the substantial correctness of the theory, yet considered these confirmations of it insufficient.

A hobby of his, it seems, first placed in his hands the means of discovering more tenable ones. Being an Englishman, and an English landowner, he was a pigeon-fancier; and as such he endeavoured to procure all possible varieties of this fowl, as well as to breed such himself. In this way he discovered, that forms of development which at first sight so widely diverge as to appear to belong to different species, may yet, in the course of several generations, be produced from a simple aboriginal stock by artificial breeding. The fancier, for example, finds amongst his common pigeons one specimen which possesses an additional feather in its tail, or a somewhat larger crop than the rest; immediately he looks out for a second specimen for each of these, in the other sex, in which the same deviation may have occurred; he pairs both of these couples; and it would be strange if amongst their progeny specimens should not appear, in time, with their tail-feathers still further multiplied, perhaps also enlarged, and crops more markedly inflated. Thus, in the course of many years and generations, the fan-tail on the one hand, the pouter on the other, as well as all the other varieties, have been bred from a simple aboriginal stock; the variations extending at last, from plumage and colour, to the structure of the bones, and the habits of life.

Similar results are notoriously produced by a like procedure in the case of other domestic animals, such as horses, dogs, sheep, and cattle, as well as with plants, especially flowers. This is rendered possible by the law of Nature, already adverted to, that organic types, with all their immutability in the whole, are yet mutable in their parts, and that those deviations are inherited by their descendants; but those striking results—I mean the astonishing diversity of the selected varieties from the parent-stock—are actually produced by the arbitrary interference of man, by pairing specimens which answer his purposes, and preventing their intercrossing with others. Man by artificial selection, produces varieties in regard to which it at last becomes a mere dispute about words to refuse recognition as new species: if something similar to this selection could be proved to have taken place in the domain of unfettered Nature, we should see our way to explain the ramification of organic life into the diverse forms and species that we have before our eyes.

54.

Is there, then, something in Nature causing the variations which have arisen in generations of plants and animals to be preserved and increased? causing, further, as a consequence of this, certain specially organized individuals to propagate themselves in the course of generations? and where are we to ask for this principle, this universal leaven?

The direction in which the Englishman searched for and found this is very characteristic. He was under no necessity to search for it at all, as everywhere in his native land he saw around him energetic industry, and the astonishing effects of his principle. He only needed to transfer competition from the world of man into the household of Nature. Darwin's "Struggle for Existence" is nothing else but the expansion of that into a law of Nature, which we have long since recognized as a law of our social and industrial life. We see organic beings possessing the impulse and capacity to produce a far greater number of offspring than can in the long run find adequate subsistence. Not only is there competition between animals for the pasture, but even between grapes and trees for the soil and the sun. If all cannot subsist, but only some, those few will, as a rule, be the stronger, more efficient and dexterous ones. If the weaker the clumsier, perish early, the better-equipped will be the principal propagators of their kind. If this process goes on uninterruptedly for several generations, more and more variation will continue to present itself among the descendants from the parent-stock.

In this way races of animals may acquire limbs, weapons, or even ornaments, not possessed by the progenitors. Goethe says, that in future it will no longer be asserted that the horns of the bull were given him to butt with, but that we shall enquire, rather, how he came by horns wherewith to butt? Lamarck taught that the horns of the bull were owing to his love and habit of butting. According to Darwin, this does not take place in quite so simple a fashion. He interpolates his "Struggle for Existence." Let us suppose a herd of cattle of primæval time to be still destitute of horns—only possessed of powerful necks and protruding foreheads.

The herd is attacked by beasts of prey; it defends itself by running against them and butting with the head. This butting will be the more vigorous, the fitter the bull to resist the beasts of prey, the harder the forehead with which he butts. Should this hardening in any individual have developed to an incipient horny accretion, then such an individual would have the best chance of preserving its existence. If the less well-equipped bulls of such a herd were torn to pieces, then the individual thus equipped would propagate the species. Unquestionably there would be some, at least, among its descendants in whose case the paternal equipment would be repeated; and if on renewed attacks these very ones again survived, then, little by little, by transmission of this weapon to the other sex also, a completely horned species would be formed; especially if this other sex would, of its own accord, give the preference to males thus ornamented : and here Darwin's theory of natural selection is supplemented by the so-called sexual selection, to which he recently has devoted a special work.

55.

This, in the first place, however, seems to point to a development and improvement within the limits of a given species, not to a differentiation into many. But in the domain of industry, competition impels energy not only vertically, but laterally as well. If all the English manufacturers devoted themselves exclusively to the manufacture of cotton, they would realize but poor profits. On that account some have taken to wool, others to silk, others again to iron or steel. The increasing competition among physicians is the cause that the rising men have more and more confined themselves to specialities, the one making this, the other that special organ of the human body his branch of study.

It is not otherwise in Nature. Suppose a crowd of competitors to drive a certain number of herbivorous animals from a rich plain on to the hills; the ousted ones grow more or less accustomed to the scantier food, the stony soil, the keener air; after the lapse of generations, they have come to be thoroughly at home in their new circumstances, but this has been accompanied by corresponding alterations in their structure: they have grown slimmer, fitter for climbing and leaping, keener of

sight; finally, a new species will have been evolved,
Or let us take one of the species of birds. The
genus of crossbills is divided, as we know, into fir-
crossbills and pine-crossbills; the former a more
vigorous species, which feeds on the seeds it painfully secures from the fir-cones, the latter a feebler
kind, which, by reason of its weaker beak, finds itself
consigned to the more delicate pine-cones. Here
the supposition arises that the more robust species
developed itself in tracts of country where only
the coarser kind of food was found; but we may
also assume that the want produced by too great a
competition induced the stronger individuals of the
entire species to struggle for the most difficult prize,
which those weaklings could dispute with them less
and less in every successive generation.

56.

So far, so good; but as long as the now improved
variety inhabits the same forest, the same plain, as
the old stock, specimens of the one must perpetually
be pairing with specimens of the other, in consequence of which the descendants will always revert
to the type of the original species, thus impeding
the independent evolution of the new type. The
separation of the individuals in which a tendency

to variation from the common kind has manifested itself, this isolation, by which alone artificial selection can attain its results, seems to be wanting in Nature, and similar results, in consequence, impossible with her.

" It is not wanting in Nature," remarked a German naturalist, but here is a gap in the theory. Unquestionably the origin of new species is not possible without isolation; but Nature possesses barriers enough and to spare by which she renders this possible. Moritz Wagner, our great traveller, remembered having observed in Algeria that the rivers which run from the Atlas range to the Mediterranean, without being very broad, nevertheless serve as distinct barriers. He found certain of the smaller rodents and reptiles, certain species of beetles and snails, to be confined by the river Schelif, which they never crossed. Broader streams, such as the Euphrates, the Mississippi, or a marine channel like the Strait of Gibraltar, exercise a yet more potent influence; but the most formidable barriers of all are compact mountain ranges, such as the Pyrenees, or the Caucasus. Here, on the one side and the other—save for the species which man has arbitrarily transplanted or involuntarily taken with him—a marked difference is perceptible in

the less mobile species, and even the flora participate in the variations of the fauna. For the seeds
of plants as well as animals (excepting the light-
winged of both kinds) but rarely and casually, and
then with great difficulty, succeed in crossing an arm
of the sea, or surmounting a towering range of mountains. But the instinct to do this is in them: the
migratory instinct is possessed by animals as well
as man; that of dissemination by plants: and with
all of them this is the result of the struggle for
existence. Competition, with chance superadded,
which now and again casts one or more individuals
into remote districts, is the true founder of colonies.
Let us imagine, for example, a pair of beetles trans-
ported by a tempest or a boat across the Schelif
or the Euphrates; or again, a couple of reptiles—or
but a pregnant female of each kind—surmounting
the Andes, the Pyrenees. The wanderers bring
their individual peculiarities with them, which
everywhere distinguish every single being from
every other in the world of life, and henceforth are
able to develop uncrossed; and as the new abode
usually entails at the same time climatic differences
and partial changes of food, variations from the
species which remained in the original home must
in the long run occur. But the intervening barriers

prevent specimens of the latter from following those which have migrated. Generations must elapse ere a second couple is successful enough to follow the first; and in the meanwhile the descendants of that first migrating pair have long ago developed into a new species. Only thus are we able, Wagner thinks, to account for the fact that the same species do not occur on the farther side of such boundaries, but in their stead very similar representative species.

Means and ways of this sort, which were and are still employed by Nature to differentiate herself—or, to express it subjectively, such explanations of the variety of organic forms on the earth—will be found more and more as the investigation of Nature proceeds; they do not exclude one another, but tend all together to the solution of the great enigma.

END OF VOL I.

THE OLD FAITH AND THE NEW.

57.

In primæval times a chief cause of those variations lay, doubtless, in the evolutions which the surface of our planet underwent, during long periods of time, in regard to temperature, its atmospherical constitution, and the distribution of water and land.

The documentary history of these changes, of the development of the earth's surface, is, as we know, preserved in the succession of her strata, and the remains of extinct plants and animals contained in them. These histories, indeed, like those of a Livy or a Tacitus, up to the present time lie before us in a very fragmentary condition, and full of considerable breaks, partly because many of the organic remains have actually perished on account of their innate fragility, partly because the archives of the earth have been consulted—or the soil, in other words, examined below the surface—in only a few spots.

Their succession of allied forms, nevertheless, **not** only confirms the theory of evolution as **a** whole, but reveals to **us** also, if only we do not suffer ourselves to be led astray by apparent deviations, **a** generally progressive development.

Cuvier already perceived that the difference between the fossil and existing species of animals increases with the depth of the strata in which the former are deposited. But that the later forms of plants, as well as of animals, are in general more perfect (although some of the earlier ones surpassed them in bulk and power, and some few actually retrograde formátions are not wanting) may be verified by ocular inspection, as we ascend from stratum to stratum. Thus, as regards the primæval flora, we find that the original algæ, or seaweed, are followed first by fern-like bloomless shrubs, then, among flowering plants, first by the more imperfect species of fir, finally by foliated trees and other perfect flowering plants. Thus also, as regards animals, we find only the most inferior kinds in the lowest strata; but as we ascend, mollusca in continuously progressive development; after these crustacea; then among vertebrates, successively fish, reptiles, birds, and at last mammals; and these classes, moreover, so arranged that here also the less perfect forms precede the more perfect, till at last, in the highest strata, we find vestiges of man.

Man, it is true, did not come on the scene quite so late as until recently was taken for granted. His first appearance was not at the present era of the earth's development, and with the present fauna. The discoveries which have been recently made in various caves of France, Belgium, England, and Germany, no longer permit any doubt of man's existence in primæval times, as a contemporary of the mammoth, the cave-bear, and extinct species of the hyæna and rhinoceros. But on this account also he first appears in an extremely imperfect condition : the oldest of the human skulls that have been discovered show a formation approximating to the brute, and are surrounded by miserable flint tools, and human as well as animal bones, whose cloven condition makes it probable that these our ancestors not only feasted on the marrow and flesh of the animals, but also on those of the men they had slain. And if we consider that it is but yesterday that these discoveries concerning man's greater antiquity and primitive condition have been made, it becomes highly probable that we have not yet by a long way reached the end of these revelations ; that in future we may discover him at perhaps a still lower

stage of his development, and much more nearly
akin to his four-footed progenitors.

58.

For after the enumeration of the preceding facts,
no doubt can be entertained as to the derivation
of mankind from a lower order of existence; and if
we now look around us for that species which, by
presenting the closest affinities to man, offers at the
same time the smallest chasm to bridge, we shall
inevitably find ourselves confronted with the higher
species of apes.

Thus at last **we** arrive at the much decried
doctrine of the descent of man from the monkey,
the *sauve qui peut* not only of the orthodox and
the sensitive, but also of many an otherwise toler-
ably unprejudiced man. He who does not find
this doctrine godless, yet finds it tasteless: if not
an outrage on the dignity of revelation, it is at
least one on the dignity of man. Each to his taste:
we know there are plenty of people who prefer
a Count or a Baron, impoverished by his dissolute
life, to a citizen who has won his way by dint of
energy and talent. Our taste is the reverse; and
therefore we are also of opinion that mankind has
far more cause for pride, if from miserable brutish.

beginnings it has gradually, by the incessant labour of countless generations, worked its way up to its present standpoint, than if it is descended from a pair who, created in the image of God, were cast out of paradise, and even now is far from having attained the level from which it originally sank. As nothing is so thoroughly depressing as the certainty of never being able entirely to recover a forfeited advantage, nothing, on the other hand, is so inspiriting to enterprise as to have a path before us, the height and scope of which it is impossible to foresee.

I will quote here the very words of the theory from Darwin's latest work :—

"The greater number of naturalists," he says, "have followed Blumenbach and Cuvier, and have placed man in a separate order, under the title of the Bimana. Recently many of our best naturalists have recurred to the view first propounded by Linnæus, and have placed man in the same order with the Quadrumana, under the title of the Primates. Our great anatomist and philosopher, Professor Huxley, (Darwin is still speaking,) has fully discussed this subject, and has come to the conclusion that man in all parts of his organization differs less from the higher apes than these do from the lower members of the same group. Consequently, there is no justification for placing man in a distinct order. The anthropomorphous apes, namely, the gorilla, chimpanzee, orang, and Hylobates, are separated as a distinct sub-group from the other Old World monkeys by most naturalists. If this be admitted, we may infer that some ancient member of the anthropomorphous sub-group gave birth to man. No doubt man, in comparison with most of his allies, has undergone an extraordinary amount of modification, chiefly in consequence of his greatly-developed brain and erect position ; nevertheless we should bear in mind that he is but one of several exceptional forms of Primates. It is probable that Africa was formerly inhabited by extinct apes, closely allied to the gorilla and chimpanzee ; and as these two species are now man's nearest allies, it is more probable that our early progenitors lived on the African continent than elsewhere. We must, however, beware of assuming the identity of the original ancestor of the Simiadæ, including the human species, with any existing ape, or even a very strong resemblance between them." Darwin explains the great gap which undeniably exists between man and the higher species of apes of the present day, from the extinction of intermediate forms, and the deposition of their fossil remains in Africa or Asia, hitherto so imperfectly explored by geologists. He points out, at the same time, that this gap would have appeared yet greater if the lowest and most ape-like races of men on the one hand, and the large anthropoid apes on the other, had been entirely exterminated.

Schopenhauer also speculated on this question in the same sense; and while Darwin and his successors assume the primæval progenitor of man to have been an old extinct branch of the anthropoid group of apes, he unhesitatingly points to the chimpanzee as the common ancestor of the black African, or Æthiopian race, and to the pongo as that of the brown Asiatic, or Mongolian, while he regarded the white Caucasian as an offshoot bleached by a colder climate. The original formation of man could, according to him, only have taken place in the Old World, and, moreover, only in the tropical zone: first, because in Australia Nature never produced a monkey at all, and in America only the long-tailed, not the short-tailed, far less the highest, tail-less species of monkey; secondly, because new-formed man would have perished in the colder zones during the first winter.

59.

Shortest steps and longest periods of time, we may say, are the magic formulæ by which Natural Science at present solves the mystery of the universe; they are the two talismans by whose aid she quite naturally unlocks the portals formerly reputed to fly asunder at the sole bidding of miracle.

Thus, to begin, for example, with periods of time, the 6,000 years which were counted in the Christian schools since the so-called creation of the world and man, have long ago grown to be as many tens, if not hundreds, of thousands of years, since the formation of man alone, notwithstanding all the difficulties attendant on a correct estimation of the position of human remains beneath alluvial soil, needing long periods for its formation. This estimate rests on an incomparably surer basis than did the old one, based on the Biblical text, of the ages of the patriarchs.

The discoveries of the lake habitations, the flint tools with which men had to make a shift before they discovered the art of working in copper, and subsequently iron, open out a vista into antiquity in comparison with which that of the Egyptian Pyramids may be considered as young, and of modern date. But this stone-era already bears a certain stamp of civilization, as, in fact, must every period in which man, besides using his natural tools and weapons, his arms, nails and teeth, has recourse to such as he seizes in the external world, and further still, instead of leaving these in their original condition, as stones and branches of trees, fashions them artificially, as those flint tools alluded to. Such enormous periods of time are in due proportion to the prodigious interval which had to be measured by man from the monkey-stage to that even of the lowest savage, who devoured not only the flesh of beasts, but of men.

And this immense progress leads us to understand, on the other hand, its splitting up into a multitude of minute, imperceptible gradations of progressive development. *Divide et impera* is also the watchword here. It was doubtless no small achievement when in yon apelike horde, which we must consider as the cradle of the human race, the thoroughly erect walk became the fashion, instead of the waddle, or partially quadrupedal gait of the higher apes; but step by step it went on improving, and time, at least, was no consideration. Neither did they lack a motive for becoming accustomed to the new posture, which left the hands free, in the first place, to carry stones and clubs, next, for the fabrication and handling of artificial utensils, and became thus useful in the struggle for exis?ence. More astounding still does this progress appear from the harsh scream of the ape to articulate human speech. Nevertheless, like most of the higher animals, monkeys also possess some sort of language : they utter warning cries at the approach of danger ; and express diverse emotions by diverse sounds, which are understood by their kind. It is true, we do not perceive a further development of this capacity among any of the present species of monkeys; whatever else he may learn, if brought into contact with man, the monkey certainly does not learn to speak. But he by no means lacks the organs of speech which with his cousins have developed into language ; and besides this, there is no question here of the present ape, but of a primæval stock, which amongst its ramifications counted one whose higher capacity of development led him in time to humanity, while the remaining branches sundered into the diverse species of monkeys, in part existing at present. Ere that pre-human branch, little by little, elaborated something resembling a language, periods of immeasurable duration may have elapsed; but after he had once hit upon speech, in however imperfect a condition, the speed of his progress was vastly accelerated. The capacity of thought, which, in the proper sense, first occurs with the formation of language, must have acted on the brain, enlarged and elaborated it; and this development of the brain again reacting on all the energies of the strange intermediate creature, must have given it a decided superiority over its allied species, and thus accomplished its metamorphosis into man.

60.

Metamorphosis of the animal into the man! Strange that not only laymen, but naturalists even, should believe in the incarnation of God, but find the metamorphosis of the animal, the progressive development of monkey to man, incredible! Very different views on this subject were held by the ancients, and still obtain in the far East. The doctrine of metempsychosis knits man and beast together there, and unites the whole of Nature in one sacred and mysterious bond. The breach between the two was opened in the first place by Judaism, with its hatred of the Gods of Nature; next by the dualism of Christianity. It is remarkable that at present a deeper sympathy with the animal world should have arisen among the more civilized nations, which manifests itself here and there in societies for the prevention of cruelty to animals. It is thus apparent that what on the one hand is the product of modern science, the giving up of the spiritualistic isolation of man from Nature, reveals itself simultaneously through the channel of popular sentiment.

In spite of this, however, not only does public opinion in general, but—if the expression be permissible—orthodox science also persist in regarding the human and animal world as two separate kingdoms, the yawning chasm between which no bridge can span, for the simple reason of man only being man by reason of possessing a something *per se*, from the beginning of creation, which is and always must be wanting in the animal. According to the Mosaic cosmogony, God made the animals, so to speak, out of one piece ; as to man, however, he first formed his body of the dust of the ground, then he breathed the breath of life into his nostrils, " and man became a living soul." The living soul of the ancient Hebrew writer was, in course of time, transformed by Christianity into an immortal soul, a being of quite another kind and dignity from those common souls which it is true could not be denied to animals. Or if, peradventure, the soul was allowed to be common to animals and man, the latter had spirit superadded to it, this being the immaterial principle of the higher intellectual and moral faculties, which distinguishes him from the animal.

This, however, in the domain of science, is contradicted by the unmistakable circumstance that the capacities of animals differ from the human race only in degree, not in kind. Voltaire justly remarks that animals possess sensation, conception, memory, and on the other hand desire and motion, even as we; and yet that nobody dreams of ascribing to them an immaterial soul. Why should we, therefore, require it, because we enjoy an insignificant increase of those faculties and energies? True, this Something superadded to man is not as insignificant as Voltaire, rhetorically belittling it, would have us suppose; on the contrary, it is enormous, but nevertheless only an increase of something—not something else. Even if we take the case of animals of a very low order, it would fill a volume, says Darwin, to describe the habits and mental powers of an ant. The same is true of bees. It is, in fact, curious that the more closely the life and ways of any one species are observed, the more the observer finds himself impelled to speak of their reason. The stories relating to the memory, the judgment, the capacity of learning and developing, of the dog, the horse, the elephant, are astounding. But even the so-called wild animals show traces of similar qualities. Speaking of birds of prey, Brehm remarks, "They act after mature deliberation; they form plans, and execute them." And of the thrushes he says, " They are quick in apprehension, correct in judgment, and know especially how to make use of all ways and means to ensure their safety. Those that have grown up in the silent and solitary forests of the North are easily decoyed; experience, however, very soon sharpens their sagacity, and those that have once been taken in are not again easily deluded in the same manner. Even as regards men, whom however, they never quite trust, they yet know how to distinguish between the dangerous and the inoffensive : they suffer the shepherd to approach them more nearly than the hunter." Coinciding with this is Darwin's account of the almost incredible degree of shrewdness, caution, and cunning, which has been developed in the fur-bearing animals of North America, in consequence of the unremitting waylaying they suffer at the hands of man.

Added to their reasoning faculties, Darwin endeavours to trace, especially in the higher animals, the commencement of the moral sentiment, which he connects with their social instincts. A certain sense of honour, of conscience, can scarcely be denied to the nobler and better-kept kinds of horses and dogs. And if the dog's conscience is, not quite unjustly, traced back to the stick, we may ask, in return, whether the same holds not good of the ruder sorts of man also? But the instincts, more especially, which bear on the rearing of young, the care, the pains, the self-sacrifice there lavished, must be regarded as a deposit of the higher moral faculties in the animal kingdom. To use an expression of Goethe's to Eckermann, "In the animal that is intimated in the bud which afterwards comes to full flower in man."

61

Voltaire, with his usual good sense in such things, remarks that the power of Thought fills us with astonishment, yet that that of feeling is quite as marvellous : a divine force reveals itself in the sensations of the lowest animal as much as in the brain of a Newton. In fact, he who should explain the zoophyte's instinctive grasping after its dis-

covered prey, the convulsive shrinking of the larva
of an insect upon being pricked, would not therefore, it is true, have explained the process of
thought in man, but he would, nevertheless, be on
the right path to it, without the need of calling a
new principle to his aid. On the contrary, the
distinct division and manifold development which
have been accorded to the material apparatus of
thought and feeling in the brain and nervous
system of man and the higher animals, must render
the explanation of them easier than, for example,
are those of the social and artistic instincts of the
bee or the ant, considering their far more imperfect
structure.

" If the soul unassisted by the brain is helpless,"
says Virchow, " if all her energies are dependent on
the changes of its parts, it can hardly be asserted
that consciousness or anything else is an original
attribute of the independent soul ; " but we might
as well " declare the brain to be sentient and thinking, even could it be demonstrated that its consciousness is first aroused by something different
from itself." From this dependence of mental
activity on the brain,—with whose growth and
development it unfolds itself, decreasing again as
the latter dwindles away in old age, and likewise

participating in any affection caused by its disease or injury,—Carl Vogt especially (with whom, although usually at issue, I thoroughly agree here) has undauntedly concluded that the admission of a special spiritual substance " is a pure hypothesis; that not a single fact points to the existence of such a substance; and that, moreover, the introduction of this hypothesis is utterly useless, as it explains nothing, brings nothing more forcibly before us."

On the contrary, many of the difficulties environing the problem of thought and feeling in man entirely proceed from this assumption of a psychical essence, distinct from the corporeal organs. How from an extended, non-thinking thing, such as the human body, impressions can be conveyed to a non-extended, thinking thing, such as the soul is alleged to be; how impulses are re-transmitted from the second to the first; in short, how any communion is possible between them,—this no philosophy has yet explained, and none ever will. The matter must, in any case, be much more intelligible, if we have only to do with one and the same being, of which in one respect extension is predicable, in another, thought. Of course we shall be told, such a being is not possible. We reply, It exists: we ourselves are all such beings.

It is astonishing how stubbornly men, even scientific men, will sit down for centuries in the face of such a problem, and for that very reason find it insoluble. It certainly is not so very long since the law of the Persistence of Force has been discovered, and it will still cost much labour to clearly explain, and determine it more precisely in its nearest relations, as concerns the transformation of heat into motion, and *vice versâ*. But the time cannot be very distant now when the law will be applied to the problem of thought and sensation. If, under certain conditions, motion is transformed into heat, why may it not, under other conditions, be transformed into sensation ? The conditions, the requisite apparatus, exist in the brain and nervous system of the higher animals, and in those organs which represent these among the lower orders. On the one side an internal motion is occasioned by contact with a nerve ; on the other an idea is roused by a sensation or a perception ; and *vice versâ*, on their way from within outwards, sensation and thought are transformed into bodily motion. " If," Helmholtz says, " in the production of heat by friction and percussion, the motion of the whole mass is transformed into motion of its minutest particles ; and on the other hand, in the production of motive force by heat, the motion of the minutest particles is again transformed into one of the whole mass,"—then I ask: Is this something essentially different? Is the above not its unavoidable corollary?

I shall be told that I am here speaking of things I understand nothing about. Very well; but others will come who will understand them, and who will also have understood me.

62.

If this be considered pure unmitigated materialism, I will not dispute it. In fact, I have always tacitly regarded the contrast so loudly proclaimed between materialism and idealism (or by whatever term one may designate the view opposed to the former), as a mere quarrel about words. They have a common foe in the dualism which pervaded the conception of the world throughout the Christian era, dividing man into body and soul, his existence into time and eternity, and opposing an eternal Creator to a created and perishable universe. Materialism, as well as idealism, may, in comparison with this dualistic conception, be regarded as Monism; *i.e.*, they endeavour to derive the totality of phenomena from a single principle—to construct the universe and life from the same block. In this endeavour one theory starts from above, the other from below; the latter constructs the universe from atoms and atomic forces, the former from ideas and idealistic forces. But if they would fulfil their tasks, the one must lead from its heights down to the very lowest circles of Nature, and to this end place itself under the control of careful observation; while the other must take into account the higher intellectual and ethical problems.

Moreover, we soon discover that each of these modes of conception, if rigorously applied, leads to the other. "It is just as true," says Schopenhauer, "that the percipient is a product of matter as that matter is a mere conception of the percipient, but the proposition is equally one-sided." "We are justified," says the author of the "History of Materialism," more explicitly, "in assuming physical conditions for everything, even for the mechanism of thought; but we are equally justified in considering not only the external world, but the organs, also, with which we perceive it, as mere images of that which actually exists." But the fact always remains, that we must not ascribe one part of the functions of our being to a physical, the other to a spiritual cause, but all of them to one and the same, which may be viewed in either aspect.

I am therefore of opinion that both systems should reserve their weapons for that other veritable and still formidable foe, while treating each other with the respect, or at least the politeness, of allies. The overbearing, half-lecturing, half-incriminating tone which some philosophers love to assume towards the materialism of the natural sciences, is quite as blameable, and even unwise, as is, on the other hand, the rude abuse of philosophy with which materialists are so fond of amusing, if not of edifying us. And the misapprehension is almost more stubborn on the side of the latter than the former. That knowledge of the natural sciences is indispensable to the philosopher, that familiarity with the latest discoveries in chemistry, physiology, etc., is absolutely requisite to him, is hardly now denied by anyone of philosophical pretensions; we far more frequently see the representatives of the exact sciences disposed to relegate philosophy into the lumber-room, with astrology and alchemy. For a good while it certainly did act as if it deserved it; but these gentlemen, as naturalists, ought surely to be able to distinguish between moulting of the outer covering and a mortal distemper of the whole system. That philosophy has for some time past been in this state of transition, is only too evident ; but its plumage will grow again. The token of a healthy crisis is the regimen in now observes. It occupies itself chiefly with its own history; and in this department can point to productions which, for thoroughness and insight, far outstrip every work of former times. This is clearly the safest way of arriving at the conclusion as to what its capabilities are, what it should do, and, still better, what it should leave alone. And if anything has good cause to wish it success in its endeavours, it is Natural Science. For the accurate formation of those most delicate instruments which are hourly wielded by the naturalist, the ideas of force and matter, essence and phenomena, cause and effect, can only be taught him by philosophy and metaphysics, and their accurate application by philosophy as logic ; the Ariadne-clue, which shall lead him through the labyrinth of the daily increasing mass of single observations, he can solely expect from the hand of philosophy. In regard, however, to the ultimate problems of beginning and end, limitation or infinity, purpose or fortuitousness of the universe, philosophy alone can afford him the one kind of information which is at all possible in those regions.

But science is beginning to show signs of a better

appreciation of philosophy, and of repenting its former coyness. For what, at bottom, underlies the general interest which the Darwinian theory has aroused in its circles, but the philosophical interests which, far transcending the isolated facts, looks to the infinite perspective which it has disclosed? Undoubedly our so-called philosophy of Nature has embraced a cloud instead of Juno, and begotten nothing in consequence; but the Darwinian theory is the first child of the true, though as yet clandestine, union of science and philosophy.

63.

"Darwin's theory shows how the adaptation of structure in organisms may be effected, without any interference of intelligence, by the blind operation of a natural law." If Helmholtz in these words describes the English naturalist as he who has removed the idea of design from our explanation of Nature, we, on the other hand, have already praised him as having effaced miracle from our conception of the world. For design is the magician of Nature; he it is who turns the world topsy-turvy, and, to quote Spinoza, "makes the hindmost the foremost, makes the effect a cause, and thus entirely destroys the conception of Nature." It is the adaptation in Nature, especially in the domain of organic life, which has always been appealed to by those who have contended that the Cosmos could not be understood by itself, but only as the work of an intelligent creator.

"If the eye," says Trendelenburg, "in the course of formation were turned towards the light, we should at first suspect that this precious organ was formed by contact with the luminous ray. We should seek the efficient cause in the force of light. But the eye develops in the obscurity of the womb, in order to correspond, when born, to the light. The same holds good of the other senses. There is a pre-established harmony between the light and the eye, sound and the ear; and this seems to point to a power enveloping the different members, of which the Alpha and Omega is the idea."

Similar arguments are derived from the instincts of animals. "We observe in all animals" (these words of H. S. Reimarus are even now a classical expression for the teleological mode of conception) "certain natural impulses, instincts, or efforts, which enable them from their birth to perform admirably and with hereditary finished art, that which the highest reason might have indicated as most conducive to their well being. This they do without any thought, experience, or practice whatever

on their own part, or any instruction, example, or
pattern. But as little as it is possible for art, science,
and cleverness to exist without intelligence and
deliberate action, so little can we ascribe all this to
the irrational creatures themselves. It is the revelation of an infinite intelligence, which is the original
fountain of all possible invention and science, and
which found the means of implanting as an innate
capacity in the blind nature of all these creatures,
that part of itself which they needed."

The intelligent artificer of organisms, the personal
inspirer of instincts, could not well be retained by that
modern thought which has been developed by the
progress of the Natural Science. It had been too
clearly apprehended that our consciousness of both
the outer and inner worlds is first rendered possible
on the substratum of the senses, that our thought depends on a physical apparatus, especially on the brain
and the nervous system, and is in consequence conditioned by a limit, but all limit must be withheld from
the absolute being. This has inspired the author of
" The Philosophy of the Unconscious" with his
theory of an unconscious Absolute, which, acting in
all atoms and organisms as a universal soul, deter-
mines the contents of creation, and the evolution of
the universe, by a "clairvoyant wisdom superior to

all consciousness." At the same time, the unconscious
sets to work in the same manner as did formerly
the conscious and personal Absolute: it pursues a
plan, and chooses the most appropriate means, only
nominally without consciousness; the explanations
which E. von Hartmann gives of the adaptation
of Nature, are exactly like those of old Reimarus;
neither the effect nor the mode of operation is
differently conceived, but only the operating subject. But this is the alteration of a word, not the
solution of the problem. If formerly the contradiction lay in the subject, in the relation of its incompatible attributes of absoluteness and personality,
it now lies in the relation of the subject to its
activity; performances and actions are ascribed to
an unconscious which can only belong to a conscious being.

64.

If an unconscious something is to have accomplished what appears to us in Nature as an
adaptation of means to ends, then I must be able
to conceive of its action being such as is adapted to
the unconscious; it must, to speak with Helmholtz,
have acted as a blind force of Nature, and yet have
accomplished something which corresponds to a

design. We have been led to the summit of this standpoint by the recent investigation of Nature in Darwin.

If Reimarus, speaking of instincts, says, "they are skill implanted by God in the souls of animals," while Darwin, on the other hand, regards them simply as "inherited habits," the chasm is fully revealed which separates the new Cosmic conception from the old, and the progress is shown which, during the last century, has been made in the comprehension of Nature. Trendelenburg insists on the fact that the eye is not formed *in* light—in consequence, not *by* light, yet, nevertheless, in the obscurity of the womb *for* light; and he concludes from this adaptation, not at the same time comprehending a causative one, that there must be an absolute Intelligence which makes and carries out an aim. But the eye of the embryo is only formed in the womb of a being whose eye has been, during the whole course of its existence, subject to the influence of light, and which transmits the modifications effected in the eye by light to its offspring. It is not, of course, the seeing human individual which forms its own or its offspring's eye by acting in concert with light; but it does not follow that it must therefore have been made by an

artificer external to itself: the individual finds itself
put in possession of an instrument which its
predecessors, since immemorial times, have gradually
brought to an ever higher grade of perfection
Helmholtz remarks especially of the eye,—what,
however, applies equally to every organ,—that here
" that which can be effected by the labour of countless successions of generations, under the influence
of the Darwinian law of development, tallies with
that which it would be possible for the forethought
of the highest wisdom to plan." Among these
ancestors and generations we are naturally not
merely to understand human ones, which have all
inherited the eye in its already finished condition.
Even beyond the renowned amphioxus, we must
ascend to the very beginnings of life, where an
obscure general diffusion of sensation is gradually
differentiated into the various senses, whose organs
have slowly perfected themselves under the
pressure of necessity ; in all of which mere individuals take the smallest share, although the organs
are strengthened by habit: but inasmuch as those
individuals which, in consequence of casual variation,
possess the life-promoting organ in a more perfect
condition, are better adapted to succeed and propagate their kind than the others, the organ is perfected

in the course of generations. The same is the case
with animal instincts. It is not our present bee
which plans its skilful constructions, neither is
it instructed in them by a deity; but in the lapse
of thousands of years, since the lowest insects have
gradually developed into the various genera of the
Hymenoptera, the increasing needs induced by
the struggle for existence have gradually fashioned
those arts which are now transmitted without effort
as heirlooms to the present generations.

Let us call to mind the Kantian "Give me
matter; I will show you how a world shall be evolved
thence;" an undertaking which, although considered
possible to carry out in regard to the world of
inorganic matter, he said must yet necessarily be
wrecked upon a caterpillar. Modern science,
although it has not as yet achieved this, has yet
found the right direction in which it will one day
be able to achieve, not merely the caterpillar, but
even man.

65.

Only as long as a personal deity was assumed,
and the creation of the world regarded as a free act
of his will, could there, properly speaking, be any
question either of isolated aims of Nature, or gene-

rally, of the aim of the world or creation. Starting from this standpoint, ancient theologians and philosophers sometimes defined the end of the creation as the glory of God, sometimes as the happiness of the creature, while, at the same time, they sternly insisted on the fact that God had had no need of the world, that it added nothing to his perfection and beatitude.

It is singular how it has fared with this assertion during the last stage of modern philosophy. Schelling says, that if God had already been in possession of the highest perfection without the creation of the world, he would have had no motive for the production of so many things, by which, if incapable of attaining to a higher degree of perfection, he could only have diminished the perfection he already possessed ; and that such a strangely tangled though orderly whole as the world, could not be explained as having been produced by a clear and perspicuous intelligence, such as Theism commonly attributed to the divine Being before the creation of the universe. According to Hegel also, the Supreme Spirit could only have had the patience to undertake the enormous labour of the world's history, from inability of enjoying any intellectual activity in any other manner.

Schopenhauer and his adherents express themselves much more coarsely concerning this question.
"It must be an ill-advised God," says the former,
in controverting Pantheism, "who should be able to
devise no better pastime than to transform himself
into so hungry a world as ours, to appear in the
form of innumerable millions of living, but at the
same time terrified and tormented beings, who can
only exist for a space by mutually devouring each
other, and enduring measureless and objectless ills
of anguish, misery, and death." And thus the author
of "The Philosophy of the Unconscious," who, if possible, outdoes the master, says that "if God, previous
to the creation, had been aware what he was doing,
creation would have been an inexpiable crime; its
existence is only pardonable as the result of blind
will; the entire Cosmic process would be an equally
unfathomable folly, if its only possible aim—self development, had existed without it." Maxims, of which
the first reminds one of Schelling's doctrine of the
creation as being the work of an undeveloped reason
in God, the second, of Hegel's remark on the significance of universal history.

If we enquire what it is that renders this world
unworthy of a divine creator, Schopenhauer answers: Pain and death cannot exist in a divinely

ordered universe. It is especially the struggle for existence, with its sufferings and horrors without end, which for him bars the way to a satisfactory conception of the universe. But it is this very struggle for existence which we have already recognized as being the leaven which alone introduces motion and progress into the world; and strangely enough, this perception is not wanting in Schopenhauer. "To take trouble upon himself," he says somewhere, "and struggle against that which resists him, is as natural to man as burrowing is to the mole. The calm which the satisfaction of an abiding enjoyment would bring with it, would be unbearable to him. The fullest enjoyment of his existence consists in the conquest of obstacles, whether of a material or a mental nature; to combat them and to overcome them are the conditions of felicity. If all such opportunity be wanting to him, he creates it as best he may, if only to put an end to the intolerable state of rest." Schopenhauer, however, would seek to nullify this concession by reckoning this peculiarity of human nature he has described as itself a proof of the perversity of the whole Cosmic system. Nevertheless, it would not be difficult to refute his pessimism by its help. "Every movement," says Lessing, "develops and

destroys, brings life and death ; brings death to one
creature in bringing life to another. Would we
rather have no death and no motion ? or rather
death and motion ? "

And that other saying of Lessing—" If God, holding truth in his right hand, and in his left only the
ever living desire for truth, although on condition of
perpetual error, should leave me the choice of the
two, I would humbly point to the left hand, and say
' Father, give! Pure Truth is for thee alone.' " This
saying of Lessing has always been accounted one of
the most magnificent which he has left us. It completely expresses his restless love of enquiry
and activity. The saying has always made quite a
special impression upon me, because behind its subjective meaning I still seemed to hear the faint ring
of an objective one of infinite import. For does it
not contain the best possible answer to the rude
speech of Schopenhauer, respecting the ill-advised
god who had nothing better to do than to transform
himself into this miserable world ? if, for example,
the Creator himself had shared Lessing's conviction
of the superiority of struggle to tranquil possession ?

From our present standpoint, which no longer recognizes a self-conscious creator of the universe,
these suppositions may appear to us as the dalliance

of fancy; but we may easily retain the significance
of them without applying them to a personal God.
If we can no longer transfer to God the choice between an existence in the first place devoid of pain
and death, but likewise of motion and life, or one in
the second place wherein life and motion are bought
by pain and death, we have, nevertheless, the choice
whether we will try to understand the second, or
whether, in fruitless negation of what actually exists, we insist on preferring the first.

66.

In so far, therefore, as we still speak of a purpose
in the universe, we are clearly conscious that we are
expressing ourselves subjectively, and that we only
express by it what we seem to recognize as the
general result of the co-operation of the active
forces in the world.

We imported from our preceding section the
conception of the Cosmos, instead of that of a personal God, as the finality to which we are led by
perception and thought, or as the ultimate fact
beyond which we could not proceed. In the course
of further investigation, this assumed the more definite shape of matter infinitely agitated, which, by

differentiation and integration, developed itself to
ever higher forms and functions, and described an
everlasting circle by evolution, dissolution and then
fresh evolution. The general deduction from the existence of the universe appears to us to be, as a whole,
the most varied motion, or the greatest abundance
of life; this motion or life specialized as one developing itself morally as well as physically, strug-
gling outwards and upwards, and even in the decline
of the individual only preparing a new uprising.

The old religious conception of the universe
regarded the attainment of its aim as placed at the
end of the world. There as many human souls
as possible, or as was predestined, are saved; the
others, including the devils, are delivered unto
merited punishment; the spiritual beings are completed and continue, while Nature, which only served
as the basis for their development, may perish.
From our standpoint also, the object of the terrene
development seems much nearer its attainment
now, when the earth is filled by men and their
works, and partly inhabited by nations of a high
mental and moral civilization, than many hundreds
of thousands of years ago, when she was still exclusively occupied by mollusca or crustacea, to which
fish were added later, then the mighty Saurians,

with their allied species, and finally, the primæval mammals, but still without man.

Nevertheless, a time must come when the earth will be no longer inhabited,—nay, when she will have ceased to exist as a planet. Then all that which, in the course of her development, was produced and in a manner accomplished by her—all living and rational beings, and all their productions, all political organizations, all works of art and science— will not only have necessarily vanished from existence, without a trace, but even the memory of them will survive in no mind, as the history of the earth must naturally perish with her. Either the earth has missed her aim here—no result has been produced by her protracted existence ; or this aim did not consist in something which was intended to endure, but has been attained at every moment of her development. The sum of the terrestrial events, however, which remained constant in all stages of the earth's development was only in part the richest expansion and motion of life in general, in part specially the ascending direction of this motion, which in its ascension oversoared the decline of the individual.

The fact is, that ascent and decline are only relative conceptions. The life of the earth, for

example, is at the present period quite as certainly
waning in one respect as it is waxing in another.
The brooding warmth, the luxurious fruitfulness,
the vast creative power, have decreased; while the
delicacy, the elaboration, the spiritualization have
increased. It is probable that a time will come in
the distant future, when the earth will grow yet
colder, dryer, and more sterile than she is at
present; we may feel inclined to conceive of the
men of that period as debased, decrepid, Samoyed-
like; but it is quite as conceivable, at least, that
the more unfavourable conditions of existence will
open out new mental resources, sharpen their in-
ventive faculties, and strengthen their mastery of
themselves and of Nature.

For if we must hold fast by the idea that each
individual part of the universe, such as the life
of our earth, attains, indeed, its end in ever higher
manifestations, yet is at every moment complete in
itself; the latter alone holds good of the universe
as the infinite Whole. The All is in no succeeding
moment more perfect than in the preceding one,
nor *vice versâ :* there exists in it, in fact, no such
distinction of sooner or later, because all gradations
and stages of contraction and expansion, ascent
and decline, becoming and perishing, exist side by

side in it, mutually supplementing each other **to** infinity.

Nevertheless the general object or result of the world is specially conditioned for every part, every class of beings. Although the variety of life, the struggle of forces, the progressive tendency, will be the same on one planet as on another, they will, nevertheless, in each be subjected to different rules of action, different forms of manifestation. And in like manner, the result will assume different proportions among the different organisms on the earth. The development of the dog or cat genus will produce, and humanly speaking, be intended to produce, a different result from that of the development of mankind.

What the result of the latter ought to be, and is, we hope will become plain to us, if finally we still endeavour to answer the last of the questions **we** have proposed, namely, the question :

IV.

WHAT IS OUR RULE OF LIFE?

67.

THE path by which we have reached man, the process of development whence we have seen him evolved, has, as regards the conception of his destiny and the tasks of his terrestrial existence, naturally given us a standpoint different from that of Christian theology. For as man did not come forth from the hand of God, but arose from depths of Nature, his first estate was not paradisaical, but almost brutal. Neither, of course, did he in our eyes fall with the first step, and thus forfeit Paradise. He did not begin his career on a great elevation, to sink very low immediately afterwards; on the contrary, he began very low, to rise, although very slowly, yet gradually to ever greater heights. By this means alone he is included in the universal law of development, from which the Christian conception withdraws him at the very first.

We know at present that the beginnings of man

were so low that, even after his ejection from **Para-**
dise, he is still placed too high by the biblical
narrative. He is described as having cultivated
his field; but primæval man, an offshoot of the
primæval ape, was yet far from having attained
this stage. A truer discernment may be found in
the story of the coats of skins; but alas, these were
not made for him by a god: he himself was forced
to combat and destroy the monsters in order to
flay them. He appears, in the first stage of his
development, as a famished huntsman, a sullen
inmate of caves,—nay, as a cannibal and devourer
of his fellows. Of vegetable food he partook, along
with the flesh and marrow of the bear or rhinoceros,
of such fruits as the tree or shrub offered spontaneously, or of such edible roots as he found in the
earth. How many millenniums may have elapsed
ere he learnt to domesticate the goat, sheep, and ox,
to grow corn on a spot of ground, to kindle a fire,
and roast his meat by it, to triturate grain, and
make his cake more palatable by the aid of fire!

But however miserable we may be compelled to
conceive the condition of primæval man, one quality,
at least, we may assume him to have possessed,
which was likely to help him forward on his way:
sociability. Besides other higher animals, those

are especially social in the state of Nature whose acquaintance we have already made as being man's nearest relatives. Now, it is true, animals are not further developed by sociability; it aids them in discovering food and protecting themselves against enemies, but in other respects they remain as they were. That group of animals, however, which was destined to develop into man, possessed, besides its sociability, a pliability both of the external limbs and more especially, of the organs of speech and of the brain. In conjunction with these the social qualities could achieve specially high results.

As in the combinations of matter in the domain of inorganic Nature we distinguish between forces of attraction and repulsion, centripetal and centrifugal impulses, thus we remark the same double action in the social aggregation of living beings. The repulsive force consists in the egotism of those to be united : one pulls one way, the other another— some two or more fighting for the same object, as for example a piece of meat ; to which is superadded what always was a chief cause of war, not only, as the poet deems, before Helen of Troy, but even before Eve, among the brute creation of primæval times—contention concerning females. The attractive, or centripetal force, on the other hand, manifests itself from within outwards, as the social impulse; and man is also impelled in the same direction by the pressure which is exercised from without by famine and the attack of the inimical forces of elemental as well as of organic Nature. The latter motive was naturally all the more potent with man, the more feeble his physical organization, especially as compared with the terrible beasts of prey, and the less he could hope to resist them except by united force.

And as everywhere else, so here, we see order arise from the collision of forces. Already among animals—and the higher we ascend the more we shall find it—no one individual is quite like another, either in the perfection of its parts or the efficacy of its performances. This, as well as the difference of age, is the reason why there is always one animal of superior strength and sagacity at the head of the herd. Now, however akin to the bestial we may consider the first human horde to have been, they must, nevertheless, soon have discovered one or another to be bolder in repelling the enemy from without, or to be more peaceably inclined towards the members of the horde itself at home. But in these half bestial beginnings, we already see the dawn of two qualities, which as they develop, will appear as two of the cardinal virtues of humanity: courage and justice. And where these have once taken root, the other two, perseverance and prudence, will infallibly soon branch out of them. At the same time we perceive that moral qualities can only be developed in society.

Not all the members of the community possess these virtues; but in order that the community may prosper they ought to possess them, or at least, not the opposite faults. Where the latter predominate and increase, especially in the mutual relations of the members of the community, there society is threatened with decline and dissolution. Here we may catch glimpses of the history of savage and protracted struggles, during which much violence and suffering was inflicted and borne by the various human hordes, and much knowledge stored up likewise. Experience taught them, in every shape and by countless repetitions, what might be expected of a human community in which there was no security for life, acquired booty, or legitimate property,—and in the relation of the sexes, no limit imposed on rude desire. From the dear and blood-purchased experience of what is noxious and what useful, there arise gradually among the various races of mankind, first customs, then laws, at last a code of duties.

68.

We possess various compilations of such primal laws of nations, belonging to the Aryan as well as to the Semitic races; the one which is most familiar to us is the Mosaic Decalogue, which, although not from the oldest period, yet dates from a very ancient one. It consists chiefly, apart from the precepts relating to the Hebrew religion, of maxims affecting human rights, forbidding murder, theft, and adultery. Certain actions are here forbidden which, although society cannot prevent by the penalties it attaches to them, it can yet render of less frequent occurrence. The precept to honour father and mother, also one of the laws, reaches higher already; it could not, like the others, be enforced by the menace of punishment, and the lawgiver therefore attempts this by the promise of a divine recompense. But lying quite beyond the reach of mere law, touching on the inner spirit, are the two remarkable appended commandments, which forbid man to covet the wife or goods of his neighbour. Here the experience manifests itself already, that the surest means of preventing certain external actions is to stop up their sources in the mind of man.

To the two questions : How did men come by laws of this kind ? and Whence do they derive their validity ? legend everywhere returns the same answer—they were given by God, and are therefore binding on men. The Bible gives a minute description of the scene on Mount Sinai, where Jehovah, amidst thunderings and lightnings, handed the tables of the law to the leader of the Israelitish people. At a later period the prophets also, in uttering their warnings, appealed to an immediate divine command ; and finally Jesus, according to the Gospels, enforces his doctrine by his Messianic dignity, and especially his intimate relations with his heavenly Father. From our point of view, these mythical supports have decayed, and these precepts can only rely on their own intrinsic authority.

We acknowledge the laws of the Decalogue, just quoted, to have been the product of a necessity for such in human society, gradually taught by experience; and herein also lies the reason of their unalterable obligation. Nevertheless, we cannot quite overlook the loss entailed by this exchange : the doctrine of their divine origin hallowed the laws, while our view of their growth seems to admit merely their utility, or at most, their ex-

ternal necessity. They could only fully recover
their sanctity, if it were possible likewise to discover their internal necessity—their derivation,
not only from social wants, but from the nature or
essence of man.

If Jesus gave his disciples the precept, Do unto
others as ye would be done by, this precept
possesses an immediate divine sanction for the
believer, by reason of the divine dignity of Christ's
person. For us, on the contrary, the authority
which we also still concede to this person consists
in his having enforced more precepts, uttered more
thoughts of the same kind, from which we cannot
withhold our assent, it making no difference to
the value of those thoughts whether they had
spontaneously sprung up in Christ's mind and
heart, or he was indebted for them to some tradition. Moreover, in the moral precept here in question, the influence of a time cannot be overlooked
when, in consequence of the world-wide Roman
rule, even the exclusive Jewish people saw their
own horizon expanding into that of humanity in general.

Jesus was no philosopher, and has not therefore
given any further reasons for this precept than for
so many others. But the precept itself is in a

manner philosophical. It does not appeal to a divine injunction, but in order to find a rule for human action, abides on the basis of human nature (and yet not solely on that of a merely external requirement). But this is exactly the fundamental position which philosophy has always taken.

69.

The most distinguished practical philosophers we may consider to have been the Stoics, in the ancient world, and in the modern, Kant. The leading moral doctrine of the Stoics was to live according to Nature. If they were asked, to what Nature? some answered, according to the human, others to the general Nature, or universal law. Now, human nature is adapted to the dominion of reason over the desires; therefore the philosophical emperor wrote that, to the reasonable being, acting naturally was equivalent to acting reasonably. And as the same reason, moreover, which is said to reign in man is also the divine principle pervading the whole universe, according to the doctrine of the Stoics, the man acting in consonance with his own reason, acts also consonantly with universal reason. And as by this same reason he knows himself to be part of the world, and especially a member of the great community of rational beings, he recognizes it as his duty to live, not only to himself, but also for the general good.

The following maxim is laid down by Kant as the fundamental law of practical reason : " So act that the dictate of thy will may always pass at the same time for the principle of a general legislation." That is to say, that whenever we are about to act, we ought first to make clear to ourselves the principle we are going to act upon, asking ourselves how it would be if everybody were guided by the same principle,—not how the world thus produced would please us ; our relish or disrelish is to be put entirely aside in this case ; but whether anything at all harmonious could be thus produced. He uses the example of a deposit, which some one, on the death of the depositor, and in the certainty of there being no proofs against him, might feel himself inclined to retain. He would then, according to Kant, have to make clear to himself the principle upon which he is tempted to act: that everybody might deny the receipt of a deposit which nobody could prove to have been entrusted to him. But as soon as he begins to think of this as a generally accepted principle, he must see that it annihilates itself; for nobody in that case would feel inclined to make a deposit. It is clear that Kant wants to go beyond the Do as ye would be done by; for this appeals to inclination; while Kant wishes to constitute reason its own lawgiver, its test being that nothing self-contradictory can be deduced from its precepts.

But Schopenhauer not unjustly points out that a moral imperative must not be spun together out of abstract ideas, but be connected with an actually existing impulse of human nature. Besides selfishness (and malice, which, however, is more properly subordinated to it, as an extreme or degeneracy of selfishness), Schopenhauer considers compassion to be the spring of human actions, and this latter is, in his eyes, the exclusive source of moral action. If we may further conceive compassion to include also sympathy, we shall arrive at that principle of benevolence which it was the custom, especially of the Scotch moralists in the last century, to oppose to that of self-love. But that it may also be thus conceived in the sense in which it is used by Schopenhauer, is apparent from the manner in which he classifies the actions which have compassion for their source. For he makes a distinction between actions in which the (negative) will is manifested not to injure others, or actions of justice, and such in which the (positive) will is shown to assist others, or actions of philanthropy.

By this reasoning Schopenhauer naturally only obtains duties towards others, and he endeavours to prove at much length that man can have no duties towards himself, such as were still admitted by Kant. He may frequently be right as regards individual facts, but his deduction does not seem to cover the whole field. Let us take, for example, a young man whose duty it is to cultivate his faculties: can compassion, in his case, be the spring of action which shall make him industrious? Let us call it sympathy, as we said, and conceive it as consideration for society, of which he is in future to be a useful member; for Schopenhauer only recognizes, as a moral spring of action, that which manifests itself as such in actual life; but it is certainly only in exceptional cases that a young man's incentive to industry and learning is the duty which he owes to society. Consideration even for his parents, who feel pleasure at his industry and progress, and pain at the reverse, may indeed influence him to some extent, but cannot be regarded as the real motive. This can only be the impulse of his mental energies to expand and exert themselves. Should it be objected that this is not a moral but a distinctly selfish motive, the following considerations would have to be regarded. Besides his intellectual and moral capacities, the young man is conscious in himself of sensuous forces insisting on being exercised and developed, and that, moreover, with an energy and a violence which that higher impulse is not capable of displaying. But if, nevertheless, he gives free play to those sensuous impulses only so far as they do not interfere with the development of his higher energies, we must call this an ethical action, not deducible from pity—not, in fact, manifesting itself in the moral relations of one man towards others, but towards himself.

70.

I should say, that all moral action arises from the individual's acting in consonance with the idea of kind. To realize this, in the first place, and to bring himself, as an individual, into abiding concord with the idea and the destiny of mankind, is the essence of the duties which man owes to himself. But in the second place, to practically recognize, and promote in all other individuals also, this permanently enduring kind, is the essence of our duties to others; where we must draw a distinction between the negative obligation of abstaining from injuring others in their equal rights, and the positive one of assisting all to the extent of our ability, or between duties of justice and of philanthropy.

According to the narrower or wider circles which humanity draws round us, these duties to our neighbours will be subject to further subdivisions, defined according to the various obligations incumbent upon us in our relation to each of these circles. In the narrowest, but also most intimate of these—the family—we must sustain and transmit what we have received from it : kindly nurture of life, and education to humanity. To the State we owe the firm basis for our existence, the security of life and property ; and by means of the school our fitness for living in a human community : it is incumbent on every one of its members to do all which their position in society enables them, to ensure its stability and prosperity. From the nation we have received our language, and the entire culture connected with language and literature; nationality and language form the inmost bond of the State ; national habits are also the basis of family life : to the nation we must be ready to consecrate our best energies—if need be, our lives. But we must recognize our own nation to be but one member of the body of humanity, of which we must not wish any other member, any other nation, to be mutilated or stunted; as humanity can only flourish as a whole in the harmonious development of all her members; as again, her stamp is to be recognized and respected in every single individual, to whatever nation he may belong.

On the other hand, the duties of man vary according to the position which he occupies in the human community; besides the universally human, there are also special professional, or class duties. The individual's class is in many instances determined for him; his profession, on the other hand, being usually a matter of free choice, and this again an object of moral determination. Choose that profession, runs the precept here, by means of which, in the measure of your special endowment, you can render the best services to the commonwealth, and find the greatest satisfaction for yourself.

What is chiefly meant here, is an internal satisfaction, which each living being finds when it develops and acts in consonance with the peculiar set of capacities of which its individual form is a manifestation; for the moral being, or man, too, this is about all the truth there is in what is still very crudely called the reward of virtue or piety. This so-called reward is also usually brought into such a merely external relation with that of which it is to be the recompense that a deity is necessary to connect the two; nay, this necessity is even made an argument for the existence of God. From our standpoint, so inseparable from moral action is its reflex in feeling, or beatitude, that at most it can but take color from external circumstances but can never lose its value as beatitude.

If morality is the relation of man to the idea of his kind, which in part he endeavours to realize in himself, in part recognizes and seeks to promote in others, religion, on the other hand, is his relation to the idea of the universe, the ultimate source of all life and being. So far, it may be said that religion is above morality; as it springs from a still profounder source, reaches back into still more primitive ground.

Ever remember that thou art human, not merely a natural production; ever remember that all others are human also, and, with all individual differences, the same as thou, having the same needs and claims as thyself: this is the sum and substance of morality.

Ever remember that thou, and everything thou beholdest within and around thee, all that befals thee and others, is no disjointed fragment, no wild chaos of atoms or casualties, but that it all springs, according to eternal laws, from the one primal source of all life, all reason, and all good : this is the essence of religion.

That thou art human—what, after all, means this How shall we so define man, that we not merely catch hold of empty phrases, but combine the results of actual experience into one distinct conception?

71.

" The most important general result," says Moritz Wagner, " which comparative Geology and Palæontology"—and the Natural Sciences in general, we may add—" reveal to us, is the great law of progress pervading all Nature. From the oldest times of the earth's history of which any traces of organic life survive, up to the present creation, this continuous progress is a matter of fact established by the experience of the appearance of more highly-developed beings than the past had to show. And this fact is perhaps the most consolatory of all the truths ever discovered by science. In this inherent aspiration of Nature after an unceasingly progressive improvement and refinement of her organic forms, consists also the real proof of her divinity. A noble utterance," adds Wagner, " which the naturalist, however, interprets in an essentially different sense from the priest of a so-called revealed religion."

In this cumulative progression of life man is also comprised, and moreover, in such wise that the organic plasticity of our planet (provisionally, say some naturalists, that we may fairly leave an open question), culminates in him. As Nature cannot go higher, she would go inwards. To be reflected within itself was a very good expression of Hegel's. Nature felt herself already in the animal, but she wished to know herself also.

Here is that legitimation of man's impulse and activity in exploring and understanding Nature, which we miss in Christianity. Man is labouring in his own especial vocation if not one of Nature's creatures appears to him too insignificant for the investigation of its structure and habits, but neither any star too remote to be drawn within the sphere of his observation, for the calculation of its motions and its course. From the Christian point of view, this, as well as the pursuit of wealth, appears a waste of time and energy, which ought to be exclusively devoted to securing the weal of the soul. It was already during the transition to a new era, when the poet of the Messiah sang the beautiful task, "to think once more the great thought of the Creation," even the creation of Mother Nature herself.

In man, Nature endeavoured not merely to exalt, but to transcend herself. He must not, therefore, be merely an animal repeated; he must be something more, something better. He ought, because he can. The sensual efforts and enjoyments are already fully developed and exhausted in the animal kingdom; it is not for their sakes that man exists; as, in fact, no creature exists for the sake of that which was already attained on lower stages of existence, but for that which has been newly conquered through itself. Thus, man must interpenetrate and rule the animal in him, by his higher faculties, by the qualities which distinguish him from the brute. The wild savage struggle for existence has already had abundant play in the brute world. Man cannot entirely avoid it, in so far as he is still a mere product of Nature; but in the measure of his higher faculties, he should know how to ennoble it, and in regard to his fellow-men should mitigate it, especially by the consciousness of their kindred and the mutual obligation of race. The wild turbulence of Nature must be appeased in mankind; man must be, so to speak, the *placidum*

caput, the Virgil's Neptune reared above the
tumultuous waves, in order to calm them.

Man not only can and should know Nature, but
rule both external Nature, as far as his powers admit,
and the natural within himself. Here again a most
important and productive field of human activity
finds the recognition and the sanction denied it by
Christianity. Not only the inventor of printing—
which, among other things, was also a powerful agent
in the dissemination of the Bible—but those, too,
who taught the steam-engine to shoot along the iron
road, thought and speech to flash along the electric
wire—works of the devil, according to the consistent view of our pietists—are from our standpoint
fellow-labourers in the kingdom of God. Technical
and industrial arts, although they promote luxury,
which is, however, a relative notion, promote humanity also.

I would add one thing more. Man ought to rule
the Nature around him—not like a fierce tyrant
however, but like a man. Part of the Nature whose
forces he constrains to his service consists of sentient
beings. The brute is cruel to the brute, because,
although having very strong sensations of its own
hunger or fury, it has not an equally distinct conception of the pain its treatment inflicts on others.

Man possesses this distinct conception, or, at least, is capable of possessing it. He knows that the animal is as much a sentient being as he is himself. Notwithstanding, he is convinced—and not unjustly, we consider—that in order to maintain his position in the world, he cannot do otherwise than inflict pain on some animals. Some he must seek to exterminate, because they are dangerous or offensive ; others he must kill, because he requires their flesh as food, their skins for clothing ; others, again, he must subjugate, and compel to manifold toils, because he cannot dispense with their assistance in his traffic, his labour. As a being, however, who is cognizant of the pain which the animal suffers in the process, and who can reconstruct it in himself as sympathy, he should endeavour to bring all this upon animals so as to involve the least possible amount of suffering. In one case, therefore, he should expedite slaughter as much as possible ; in the other, render service as tolerable as may be. Man pays heavily for the violation of these duties, as it blunts his feeling. Criminal history shows us how many torturers of men, and murderers, have first been torturers of animals. The manner in which a nation in the aggregate treats animals, is one chief measure of its real civilization. The

Latin races, as we know, come forth badly from this examination; we Germans, not half well enough. Buddhism has done more in this direction than Christianity, and Schopenhauer more than all ancient and modern philosophers together. The warm sympathy with sentient Nature which pervades all the writings of Schopenhauer, is one of the most pleasing aspects of his thoroughly intellectual, yet often unhealthy and unprofitable philosophy.

72.

Man ought, we said, to rule Nature within as well as without him. Nature in man is his sensuousness. This he should essay to rule, not to mortify, so surely as Nature in him did not forsake, but transcend herself.

Sensualism we call that disposition of a being by means of which it feels external influences, these feelings inciting it to action. The higher the animal, the less immediately is every special influence followed by action. The higher animal remembers what it did on occasion of a similar influence, and what consequences were thereby entailed, and shapes its present conduct accordingly. On this rests the animal's capacity for education. If the dog, the horse, invariably suffer pain after

any action to which they were led by a special
influence, they will omit the action even upon the
recurrence of the same influence. But wild animals,
also, as we have already said, have experiences, and
make use of them. The fox, the marten, are rarely
enticed a second time into a trap from which they
have once made good their escape. The animal
remembers, compares several cases, and acts accordingly; but it is incapable of deriving thence a
general principle, an actual idea. The same may
be said of its cognition of the kind, the species, to
which it belongs. The cock-pigeon will not mistake a hen for a pigeon, yet will be incapable of
forming the conception of a pigeon-species.

Man's development of this capacity within himself, by means of language, gives him, from a
practical point of view, also, an enormous start of
the animal. It is naturally the more unseemly in
him to allow his actions to be determined by the impulse of the moment. If he compares the individual
case with others which have preceded it, and is
guided by the experience he has gathered thence,
he has still merely put himself on a par with the
higher animals. It is only when he has deduced a
principle from his experiences, conceived this as an
idea, and regulated his actions accordingly, that he

has raised himself to the height of humanity. A rude peasant lad or workman is ready with a stab at the slightest blow, or even at an unpleasant word; he is no better than a brute, and a very ignoble brute too. Another remembers, on a like irritation, how stabbing has been the cause of this or that man being locked up in gaol : he forbears, therefore, and is in consequence as good as a well-trained dog, or a fox made shrewd by experience. A third has thought the matter over; he has formed the principle, or learnt at school, that the life of man ought to be sacred to man; he is the first who behaves humanly; it will not even occur to him to grasp his knife. So potent a protection against the power of sensualism has man in his intelligence !

The perception of kind acts as sensation in the brute, as well as in man; but with man alone it is a conscious principle of action. The fellow-feeling of kind does not prevent beasts of prey from rending others of their species, does not prevent the he-cat from occasionally devouring its own young; as neither does it prevent human beings from mutually slaughtering each other. The consciousness of kind certainly does not interfere with their doing so. Were our lives always secure with every one capable of formulating in his mind the conception of kind, including us in it as well as himself, it would be well with us. But there are various ways of formulating this conception, and the point is just this,—that we lead men to formulate it in the right manner. In the first place, of course, it is nothing but a name, an empty-sounding phrase, which can have no sort of effect. To become effective, it must be filled with the whole meaning of which it is capable. It is men's conception of man that ensures them their position on the summit of Nature, and enables them, by comparison and reflection, to resist the promptings of sense. But in the next place, the solidarity of mankind consists not only in a common descent and resemblance of organic structure, such as also forms the bond of every brute species; but is of such a nature, that man can only come to be a man by the co-operation of men, mankind forming a consolidated united community in a sense quite other from that of any species of animal. It is only by the help of man that man has been able to raise himself above Nature; and only in so far as he acknowledges and treats others as his equals, as he respects the institutions of the family, the state, can he maintain himself at this height, and develop himself still further. At the same time, it is of the highest importance that this knowledge should be retransmitted, and enkindled by emotion,—that the moral principles thus acquired should become man's second nature. Thus the sentiment of human dignity should grow into a habit in his relation to himself, and sympathy in its various gradations in his relation to others; and every violation of the one or the other should find its echo in the moral verdict of the conscience.

We need not here enter on a discussion of the question of free-will. Every philosophy deserving the name, has always considered the reputed indifferent freedom of choice as an empty phantom; but the moral worth of human principles and actions remains untouched by that question.

73.

One of the most potent of the seductions of sense is the sexual instinct; on which account sensuousness is frequently understood only as that which is connected with this impulse in man.

Antiquity, as is known to all, regarded this impulse in a different light from our modern Christian era. It judged and treated it with an ingenuousness which sometimes appears to us as immodesty It claimed for it the fullest right of existence and activity. In the ancient religions, especially of Asia Minor, we find this tendency expressed in the most monstrous of forms and usages. The Greeks, during their best age, knew at least how to restrain it within the forms of the humanly beautiful; while the Romans, after a greater display of austerity in the first instance, ended by making their capital not only the emporium of the treasures of the conquered East, but imported into it also all the unbridled extravagance of its licentiousness. The detestation in which the Jews held the religion of their Syrian neighbours preserved them likewise from their excesses; while, on the other hand, marriage and the begetting of children were held in high esteem among them. But they could not repel the universal moral corruption which overtook the ancient world, towards the decline of the Roman Republic and the beginning of the Empire, and in which the demoralization of the sexual relations played an important part.

Men were satiated with pleasures of all kinds; they were seized with nausea, and the world was overcome by such a mood as, according to the "West-Oestlicher Divan," Persians call *bidamag buden*, and Germans *katzenjammer*—cat-sickness—a result of being out late at night and concomitant practices. It had had an over-dose of sensuality.

disgust and abhorrence succeeded in their turn.
Here and there in the Roman Empire, dualistic ideas
and ascetic tendencies began to manifest themselves.
An aversion to the world of sense is already observable among the so-called Neo-Pythagoreans; and
now even among the Jews—lovers of children and
marriage as they were—sprang up the sect of Essenes whose stricter notions impelled them to reject
marriage, as well as the use of wine and meat.

The same spirit influenced the beginnings of
Christianity, whose connection with the Essene
doctrines continues to be an hypothesis as irrefutable
as it is indemonstrable.   We cannot fail to recognize an ascetic tendency in the Apostle Paul, nay, in
Jesus himself, especially as regards the relation of
the sexes.   The apostle of the Gentiles only toler-
ates marriage as being the lesser evil in comparison
with licentious desires, while he considers celibacy as
being the only state in which it was possible to serve
God with an undivided heart.   But Jesus teaches,
in his Sermon on the Mount, that he who looked
upon a woman to desire her, had already committed
adultery with her in his heart.   It is true that here
there is considerable doubt as to the true exegesis,
and it may be more correct to consider the text as
referring solely to the wife of another, thus only

inculcating anew the ninth commandment. **If it** be inward adultery, however, to lust after the wife of another, the same feeling for an unmarried woman, who is not yet mine, must be inward fornication: this, then, must have preceded all marriages, except such as were contracted for the sake of position, etc.

In the entire Christian conception of man, sensualism in the sense in which we here understand it, is something which positively ought not to have existed, which first came into the world by the fall of man. It is true that, according to the old Hebrew narrative, Adam and Eve, when still in Paradise, were also to beget children and multiply ; but this, according to the Fathers of the Church, was to be without desire and gratification, in which case mankind must have died out, even as it would starve, **if** eating were not pleasant, nor hunger painful.

On the contrary, these sensuous impulses lie **in** the normal disposition of human nature, because in fact they are comprised within the laws of animal life where man's belong. Only with man they should not, as with the brute, constitute the whole stimulus, but be ennobled with human sympathies. One of these ennobling factors consists, in the first instance, in the æsthetic impulse, the sense of the beautiful, which plays a more or less important part, according to the degree of culture of each individual. But it does not suffice by itself. In no nation was the sense of the beautiful more developed than with the Greeks, especially in regard to the relation of the sexes; and yet at last this degenerated to the uttermost. The ethico-emotional factor was wanting—such as ought to unfold itself in marriage. Poetry has handed down to us two beautiful pictures of Greek marriage in the heroic age; but just at the culminating period of the political and social life of this people, the almost orientally secluded wife was effaced behind the cultivated *hetæræ*. The matron at first was held in high esteem by the Romans, but the harshness of the Roman character at last revealed itself in this relation; and thus, in the later times of the Empire, it ended in utter licentiousness.

It is disputed whether Christianity or the Teutonic race ennobled marriage by infusing an emotional element into it, and thus imparting to it a higher ethical sanction. It is historically demonstrable, that with the advent of Christianity, and its admittance into the circles of heathen society favourable to it, the redundance of the sensuous element was pruned away, while the conjugal and, in fact, the domestic relations generally, gained in sweetness and depth; but asceticism made its appearance at the same time, and hypocrisy tarried not to follow in its wake. The healthy Teutonic mind needed much time, and the aid of classical antiquity through the study of the humanities, before in the Reformation it succeeded in casting off at least asceticism without, however, on account of its perverted conception of the sensuous, being able to radically free itself of hypocrisy and sanctimoniousness.

Monogamy was the established custom in nearly the whole of the circle where Christianity was first adopted; especially so among the Germanic nations; and this has, as contrasted with polygamy, to which Islamism imparted a fresh impetus, proved itself to be the higher form, from the fact that polygamous nations, even after the most promising beginnings, have yet invariably remained stationary at much lower stages of civilization. The chief reason of this lies, doubtless, in the difficulties which are attendant on education in the polygamous state. But we cannot recognize the fact of Christianity now declaring its monogamous marriage indissoluble, with the exception of one single ground of divorce, as having been a laudable achievement,

either in the cause of marriage or mankind. In
opposition to the prevalent abuse, according to
which the Jewish husband could quite arbitrarily
divorce his wife, Jesus, as an idealist, went to the
other extreme, in declaring marriage morally indissoluble, save in the case of the adultery of one of
the parties. The question of divorce, however, is
one of such complex practical bearing, that a
solution of it is only possible by the most varied
experience, and not by mere feeling, however
highly pitched, or at the dictum of a single general
principle. Such experience, however, was not
possible to Christ, not only because he himself was
unmarried, but also because, on his own showing, he
was adverse to interfering with the family concerns
of others. To this may be added, that although in
ruder times and conditions, adultery only might
have been a sufficient cause of divorce, yet with the
progress of civilization, a multitude of subtler distinctions have been superadded, which may render
a beneficial continuation of conjugal life as impossible as adultery.

The problem of the marriage law is only to be
solved by a compromise. It is necessary, on the
one hand, to resist caprice and to uphold marriage,
not only as a thing of sensuous desire or æsthetic

pleasure, but of rational will, and moral duty. Especially must it be upheld on account of the children, whose existence or non-existence must materially modify the state of the case. But this must be done without, on the other hand, making it too difficult to unloose the knot, when prolonged experience and careful examination have proved the impossibility of an advantageous union.

74.

After these general ethical speculations, however, we must bethink ourselves of the real ground on which all moral relations are formed.

According to a law pervading the whole of Nature, mankind is divided into races, as it furthermore, in accord with the configuration of the earth's surface and the course of history, coalesces into families and nations. The subdivisions have not been the same at all times: sometimes smaller aggregations have combined into larger masses; sometimes a greater mass has again resolved itself into smaller groups. The external circumstances have undergone similar changes: sometimes the tribes have migrated into remote regions, or at other times they have at least modified their respective boundaries. More and more, in the course of time, did seas or mountains, deserts or steppes, assert their influence as permanent barriers, within whose precincts the nations began to establish themselves, each with its own language and customs. These boundaries, nevertheless, are not of an immutable character, especially as they are not everywhere marked out very distinctly; even after the human multitudes have become fairly settled there is yet a perpetual pushing and pressing, encroachment and defence taking place on a smaller scale.

So far, History consists in the internal development of these races, their friction and intermingling, and the subjugation of one by the other, and at last, of many by one; next, in the fall of great empires, and subsequent formation of smaller states; and all this accompanied by a continual transformation of manners and customs, an increase of knowledge and aptitudes, a refinement of culture and sentiment,—a progress often interrupted, however, partly by gradual retrogression, partly also by sudden relapses. We see, at the same time, how the horizon of mankind is gradually enlarged, and especially how the harshest and most violent of those changes—the attempts at founding universal empires—although destructive of much individual happiness and affluence, nevertheless serve essentially to promote the progress of the race.

No one was so decried by the advocates of civilization and culture in the last century, as a conqueror: the godless author of the Pucelle and the god-inspired chanter of the Messiah vied with each other in expressing their abhorrence of these sanguinary persons; and if the first could not forgive the great Frederic his Silesian war, the other entirely forgot that we could scarcely have had Christianity without the invasion of Asia by Alexander the Great. We have since then been taught, by a profounder consideration of history, that it is the impulse towards development in nations and mankind which acts through the personal motives—the love of glory or the love of sway—of these individuals, only assuming different shapes in them according to their individual and national peculiarities, on which depend their various degrees of intrinsic merit. But whatever the difference between the intellectual and moral worth, as well as the military and political importance of an Alexander and an Attila, a Cæsar and a Napoleon, it must be admitted that they were all agents in the world's history ; we cannot imagine the

development of mankind, the progress of civilization, as taking place without their intervention.

Inasmuch as war is the method of the conqueroi
and it is this iron instrument which inflicts such
sanguinary wounds on the nations, the humanitarian zeal of our time has declared itself against
war. It is absolutely condemned, and societies are
formed, conferences held, in order to ensure its
complete abolition. Why do they not also agitate
for the abolition of thunderstorms? I must always
repeat. The one is not only just as impossible, but,
as things are, as undesirable as the other. Just as
electricity will always be accumulating in the
clouds, so from time to time causes of war will
always be accumulating in the nations. The boundaries of the various nations and states of the
earth will never be so equally balanced as exactly
to meet their wants and wishes; and in the interior
life of the different states, there will likewise occur
dislocations, obstructions, and stagnations, proving
intolerable in the long run. Within the party
conflicts of the same nation, recourse can usually be
had to pacific arrangements; inferior points of dispute between two nations may admit of settlement
by means of a freely-chosen umpire; in the
differences, however, which arise concerning ques-

tions vitally affecting their existence or power, although for a time they may endeavour to come to an agreement, yet, as a rule, this will be nothing but an armistice till one of the parties feels strong enough by itself, or with the assistance of allies, to break the peace. Cannon will continue to be the *ultima ratio* of nations, as once of princes.

I say, once of princes. For we must endeavour in every way, (although it is partly being adjusted of itself) that the commencement of war shall be less and less in the power of the capricious ambition of princes.

Napoleon III. would not have declared the last war, had he not known that he was supported in it by his vain and restless people—nay, if he had not felt himself impelled by them; and King William would have tried to avoid the war, had he not been conscious that, in accepting it, he was acting according to the spirit and feeling of the brave German nation. The acceptance of the war was, then, on the part of the Germans, a purely rational action: had Kant himself been the minister of the King of Prussia, he could have advised nothing else. But all this of necessity presupposes the existence of unreasoning passion, and it will never be wanting in nations or individuals, as long as men are men.

War will come to be of rarer occurrence, but not cease altogether.

The ladies and gentlemen who spoke at the famous Peace Congress at Lausanne could hardly be expected to know the Odes of Horace by heart; or else one might have reminded them of the verse about the fury of the savage lion, a piece of which, it says, the man-shaper, Prometheus, added to the human heart. But, in fact, the theory of their neighbour Carl Vogt, which doubtless has their full assent, ought to have led them to the same conviction. If man is descended from the animal, even as its highest, most refined offshoot, then he is originally an irrational being; and in spite of his intellectual and scientific progress, Nature, as desire and anger, must continue to exercise great power over him; and—Do you know, ladies and gentlemen, when you will bring mankind to the point of settling its disputes by pacific convocation? On the day when you shall have arranged that it shall only propagate itself by intellectual converse.

75.

If in former times the chief cause of war was the desire of the various nations and their rulers to subjugate and plunder other nations, and at the same time to extend their own power beyond its natural frontiers, at the present time, on the other hand—if we exclude the wars of European nations on other continents—the most frequent cause of war is the wish of nations to regain their natural and national frontiers, *i.e.*, either to cast down the limits where a people speaking the same language is divided into different states, or to win back those portions of the race, speaking the same language, which have been incorporated with their state by nations of a different stock. This is the so-called principle of nationality, which began to play an important part in the present century. It began as a reaction against the ambitious schemes of the first Napoleon. Within the last twenty years it had transformed both Italy, under the vacillating protection of the third Napoleon, and Germany in the war with him.

Now, if we in Germany have made this principle thoroughly welcome, and appropriated it, without, however, being minded to carry it out to the utter-most; and if now—satisfied with having given that extension to our body politic which not only makes it a living organism, but gives it strength to repel aggression—we do not dream of enforcing

the restitution of the German-speaking portions of
Switzerland, or the Baltic provinces of Russia, or
even the German provinces of Austria: it indicates
that there is now growing up around us—and moreover, in close connection with those erroneous preach-
ings of peace—a certain doctrine which declares itself
opposed to the principle of nationality, and has more
care for the establishment of some particular form of
political and social organization than for national
unity. It would have the large consolidated states
resolve themselves into groups of small confederated
republics, organized on the socialistic principle, between which, thenceforth, differences of language
and nationality could no longer act as barriers, or
prove the causes of strife.

This calls itself, indeed, cosmopolitanism, and gives
itself airs, as being a progress from the confined national standpoint to the universal standpoint of humanity. But we know, that in every appeal, the
sequence of procedure must be observed. Now the
mean tribunal between the individual and humanity
is the nation. He who ignores his nation does not
thereby become a cosmopolitan, but continues an ego-
tist. Patriotism is the sole ascent to humanitarian-
ism. The nation, swith their peculiarities, are the
divinely-ordained—that is to say, the natural forms

through which mankind manifests itself, which no man of sense may overlook, from which no man of courage may withdraw himself. Among the ills which the people of the United States are suffering from, one of the deepest is the want of national character. Our European nations consist also of mixed races: Celtic, Teutonic, Latin, and Sclavonian elements, have at various times been heaped up one above the other, and have become strangely blended in Germany and France and England. But they have ended by assimilating and crystallizing (excepting certain frontier lines) into a new formation—that of the present nationality of those peoples. But in the United States the cauldron continues to bubble and ferment, in consequence of the perpetual addition of new ingredients; the mixture remains a mixture, and cannot combine into a living whole. The interest in a common state cannot replace the national interest; as sufficiently proved by facts, it is impotent to exalt individuals above the narrow sphere of their egotism and their hurry to be rich, to the height of ideal aspirations; without patriotism, there simply can be no deep feeling.

We have not forgotten that the national limits at times grew too narrow also for our own great spirits of the last century, a Lessing, Goethe, Schiller.

They felt themselves to be citizens of the world, not of the German Empire, much less still Saxons or Suabians; nor did it suffice them to meditate and create in the spirit of one nation. Klopstock, with his enthusiasm for German nationality and language, almost appeared eccentric. Schiller, nevertheless, knew and expressed with the whole force of his sterling judgment, that the individual must "attach himself closely to his own native land," because here only lay "the strong roots of his energy; and there are abundant utterances of the two other great men also, which sufficiently prove that cosmopolitanism did not with them exclude patriotism. Now let us examine in what did their cosmopolitanism consist. They embraced the whole of humanity in their sympathy, they longed to behold their ideas of ethical beauty and national freedom gradually realized among all nations. What, however, is the desire of our present preachers of national fraternity—the International? They desire, above everything, the equal distribution of the material conditions of human existence, the means of life and enjoyment; the intellectual only occupies a secondary rank, and is chiefly esteemed as the means of procuring those enjoyments; and the effort at equalization is made at a sorry mean,

in comparison with which higher things are regarded with indifference, if not with distrust. No;
this sort of cosmopolitans must not appeal to Goethe
and Schiller.

The people they really go along with,—the fact
has long been patent to all eyes, let them be inhabitants of Germany or Italy, England or America,
—are those whose real home is the Vatican. These
have no wish for a national state, because it limits
their universal hierarchy; just as those others have
no wish for it, because it interferes with their individual state—the separation of mankind into feebly
organized and loosely connected federal republics.
Just as the Ultramontane party only prepares
man's intellectual subjection, although not unfre-
quently in the guise of invoking political rights,
even so the higher intellectual interests are endangered by the Internationals, through the supreme
position they allot to the individual, and his material
wants and requirements. Only in its natural division
into nations may mankind approach the goal of its
destiny; he who despises this division, who has no
reverence for what is national, we may fairly point
to as *hic niger est,* whether he wear the black cowl
or the red cap

76.

As regards the various forms of government, we may consider the prevailing opinion with us in Germany to be, that although a republican form of government is the best in itself, yet con sidering the actual circumstances and conditions of the European powers, the time for it has not yet come, and therefore, monarchy, made as little objectionable as possible, is to be tolerated for the present, and for a period as yet indeterminate. This shows at least a progress of insight, in comparison with twenty-four years ago : a numerous party among us then considering monarchy as a stage left definitively behind us, the republic as the goal for which we might steer forthwith.

The question, however, What is in itself the best form of government? is always a question wrongly put. It is equivalent to asking, What is the best kind of clothing?—a question which cannot be answered without, on the one hand, taking the climate and season into account, and again, the age, sex, and state of health of the individual. There cannot be an absolutely best form of government, because government is something essentially relative. The republic may be excellently suited for.

the United States, in the boundless area of North America, threatened by no neighbour, only, perhaps, by the internal conflict of parties; it may also suit Switzerland, shielded by its mountains, whose neutrality, besides, is guaranteed by the interest of the neighbouring states; and yet it might nevertheless prove pernicious to Germany, hemmed in by grasping Russia and restless France, now also brooding over her revenge.

But if the question be only to ascertain which of the different kinds of government conforms most to the dignity, or (to express it less pretentiously) to the nature and destination of man, even then it does not follow that the question must necessarily be decided in favour of republicanism. History and experience have not taught us, hitherto, that mankind has been helped on its way (and that surely can only mean that the harmonious development of its parts and capacities be promoted), or has more securely progressed towards it in republics than monarchies. That the republican institutions of antiquity count for nothing in this enquiry, is generally acknowledged, inasmuch as, by reason of the slavery which formed an integral part of their systems, they were, in fact, oligarchies of the most exclusive description. In the middle age, the republic is to be met with only in the smaller communes, chiefly towns and municipal domains; and here again, even if without actual slavery, usually accompanied by highly aristocratic institutions. In modern times, the republic appears sometimes transiently, especially in France, as an episode of violent political crisis; as an abiding institution, on the grandest scale in North America, on a smaller one in Switzerland.

It is true that these two republics, the only ones that are firmly established, apparently possess certain advantages in common,—one especially, which has secured to this form of government the favour of the multitude: the generally satisfactory condition of the finances, notwithstanding the light taxation of the citizen. Next, that there is not only a passive, relation of the citizen to he Government, but an active one distinctly defined. With this is connected the generally freer scope permitted to the indi vidual for the development of his energies and his preferences. But this has at the same time its dark side, as it leaves open every avenue for political agitation, keeping the state in a perpetual ferment, and placing it on an inclined plane, down which it must almost inevitably slide into ochlocracy, assuredly the worst of all forms of government.

But while we do not despair of the possibility of introducing into monarchy the citizen's participation in government, combined with greater liberty of action, so far as is conformable with the consistency of the State, we miss, on the other hand, in the above-mentioned republics, that flourishing condition of the higher intellectual interests which we find in Germany and, in some respects, in England. Not as though there were any lack of superior as well as inferior schools, and in part, well-organized and appointed ones too. But we miss all higher results. In Switzerland the leading cantons are German; in North America the dominant element, after the English, is also the German; and yet science and art in Switzerland and the United States are far from having put forth those native blossoms which they show in Germany and England. Switzerland possesses no classical literature of its own, but borrows it from us; as the professors at its high schools are still for the most part Germans, or at least, men educated in Germany. American literature occupies a similar position towards England; and where this is not the case, we see the science as well as education of America entirely based on the exact and practical, on utility and serviceableness. In a word, we Germans are struck

by something plebeian, something coarsely-realistic
and soberly-prosaic, in the culture of these republics;
transplanted to this soil, we miss that most subtle
spiritual atmosphere we breathed at home; besides
which, the air of the United States is infected by a
corruption of its leading classes, only to be paral-
leled in the most abandoned parts of Europe. But
as these faults, besides arising from the want of
national feeling, appear to us to stand intimately
related to the essence of the republican form of
government, we are far from unhesitatingly award-
ing to it the preference over the monarchical form.

77.

This much is certain : the institutions even of an
extensive republic are simpler, more comprehensible,
than those of a well-organized monarchy. The
Swiss constitution, not to mention that of the different cantons, is, as compared with that of England,
as a windmill to a steam-engine, as a waltz-tune or
a song to a fugue or a symphony. There is something enigmatic, nay, seemingly absurd, in monarchy;
but just in this consists the mystery of its superiority. Every mystery appears absurd; and yet
nothing profound, whether in life, in the arts, or in
the state, is devoid of mystery.

That an individual should, by the blind chance
of birth, be raised above all his fellows, and become
the determining influence in the destiny of millions
—that he, in spite of a possibly very narrow intellect,
a perverse character, should be the ruler, while so
many better and wiser men are called his subjects
—that his family, his children, should rank far above
all others,—but little intelligence is required to
find this absurd, revolting, incompatible with the
original equality of all. Such phrases have, in
consequence, always formed the chosen arena of
democratic platitudes. More patience, more self-
abnegation, deeper penetration, and keener insight,
are requisite to perceive how it is this very elevation of an individual and his family, an elevation
which places him beyond the reach of interested
party conflicts, beyond all impeachment of his title,
and exempts him from mutability, except the natural
mutation of death—in which case he is replaced,
without choice and conflict, by his successor, who has
also been naturally called to his position—it may,
I repeat, be less apparent how in this consists the
strength, the blessing, the incomparable advantage
of monarchy. And yet it is only this institution
which can preserve the State from those commotions
and corruptions which are inseparable from the

changes recurring every few years on the election
of the Government. The practice of the United
States, especially, in their presidential elections,
the inevitable corruption following in their wake,
the necessity of rewarding the accomplices by
giving them places, and then of winking at the
delinquencies of their administration, the venality
and corruption which are thus engendered in the
ruling circles,—all these deep-lying evils of the
much-vaunted republic, have been brought into such
glaring prominence within the last few years, that
the eagerness of German orators, newspaper-writers,
and poets, to go in search of their political and
even moral ideals to the other side of the Atlantic
Ocean, has suffered considerable abatement.

Neither can we altogether approve of looking for
these ideals on the other side of the Channel; but
at all events we can learn more and better things
from Englishmen than from Americans, especially a
juster appreciation of what a nation possesses in an
hereditary monarchy and dynasty. It was possible,
during these latter years, to experience alarm and
disquiet about the political soundness of England,
on account of the republican agitation which had
sprung up there; for no one with a grain of sense
can fail to perceive that the republic would be

the *finis Britanniæ.* But behold, the Prince of Wales falls dangerously ill; and although the nation objected to much in the heir-apparent's character and mode of life, the general interest, nevertheless, rises to such a pitch, that the republican agitators themselves are moved to frame an address of condolence to the Queen. What a proof this of the sound political instinct of the nation! How much cause is there here of envy to the French, who have uprooted their dynasty with irreverent precipitation, and now, between despotism and anarchy, can neither live nor die! And how greatly may we Germans congratulate ourselves that, in consequence of the deeds and events of the last years, the Hohenzollern dynasty has taken root deeply and ineradically, far beyond the Prussian limits, in all German lands and all German hearts!

That monarchy must surround itself with republican institutions, is one of those French phrases which are exploded, it is to be hoped; to raise on high the banner of parliamentary government is also still to look towards a foreign ideal. It israther to the character of the German nation, and the condition of the German Empire, that we must look, with the co-operation of the Government and the nation, for the development of such institutions as shall be best fitted to combine strength of cohesion with liberty of movement, intellectual and moral with material prosperity.

78.

I am a simple citizen, and am proud of it. The middle class, however much people may talk and sneer on both sides, must always remain the kernel of the nation, the focus of its morality—not only the producer of its wealth, but also the fosterer of its arts and sciences. The citizen who fancies himself honoured by the pursuit, or still worse, the purchase, of a patent of nobility, degrades himself in my eyes; and even if a man of merit gratefully accepts a proffered elevation to the peerage as a reward for his services, I shrug my shoulders at this display of a pitiable weakness.

At the same time, I am far from being an enemy of the aristocracy, or from desiring its abolition. The sincere supporter of monarchy must refrain from this. We have repeatedly seen in France how little is the significance of a throne amidst a society that has been reduced to a common level. On the other hand, we may see in England even now what valuable services a real aristocracy may render, both as the champion of national rights and the support of the sovereign's legal authority. An able aristocracy is an indispensable member of a constitutional monarchy, and there can be no question of abolishing it, but only of assigning it its due position. This, in the first place, is based on ample territorial possessions; and the legislation must allow the nobility—as also, of course, the opulent middle class—to maintain this property undivided, within certain limits. The constitution must also grant it an influence in proportion to that exercised by industry and intelligence on the largest scale; and if the members of the Prussian Upper House have not hitherto, by any means, used their influence for the advantage of the State, the fault consists in the as yet insufficient admixture of the representatives of industry and intelligence with the aristocratic element in that body. That the cadets of the aristocracy, however, should have an almost exclusive privilege of occupying the higher positions in the military, the diplomatic, and even the civil services, has hitherto, especially in Prussia, excited our disapprobation. We demand, in this respect, a thoroughly free competition, and this, moreover, as much in the interest of the State as the right of the entire body of citizens. We must not be deterred from our desire by the fact of members of the aristocracy having, in these last years, so admirably administered the affairs of Germany, both in the cabinet and in the field—thus earning the lasting gratitude of the nation. No doubt that simple citizens might have done the like, if they had had the opportunity. Talents arise in all classes, and develop themselves, if a career is open to them. Canning was the son of a wine-merchant, Sir Robert Peel of a cotton manufacturer, Nelson of a clergyman; and with us Germans, Scharnhorst was the son of a mere citizen; old Derfflinger, even if not himself a tailor, was yet a peasant's son. On the other hand, how much might be told of incapable generals, and blundering diplomatists, solely owing their command or portfolio to the accident of their birth! As early as the year 1807, Prussian law granted every nobleman the right of exercising a trade without prejudice to his rank—an effort to cure the prejudices of the German nobility by English policy, which was only too soon abandoned again.

But in the main it is not by these remains of aristocratic privilege, neither is it by the pressure of the fourth class from below, by which at this moment the middle class is endangered. It is rather a crisis within its own precincts—the consequence of the altered conditions of industry and life in our time. We had always, hitherto, till within the middle of the present century, considered the middle class as being based on a tardy, but safe mode of acquisition on the one hand, and on the other, on simplicity and economy of life. The workman, the tradesman, as well as the functionary or scholar, did not grudge unremitting toil for a very moderate remuneration, contented if, after several decades of industry and economy, they had been able to educate and provide for their children, and perhaps also to lay by something which they might inherit at their parents' death. These worthy old-fashioned ways have long ceased, however, to correspond to the needs or wishes of the present generation. The expectations of many members of the middle class have been unwholesomely stimulated by the examples of the astonishingly rapid and almost spontaneous accession of wealth, by means of what is called speculation, and of the luxury which has followed in its train. But even simple middle-class people find their old modes of acquisition, even with the utmost economy, less and less sufficient for their wants. The artizan finds that his handicraft scarcely supports him ; on which account some masters are driven to become manufacturers on a large scale, while others are depressed to the level of the operative. The merchant who finds his business not sufficiently lucrative, and the man of independent means in the same predicament, try their luck by speculating in the funds. The functionary of State is the worst off of all, as, in spite of all additions, his pay suffices less and less for the respectable maintenance of his family. In this direction a thorough reformation on the part of the Government is greatly needed, as its well-being is seriously endangered, along with the integrity of its functionaries; while the latter, on the other hand, should make it their own duty and that of their families to observe a dignified simplicity, and abstain from all fashionable frivolities. It is neither desirable nor even practicable to make head against the tide of the times; everybody ought to take them into account, and endeavour to do them justice; but we ought not to let ourselves be carried away by the stream, nor to lose the firm ground of the principles which have hitherto offered us a secure footing. Preaching against luxury has ever been a barren task; but Hannibal now stands at our gates, in the form of a fourth class, which, having long been only a portion of the third, has now begun to constitute itself independent, and seems disposed to violently shatter the third, together with the entire existing organization of the State and of society.

79.

It is disagreeable, although unavoidable, at this point, to speak of the so-called fourth class, because in so doing we touch on the sorest spot of modern society. And, as is well known, every wound or disease is the more difficult of right treatment the more it has been aggravated by a wrong one. Nor will it be disputed that what we call the labour question stands in this predicament. The state of the case of itself would no doubt admit of remedy, if the patient would but suffer himself to be cured, or even try to effect the cure himself in the right way. But quacks, and pre-eminently French quacks, have completely turned his head. One would have thought that the socialistic boil which has been gathering within these last decades in France had thoroughly discharged itself in the horrors of the Paris Commune—had clearly enough, in the flames of the Hotel de Ville and the Louvre, shown society of all countries whither certain principles will lead us: the partizans of these views in Germany especially must be, one would have thought, partly abashed, partly discouraged. Nothing of the sort! In meetings, in newspapers, in our very parliament, people dare to approve, nay, to praise, what is abhorrent to the common sense of every man and citizen—thus manifesting what they themselves might be capable of under certain circumstances. At the same time, they express the most utter hatred, not only against the institution of property, but even against art and science, as being the luxurious appliances of property. These are the Huns and Vandals of modern civilization, much more dangerous than the ancient, as they do not come upon us from without, but stand in our very midst.

Let us acknowledge before all things, however, that the other side may be accused of many errors, many sins, especially of omission ; human strength has been made an instrument of reckless gain ; neither has any proper care been taken for the workman's physical or moral welfare. But worthy men have arisen to instruct the workman to peacefully help himself; well-meaning masters have displayed their good-will by giving them houses, by the establishment of dining-rooms, and by the promotion amongst them of the sick and burial clubs ; in centres of industry, besides, we may now see the formation

of benevolent societies which make the building of
dwellings for workmen their especial task.   But the
true prophets have been confronted by false ones;
and, as will happen, these latter have found the greatest following among the mass.   Party watchwords,
such as that of the war of capital and labour, satirical
invectives against the detested *bourgeoisie,* as if it
were a strictly enclosed class, instead of the access to it
being free at any time to the intelligent and industrious workman, are so easily repeated and so rarely
subjected to any accurate examination.   A foreign
society, which proposes nothing less to itself than
the subversion of all our existing social conditions,
spins its threads through every country, stirs up our
artizans, and transforms their societies, originally
formed for mutual succour, into arsenals of resistance
to the masters.   The strikes perpetually breaking
out, here, there, and everywhere, more especially in
the capital of the new German Empire, are a piece
of anarchy in the midst of the state, of war in times
of peace, of conspiracy carried out undisguisedly
in broad day, the toleration of whose existence
does not redound to the credit of the Government
and the legislature, who look on in helpless inactiv-
ity.

It is true one may say to the masters: It is

in your power to help yourselves. Form yourselves into leagues as compact as those of the workmen, oppose to their refusal to work for you at
your prices the refusal to let them work for you at
their prices, and if necessary send to foreign countries
for workmen, and then let the refractory see who
will be able to hold out longest. But, other considerations apart, while these deluded fanatical masses
are being reduced to reason, the welfare of nearly
every circle of society is perceptibly injured, and not
rarely the prosperity of whole cities and districts
destroyed. The sudden and still increasing rise in
the prices of all the necessaries of life, beginning
with house-rent, is chiefly caused by the exorbitant
demands of the men upon their masters. One
would think that it must be perceived by the men
that they are making life more expensive for themselves as well; but these people do not look beyond
their immediate purpose : the minimum of work for
the maximum of wages ! And every concession
raises their demands. They first agitated in
England for ten hours' labour, then for nine hours';
and now that this has been carried in several
branches of trade, they already clamour for only
eight : it may be imagined how this will go on if the
demand is not stopped in time. Just now, too, when

in order to come up to the increased requirements of the times, the hours have had to be lengthened in the counting-house, the bureau, and the study! What may be the prospects of boards of arbitration, consisting of members of both parties, formed to settle disputed points, and agree upon what is equitable, may easily be imagined when one considers the mood of one of the parties.

Surely here is call enough upon the new German Government, to fulfil the duties of its position, and provide that the commonwealth receive no harm. True, it may be said in its excuse that it will have a difficult time of it in view of existing legislation. There has been far too much concession already. If I am not mistaken, it was Harkort, the veteran liberal, who recently reminded the workmen that the right of coalition had not been conceded them without many misgivings; it behoved them to take care that there should be no occasion to repent of it. If journeymen and factory labourers now form trades-unions for the sake of obtaining more satisfactory wages and conditions of work, and if to this end they agree to suspend all work till their demands shall have been acceded to, they are justified therein by the industrial legis lature of the North German League, that is, of the German Empire. Under the existing law, Government is only entitled to interfere in case of workmen endeavouring to coerce their fellows into joining their unions, and carrying out their plans, by threats or compulsion. But it is evident how odious and difficult of execution must be the policeman's part Government has thus taken upon itself. Whether anything can be done by indicting workmen on strike for fraudulent breach of contract, as recently suggested, remains to be seen. The influence of a foreign society, with notoriously revolutionary intentions, might also serve for a handle, as in the case of the Jesuits. But I know not how it is nobody seems inclined toward serious action. Some, and they unfortunately are the most influential, are glad of a fourth class to be displayed as a scarecrow to the third; others, who make a great to-do, are afraid of losing their popularity; while others, again, are really taken in by certain magniloquent phrases, which are made use of by the in great part very equivocal agents of the cause of labour. Only thus much I am convinced of, that if Government were to intervene here, it would be fulfilling a duty not only to the third but to the fourth class also, by severing its just claims from all connection with intentions which, by whosoever seriously loves civilization and culture, must be combated to the death.

80.

For at the back of the labour movement are those same persons, who are not only anxious, as we have shown in a preceding disquisition, to abolish all national distinctions, but eager to subvert the limits of property, this being considered by them as their task in the pretended interests of progress. Private property is to be, if not completely annulled, yet essentially limited, principally by means of the repeal of the laws of inheritance.

Hereditary property, however, is the basis of the family : to imperil its security is to lay the axe at the root of the family, and thereby at the root of society and the state. No firm national state above, no family securely based on hereditary property below : what, then, remains but the shifting sands of political atoms, of sovereign individuals combining themselves at pleasure into little communities of the laxest possible cohesion? But where, then, could any support, any stay be found ? How wildly would the sands whirl about in every breath of air, till beaten down or swept away by torrents from above that should render new consistent formations once more possible ?

Property is an indispensable basis of morality, as well as of culture. It is at once the result and the spur of industry. But to be this it must be hereditary, or else the acquisitive impulse would degenerate into mere coarse enjoyment. The producer would prefer as a rule, to squander the gains of a lifetime, if after his death they were to come into the possession of a multitude which was indifferent to him. And that very inequality in the distribution of property which socialism would exterminate, is something quite indispensable to the progress of mankind. Without wealth, without superfluity, neither science nor art could exist, because without these, their development would be impracticable, for want of leisure, and their enjoyment for want of means.

But even were property equalized, the levelling propensities of socialistic democrats would still be troubled by the inequality which exists in the power of work, in natural endowment. For the equalization of the first very pretty attempts have already been made by the vaunted English trades-unions. Although one person be capable of doing more work than another, and is also inclined to do so, yet he is not allowed. " You are strictly prohibited," say the laws of the trades-union ot bricklayers at Bradford, with reference to the hodmen, " from exerting yourselves over much, and inciting others to do the same, in order to win a smile from the masters." In the same manner the statute of the bricklayers of Manchester decrees that "any workman who is too quick, and cannot await the time till the others shall have done," is, on repetition of the offence, to be punished by increasing fines.

But as regards natural endowment, the theory may be remembered, which was still the fashion a few years ago—receiving the support, moreover, of writers otherwise respectable, who only allowed themselves to be too much carried away by the muddy current of public opinion—that mankind henceforth would no longer, as heretofore, be guided by a few eminent men, but that, as talent and judg-. ment become more and more the common property of the masses, they would know how to help themselves, and further their own interests. It had already ceased to be necessary to lift the hat to a rich man, and the authorities, as only servants ot the sovereign people to be deposed at its will, might be slighted with impunity; all that was still wanting, was exemption from the duty of reverencing greatness. Then should we have achieved the universal fraternity of the shirt-sleeve, and happily attained to the goal, the summit of civilization.

But the events of recent years have sadly marred this democratic calculation. After the apparent temporary extinction of Goethes and Humboldts, the Bismarks and Moltkes have made their appearance, and their greatness is the less open to controversy, as it manifests itself in the domain of tangible external facts. No help for it, there-fore, even the most stiff-necked and obdurate of these fellows must condescend to look up a little, if only to get a sight, be it no farther than the knees, of those august figures. No: history will continue a thorough aristocrat, although with con-victions friendly to the people; the masses, ever widening in culture and instruction, will continue to push and press on, or to support and give emphasis to ideas, thus, up to a certain point, aiding progress; but to lead and guide will always remain the prerog-ative of a few superior spirits; the Hegelian aphorism that "at the head of deeds which mould the world's history there stand individuals as the realizing sub-jectivities of the substantial, "will remain true; and,

too, in the domain of art and science, there will never
be a dearth of kings whose monumental plans will
find employment for a multitude of cartmen.

81.

What the Roman poet says of Homer : *"qui nil
molitur inepte,"* may, in a political sense, be applied
to the English. Their tact in practical affairs,
their historical instinct, preserving them from
over haste and leaps in the dark, deserve our
admiration, and still more our emulation. The
French are fascinated by phrases, and we Germans
allow the ideal, the abstraction which has been
moulded out of air instead of reality, to exercise
over us an influence far too potent, and indeed,
perilous. A Bill for the abolition of capital punishment has just now been once more thrown out of
the House of Commons, by a majority of 167 votes
against 54; in the German Parliament propositions
of this kind have already more than once had the
support of imposing majorities approximating to
unanimity. The property-qualifications entitling
to the franchise are from time to time reduced in
England, but no statesman there ever dreams of
abolishing them altogether.

A great statesman, however, has abolished all such in Germany; but I must be allowed to doubt whether the introduction of manhood suffrage will be accounted by history as one of his claims to greatness. Prince Bismark is anything but an idealist, but he is a man of very excitable temperament. This measure was a trump card to be played against the middle class, which had plagued him so sorely during the years of struggle in the Prussian Chamber, elected under a property-qualification. We can understand his indignation at seeing the means for carrying out an undertaking which he knew to be absolutely necessary for the welfare of Germany so obstinately refused him, but we can also understand the refusal of the Chamber, which was not initiated into the secret of the Minister's plans, and even if it had been, might perhaps have considered them too audacious. After the stupendous successes of his policy, it has long been evident that the Chancellor would henceforth have as little resistance to expect from the Prussian representatives of a restricted franchise as from a Parliament chosen by universal suffrage, and that in this respect, therefore, the measure was superfluous. The evil consequences which might have been apprehended have not, it is true, hitherto been realized to the anticipated extent. The pressure exercised by Government on the many inefficient electors has scarcely been perceptibly increased. Little has been gained by the democratic element; for the clerical party has in this, as always, been the chief gainer by the mistakes of the Government; and no other has manifested such great and unmitigated satisfaction with the measure. Since then, in the Catholic districts, the intelligent inhabitants of the towns are lamentably out-voted by the priest-ridden peasantry, we have to thank manhood suffrage for a considerable portion of the so-called centre in our German Parliament. Whether this will be all—whether times may not be in store for us when the democratic socialistic party will increase in Parliament, and by its coalition with the clericals create serious difficulties to Government, cannot be at present predicted with exactness.

But independently of its possible consequences, I cannot consider this measure as in itself either just or politic. The political rights accorded to the individual by the State should be in proportion to the services rendered to the State by the individual. True, it is said every German citizen is called upon to stake his life for the German State, and he ought, therefore, also to be allowed to cast his vote into the ballot-box; the universal duty of bearing arms on the one side involves the right of universal suffrage on the other. The two things are not so immediately connected, however. The military duties which the individual does by the State are compensated, in the first place, by the protection of life and property which the latter affords to him and his family, by the participation in public instruction and the possible succession to municipal or political offices which he shares in common with his fellow-citizens. But besides this the personal participation in military service is only one of those services to which the State lays claim. Another not less important one is the contribution which the citizen makes to the support of the State by the payment of taxes. The greater amount of these financial services entitles the monied elector to a proportionate increase of political power, as in this possession itself lies the greatest safeguard against the misuse of his vote. In the property of the wealthy the State possesses, as it were, a surety that the possessor will not give his vote to a candidate who might endanger the State and its institutions by wild projects through which his own security would necessarily be imperilled. The State does not profess a similar safeguard in the case of the poor elector, who may rather hope to be a gainer by a revolution, and who at any rate has not much to lose.

Lastly and chiefly, it is a mistake to be always speaking of the franchise as if it were only a right and not rather a political function imposed by the state upon the individual. A task, however, is only portioned out in proportion to the capacities of the individual. In this case the capacity consists in a certain amount of judgment, of insight into what requires to be done. A person is to be chosen who, in conjunction with others, has for a certain period of time to control the functions of the executive body, as well as in some degree to exercise an influence on their methods. But no one can judge of a person's capacity for this who has not an idea of the actual wants of the body-politic to which he belongs. We need scarcely point out here how enormous is the difference in degree with which this idea is grasped by the different members of the community, from the utter absence of it, to an instinctive perception and up to complete perspicuity of intelligence. But it does not follow that the gradation of the electoral rights must necessarily correspond to this gradation of capacity, even were that possible. But though political capacity is not capable of exact measurement, we must not conclude that the measurement may be utterly omitted. It is true, we cannot place an examining body in front of the ballot-box; we must abide by the approximate signs, which are generally patent. And we may presume, on the average, that the wealthy are better informed, more variously educated than the poor; which is self-evident as regards the professionally educated, such as all civil officers, scholars, artists. Here, then, we have at least two classes of electors, and the State, should it entrust a member of the one with an entire vote, should entrust a member of the other with only perhaps one-sixth or one-tenth of one; unless, indeed, with Stuart Mill, it prefers the so-called cumulative vote, introducing a graduated order of election. In Germany such an arrangement needs only to be restored, as it still in part exists in the Chambers of individual states: but it is the curse of precipitate action that a false step once taken can only with great difficulty be retraced.

As a drag, so to speak, against the too rapid down-hill motion of the State-engine, manhood suffrage has been accompanied by the suppression of the salaries of representatives; a regulation which, considering the low average of incomes in Germany, is oppressive, and can probably hardly be maintained for long: nevertheless, if I were a member of the House, I would persistently vote against its abrogation,—partly in order to oppose a barrier to the influx of the Bebel-Liebknecht element into the Assembly, partly because I imagine that a compromise may possibly be effected on the basis of this institution. This would be in fact, that the Assembly should concede to Government the limitation of manhood suffrage— that it should consent to the re-establishment of even a moderate property-qualification, receiving instead an allowance to be administered according to the most urgent necessity.

82.

Among the signs of the power exercised by high-sounding phrases and fashionable prejudices, I enumerate also, as already hinted, the agitation against capital punishment which we see revived at every opportunity. Capital punishment has long ago been mitigated as well as restricted : every aggravation of it has been abolished; a multitude of transgressions, and even of crimes to which the penalty of death was formerly attached, are now punished by a shorter or longer period of incarceration. Let it be still further restricted, let the act of execution, especially, be restricted within a completely enclosed space, and its infliction be reserved for the crime of premeditated assassination. But to desire its abolition even in this case, I consider to be a crime against society, and at a time like the present as sheer madness.

The ideas which have now pervaded a numerous class, which is still boldly pushing its way forward, are a luxuriant hotbed of robbery and murder. He who considers the possession of property as a wrong, hating the possessor of it as one who has wronged and is wronging him, will, by way of establishing an equilibrium, easily award to himself the right of taking his property, and should he not willingly yield it, his life also. We need only glance at a newspaper ; every week we may find a case of this kind.

I will only quote one which gives one a most vivid idea of the state of matters. In August, 1869, Antogast, a manufacturer of Freiburg, was staying at the peaceful baths of the Reuchthal. He failed to return from a solitary walk, and was immediately after found robbed and murdered in the wood. A few days afterwards, a person was arrested for creating a disturbance in a house of ill-repute at Strasburg. In his possession were found the watch and chain of the murdered man, already described in the police advertisement. He was a shoemaker from Wurtemburg, and he confessed to having committed the murder in company with another. They provided themselves with weapons at Kehl, and proceeded to the baths of the Reuch-thal with the fixed determination " to murder and rob the first person they should meet, who might be presumed to have money about him!" Before coming across this victim, they had met two persons, a lady and a priest, whom, however, they had suffered to pass, they not having the appearance of being provided with money. The other accomplice had escaped; this one was condemned to death by the jury, but pardoned by the Grand-duke of Baden. I have always felt the profoundest veneration, the warmest attachment, for the Grand-duke Frederic, as being an excellent Sovereign and a truly German Prince—the only one who, in join-ing the new German Confederation, need not have exclaimed with Schiller's Isabella, that he acted in obedience to necessity, not to his own impulse; but I have lamented this act of pardon. I believe that in this case his kind heart, his anxious conscien-tiousness, have misled him, in his desire to spare the criminal, into committing a wrong against society, which it is the first duty of a prince to de-fend. He owes to it in such a case to set an example, to erect an image of terror which the wicked may behold from afar, which may show them that not boundless desire, but justice, gives the final decision in the world. We need not endeavour to prove here, that lifelong imprisonment, whence every criminal trusts to effect his escape, exercises no such *prestige* of terror.

I am not ignorant that the majority of lawyers are now wont at their judicial congresses, and on other occasions, to declare themselves in favour of the abolition of capital punishment. I am, however, so bold as not to let myself be deterred by this, —least of all by their appeals to certain alleged statistical facts; according to which, in this or that country the number of crimes has diminished on the abolition of capital punishment. For it is but too patent that here they ascribe to this pet scheme what in reality is the result of concurrent factors,— such as the improvement of education, of the police, the general growth of prosperity,—causes which more than compensate for the mischief occasioned by the abolition of capital punishment. But neither can the momentary majority of the lawyers weigh with me as the definite judgment of professional men. The legal profession, in its strong contingent of advocates, has always one side which is too susceptible to influences of so-called public opinion, which in countless cases means nothing but that of the ruling prejudice. But, besides this, professional men are notoriously too profoundly immersed in technicalities to readily soar above them. This, however, they must do in this case : the question of capital punishment is not one for lawyers, but for legislators. The subject is in good hands with our leading German statesman : he will maintain capital punishment; but the condemned will be pardoned by his Emperor. Whereby again our case will not be mended.

83.

As regards the relation of the State to the Church, we on our part must naturally take the liveliest interest in the action of those men who have now made it their task to regulate this relation in consonance with public welfare and liberty of thought, —our wish especially in this case being that the strong and firm hand of the German Chancellor may not be hindered by the interference of weaker hands.

For our own part, however, we do not at present crave more from these movements than did Diogenes from Alexander. All we ask is, that the shadow of the Church may no longer fall across our path: that we may no longer, that is, see ourselves compelled to have any sort of relation with the Church. This, among other things, would involve the general introduction of civil marriage, for which people seem at length sufficiently emboldened. The citizen, in fact, should no longer be asked to which church he belongs, but whether he belongs or wishes to belong to any. When the great Frederick proclaimed throughout his dominions the liberty of the individual to go to heaven after his own fashion, he would perhaps have opened his eyes wide, but certainly not in anger, if one of his people, otherwise known to him as a man of honour, had given him the answer, "Pardon, Sire, but I have no desire to go to heaven at all:" for let there be no misconception of his meaning, the saying in his mouth only implied—Let every one in my kingdom be a fool to the top of his bent, so long only as his folly does not interfere with the common weal.

We do not for a moment ignore the necessity which now exists, and must long exist, of a Church for the majority of mankind; whether it will remain thus to the end of human affairs, we regard as an open question; but we look upon the

opinion as a prejudice, which deems that every individual must necessarily belong to a church; and
that he to whom the old no longer suffices, must
join a new one. This is the reason of all that
bungling meddling with the ancient Church, all
that patchwork of the so-called theology of mediation. In Lessing's time the effort was to effect
a compromise between revelation and reason; in
our day they speak of the task they have set themselves "of reconciling general culture with Christian piety." But the undertaking has not become
more reasonable or more practicable than in the
time of Lessing. It is very certain that if the old
faith was absurd, this applies doubly and trebly to
the modernized form of it, as shown in the Protestant League and the exponents of Jena. The old
creed at least was only contrary to reason, not self-
contradictory; the new belief contradicts itself at
every point: how then can it possibly be consonant
to reason?

The most consistent of all are the so-called free
congregations, who take their stand outside the
dogmatic tradition, on the ground of rational
thought, of the natural sciences and history. This
ground is, of course, firm enough, but not the basis
for a religious society. I have attended several

services of the free congregation in Berlin, and
found them terribly dry and unedifying. I quite
thirsted for an allusion to the biblical legend or the
Christian calendar, in order to get at least something
for the heart and imagination, but nothing of the kind
was forthcoming. No; this is not the way either.
After the edifice of the Church has been demolished,
to go and give a lecture on the bare, imperfectly
levelled site, is dismal to a degree that is awful.
Either everything or nothing. As a rule, these
congregations are founded by clergymen who have
seceded from the established churches, and yet are
anxious to retain a sphere of ecclesiastical activity ;
but they do not equally correspond to any demand
on the part of laymen, who, when they have
become estranged from the standpoint of their
church, prefer on the whole to retire from divine
service. And the more thoroughly the State recognizes their position in this respect, the less motive
will they have for the future to depart from this
negative attitude.

We on our part—I refer to the *We* as whose
mouthpiece I regard myself throughout this whole
disquisition—although we find ourselves annoyed, in
view of the attitude we have taken up towards the
Church, at being still forced into some sort of con-

tact with her, especially as regards certain ritualistic observances; nevertheless, feel so little the need of another church, which should be partly or entirely based on reason, that we would not become members of such a one, even if the State were liberally to endow it with all the privileges of the old churches.

84.

As if meditation were only possible in a church, edification only to be found in a sermon ! Why hold fast by an antiquated, exhausted form, at a time and in a state of culture, when there flow so many other and more abundant sources of intellectual stimulus and moral invigoration ? After all, it' is nothing but habit. It is so difficult to think of the place as empty where something used always to stand. Sunday must continue Sunday, and on Sunday one goes to church. As we have remarked at the commencement, we have no wish to quarrel with anybody; "let each act up to his own light." We would but indicate how we act, how we have acted these many years. Besides our profession—for we are members of the most various professions, and by no means exclusively consist of scholars or artists, but of military men and civil

employés, of merchants and landed proprietors
nor is the female sex unrepresented among us; and
again, as I have said already, there are not a few
of us, but many thousands, and not the worst
people in the country;—besides our profession,
then, I say, and the family life and friendly circle, we are eagerly accessible to all the higher
interests of humanity. In recent years we have
taken a vivid interest in the great national war,
and the reconstruction of the German State, and
each after his manner has participated in it, and
we have been greatly exalted by the unexpected
and glorious course which events have taken for
our much tried nation. To the end of forming
just conclusions in these things, we study history,
which has now been made easy even to the un-
learned by a number of attractively and popularly
written works; at the same time we endeavour to
enlarge our knowledge of the natural sciences, where
also there is no lack of sources of information ; and
lastly, in the writings of our great poets, in the performances of our great musicians, we find a satisfy-
ing stimulus for the intellect and the heart, and for
fancy in her deepest or most sportive moods.
" Thus we live, and hold on our way in joy."

It is objected that this must always remain an

expedient of scholars, or at least of the cultured few; that such reading and study does not suit the plain man; that he lacks the needful leisure and comprehension. Our poets, especially, it is said, are too much above him. The Bible is more suitable for him; this he can understand. He understands the Bible, does he? But how many of the theologians understand it? pretend to understand it? Yes; men think they understand the Bible, because they have grown accustomed to misunderstanding it. The modern reader also, doubtless, puts as much edification into it as he takes out of it. Not to speak even of such books as the Revelation of St. John, and most of the prophets of the Old Testament, let it not be deemed that Lessing's "Nathan," or Goethe's "Hermann and Dorothea," are more difficult of comprehension, and contain fewer "saving truths" than an epistle of Paul, or a discourse of Christ as reported by John. Let it be specially considered whether if our peasant children should be less plagued in the village school with the geography of Palestine, and the history of the Jews, with unintelligible articles of faith and indigestible precepts, there would be all the more time to educate them so as to awaken their interest in the intellectual life of their own people, and to lead them on to draw for themselves from such abundant sources of culture.

But I have just spoken of the works of our great poets and composers — of the nourishment they afford to the intellect and heart. The function of art in all its branches is, no doubt, to reveal the harmony of the universe, or at least display it to us in miniature, for though it ever maintains itself amid the apparent confusion of phenomena, it exceeds our comprehension as an infinite whole. This is the reason of the intimate connection which, with all nations, has always existed between art and religion. The great creations of the plastic arts have also in this sense a religious influence. Poetry and music, however, exert the most direct influence of this kind on our inner life; and on this point there is still something on my mind which I should like to say. But it is not meant to contain advice as to how the masters of the one art should be read, and those of the other heard; I have no wish to tyrannize over the sentiment of any one; let it only be permitted me to say how I have heard and read them, and what I felt and thought in doing so. If I should, perhaps, become more garrulous than may seem warranted in this place, let the reader be indulgent to me:

from the fullness of the heart the mouth speaketh. Let him only be assured that what he is now about to read does not consist of older materials, which I take an opportunity of inserting here, but that these remarks have been written for their present place and purpose.

Notes to Strauss's Text

Prefatory Postscript

Page xxiv   The Protestant League and the Old Catholics: see Introduction, p. xiii above.

Page xxvi   After publishing *The Doctrine of the Christian Faith* (1840–41), Strauss turned away from theology and wrote a series of biographies, including one on the Humanist Knight of the Reformation period Ulrich von Hutten. He returned to theology in 1861 with his essay on Reimarus, and in 1870 he published a study of Voltaire. On Strauss's letters to Renan, see Introduction, p. xvi above.

Page xxvii   "Rationalistic expositors": the very special sense which "rationalistic" had when Strauss wrote is explained in the Introduction, p. x above.

Page xxxii   "Lessing in section 86": This is part of an appendix on German literature, omitted in the present edition.

Page xxxvi   For "Fechtner" read "Fechner." Leibniz compared body and mind (or 'soul') to two watches which, with complete independence from each other, kept the same time.

Page xliii   "New revision of the Life of Jesus": This is the second of Strauss's two great Jesus books, the *Life of Jesus for the German People,* 1864.

Page xlv   "My 'Dogmatik' ": Strauss's *Doctrine of the Christian Faith* (1840–41).

Volume I

Page 2   "Vigorously to repel these . . . encroachments": An
                    allusion to Bismarck's anti-Catholic legislation,
                    which began with the Prussian government protect-
                    ing 'Old Catholic' priests and bishops from being
                    deprived of their office by the Vatican.

                    "The contest between Lutheran orthodoxy and the
                    Unionists": The Unionists wanted the Lutheran and
                    the 'Reformed' (Calvinist) divisions of German
                    Protestantism to join together.

Page 15   "One of the reformers condemned . . . a meritorious
                    physician": Calvin's persecution of Servetus.

Page 23   On his way to Worms to justify himself, Luther, hav-
                    ing learned that the Emperor had had his books
                    burned, was asked whether he still meant to continue
                    with his journey. "I will go," he said, "if there are as
                    many devils in Worms as there are tiles upon the
                    housetops. Though they burnt Huss, they could not
                    burn the truth."

Page 27   "The Roman historian's testimony": Tacitus, *Annals*
                    15.44.

Page 30   The Protestant Jean Calas was tortured and executed in
                    1762 on a charge of murdering his son to prevent him
                    from turning Catholic. The son had in fact committed
                    suicide. In his study of Voltaire, Strauss shows how he
                    spent three years in a passionate and devoted struggle
                    to vindicate Calas posthumously. Strauss's acknowl-
                    edgment of Voltaire's total earnestness in this matter is
                    juster than his representation of him as a characteristi-
                    cally French "scoffer" in the present book (1, 39).

Page 44   "It evaded the offence . . .": What Strauss here says is: it evaded the offensiveness which the free thinkers had found in the postulates by toning these postulates down.

Page 106   Goethe's notorious Venetian epigram: Goethe here said that he could not stand tobacco smoke, bugs, garlic and—in the German of his manuscript— "Christ." This is probably a rhetorical singular for the plural "Christen" (Christians). Printed texts of this poem invariably substitute a cross (+) for this word.

                  "Nothing but the mere form of this sign": i.e., even the mere form of this sign.

                  " 'The West-Eastern Divan' ": this title of a cycle of poems by Goethe is derived from the "Divan" or "Collection of Songs" of a Persian poet.

Page 119   "Schiller's 'Gods of Greece' ": In this poem Schiller laments the passing of the personal gods of Greece and their replacement by a deistic abstraction.

Page 125   Lord John Russell, the Prime Minister, was asked to accede to the Archbishop of Canterbury's request to appoint "a day of fasting and humiliation" because of the prevalent cattle disease. Russell declined, saying that a prayer sanctioned by the Archbishop was already in use, "by which the nation humbled itself before Almighty God and prayed for the Divine protection in consequence of the cattle plague" (Hansard's *Parliamentary Debates,* volume 181, reporting the sitting of February 8, 1866).

Pages 211–12   The passage is not, as Strauss here suggests, from Kant's *Critique of Pure Reason,* but from his later *Critique of Judgment,* para. 80.

Page 223   Moritz Wagner: In the sixth edition of the *Origin of Species,* Darwin agreed (chapter 4) that Wagner had shown that "the service rendered by isolation in preventing crosses between newly formed varieties" is considerable; but he did not accept Wagner's contention that "migration and isolation are necessary elements for the formation of new species."

Volume II

Page 20   "The author of the 'History of Materialism' ": This is F. A. Lange.

Page 47   "The philosophical emperor": Marcus Aurelius.

Page 51   "The idea of kind": i.e., moral action is action in accordance with the idea of the species 'mankind'.

Page 55   "The great law of progress": This is a misunderstanding of Darwin's theory that was common at the time, and also one of the features of Strauss's book that drew Nietzsche's scorn; cf. Introduction, p. xv above.

Pages 56–57   "The poet of the Messiah": i.e., Klopstock, the first part of whose gigantic religious epic in hexameters, *Der Messias,* was published in 1748.

Page 76   Peace societies held International Congresses in various cities from 1843.

    Carl Vogt was "neighbor" to Lausanne as his professorial chair was in Geneva.

Page 95 "The horrors of the Paris Commune": the insurrection of 1871 against the German occupation included destruction carried out by men and women with cases of petroleum (*pétroleurs* and *pétroleuses*).

Page 110 "Stuart Mill": Mill was trying to meet the objection that unqualified universal suffrage would lead to "manual laborers" forming the great majority of voters, with the resultant twofold danger of "too low a standard of political intelligence" and of "class legislation." He suggested that educated persons should have a second vote, additional to their vote as simple citizens (*Representative Government,* chapter 8).

Page 111 Bebel and Liebknecht had recently (1869) founded the Social Democratic Workers' party.

Page 113 Schiller's Isabella opens his play *Die Braut von Messina* with these words.

Page 123 The sequel here referred to comprises Strauss's two appendices on German poets and composers, not included with the present translation.